WOLFGANG
# KRAFTW

# I WAS
# A ROBOT

First edition Copyright © 2000, Wolfgang Flür
Second revised edition copyright © 2003, Wolfgang Flür

Copyright © 2017 Wolfgang Flür
This edition copyright © 2017 Omnibus Press
(A Division of Music Sales Limited)
All song lyrics © Wolfgang Flür, except 'Greed' (© Wolfgang Flür, Barbara Stollwerck
and Chris Raistrick)

Translation by Janet Porteous, 2000; additional translation by Barbara Uhling, 2017

ISBN: 978-17855-8580-7
Order No: OP57365

**Exclusive Distributors**
Music Sales Limited
14/15 Berners Street
London, W1T 3LJ

**Music Sales Pty Ltd**
Level 4 , 30–32 Carrington Street
Sydney
NSW 2000
Australia

Every effort has been made to trace the copyright holders of the photographs in this
book but one or two were unreachable. We would be grateful if the photographers
concerned would contact us.

Printed in Malta

A catalogue record for this book is available from the British Library.
Visit Omnibus Press on the web at www.omnibuspress.com

WOLFGANG FLÜR
# KRAFTWERK

# I WAS
# A ROBOT

**OMNIBUS PRESS**

London / New York / Paris / Sydney / Copenhagen / Berlin / Madrid / Tokyo

*Wolfgang Flür*
*With a foreword by Rudi Esch*

# Contents

# Letter To The Reader
## I Had Only Wanted To Be Drumming

I realised early on that music was to be a fulfilment in my life.

Although our family did not play any instruments, all day long we heard cheerful and classical music being played on the record player and on magnetic recording tapes in the homes of our parents and grandmother.

My book is about adventures and observations that influenced and changed my life. From the age of 15, all I really wanted to do was drumming. School was bullshit. For me, drumming was like playing – it was in my nature to be playful! Nothing could give me more pleasure. I was young and thin, full of self-doubts and complexes; no one had strengthened my self-esteem. I was the odd one out in my family, a dreamer. I was called the "little sensitive one", often rebelling against my weak father. Music strengthened me, especially once I was given my first part to play in a band – as a drummer. I was a somebody then, someone who created the "BEAT" the others needed. *I* was needed!

Later, others also recognised the "BEAT" in me and opened my eyes to a modern way of beating – electro music. At first Kraftwerk was just another game for me but I quickly understood that this up-to-dateness was something new and special.

In the story of my life, which has had its ups and downs, I will be relating the in-between tones and human occurrences within my bands, whom I always considered to be my family. Kraftwerk was a long chapter in my life, a very special "family".

After I had made the decision to split from Kraftwerk, life continued, albeit with a musical abstinence of ten years. This intermission was right and important and led me to my own artistic position – the story-teller. These days I no longer drum; I narrate, I write, I even give lectures. This has culminated in suddenly finding myself in the Tate Gallery in Liverpool, standing in front of a large audience, recounting my life.

It is still a good life that I lead; it has kept me happy and healthy and I am making more music than ever – my own music. I could hardly have believed this would come to pass, although it had been predicted to me by a Japanese fortune-teller.

I wish you much pleasure with this book.

Yours,

Wolfgang Flür

# *Foreword*

I often wonder who my favourite bands are. Inevitably I tend to think of British bands, especially London ones like The Who, The Kinks, The Damned and most of all The Clash. They all have a tendency to start their names with "the", with one exception: Led Zeppelin. Over the years I have learned to love The Beatles and Ramones, and I have always had a soft spot for The Troggs. All these bands have one other thing in common: they are all four-pieces that were writing music history.

Funnily enough, in my youth I never thought of German bands in this context, although there were some obvious candidates, Kraftwerk being the most prominent of that particular illustrious species. But somehow I never related to Kraftwerk in that or any other way – maybe because on the one hand they were too close to me to get noticed as something that was really good, and on the other because I never understood this working collective as a band. Not quite the four horsemen of the apocalypse, but four technocrats busying themselves with measuring amplitude signals. The idea that these people were responsible for writing internationally acclaimed music in their backroom studio near the station was just too outlandish to comprehend. As a result, in Germany and in Düsseldorf in particular, their story was told in the fashion of a surreal fairy tale, and not as it should have been: as a story of international success and acclaim.

Every morning, four distinguished gentlemen would arrive on time at the Kling Klang Studio, marked on the outside only by a mundane-looking sign that read "Elektro Müller". If you were looking for rock 'n' roll, you were looking in the wrong place. On the inside their studio resembled an engineer's laboratory – complete with knobs and dials – rather than a typical music studio. From nine to five these four honourable enthusiasts would be engaged in the serious business of music creation. They spent their evenings alone in a hermit-like existence that didn't have any space for friends or family life. Curling up on the sofa with a cup of coffee was the height of indulgence, as they were expected to start all over again, on time, the next morning. They fiddled with sounds and structures, and pursued serious engineering in the same fashion as their role models Wernher von Braun and Werner von Siemens. This kind of cool male kinship did not light my fire.

Then, at the turn of the millennium, one of the Kraftwerk members released a book that caught my attention – or, to be precise, was brought to my attention by a friend. This friend called me one day and told me that Wolfgang Flür had written a book and that the remaining members weren't best pleased with its contents. He recommended I read it. One day we went to a reading in Düsseldorf, where there was also talk of a lawsuit in connection with this. Wolfgang had been prohibited from printing a number of passages in his book, and here he was, happy as Larry, reading from the opposing party's application to the court instead. That was the last thing I would have expected a formalistic Kraftwerkian to do. Something had shifted here. Emotions had brought the cool relationship between the gentlemen to the boil in an unexpected way. It was as if the book had cracked open the surface of the uniform quartet and shone a torch into its inner sanctum. Before then I had never been able to identify who was responsible for which task. I didn't know who Florian, Wolfgang, Karl or Ralf were. Now I understood that the drummer had put himself up against his former colleagues. The robots had suddenly become rivals. This unusual Kraftwerk case turned out to be very amusing. In front of my eyes, a Faustian plot unfolded as the counterpoint to their most famous song. Someone seemed to be shouting at the top of his voice, "I am not a robot".

I have always thought that drummers play a special role in a band. There was The Who and there was Keith Moon. There is Ringo and there was The Beatles. John Bonham and Ginger Baker were and are very special individuals. Drummers often seem to be the unlikely heroes in a peculiar plot. Now we had electronic drummer Wolfgang Flür, dropout from the classic Kraftwerk quartet, and this particular plot unfolded in front of my eyes. I took an immediate liking to him.

A few years later, while working on my own book, I had to immerse myself in Kraftwerk's output with the intention of objectively discussing and presenting the electronic bands from my hometown. I carefully listened to each album and was drawn in by the almost magical effects of this music. I could only draw one conclusion: Kraftwerk had set new aesthetic standards and created their own self-contained microcosm. Kraftwerk is brilliant music, but most of all it is art! With that in mind, Wolfgang's book has gained importance over the years, because it gives a deeply personal insight into the previously unknown Kraftworld. He grants the reader a glimpse of what was going on behind the scenes.

Wolfgang and I have developed a close friendship over these past years and I am very happy that his book is available again, and to a new audience. Wolfgang is not just an author with deep roots in the Rhineland who achieved an impressive international music career, he is also a close friend of the family who always manages to amaze my kids with his stories of robots. We meet every week for lunch in the traditional pubs of Düsseldorf and chat about everything besides electronic music – usually Ringo, Macca, Moonie or the genius of Brian Wilson and The Beach Boys. He is the gregarious one of the electronic four, with a big heart, who proudly looks back on the glory days without any kind of regret. Though Kraftwerk has been around for more than 40 years at this point, they will constantly be rediscovered. This book will help you get to know Wolfgang as a person and to demystify the Kraftwerk that surrounds him to this day.

*Rudi Esch*
*March 2017*

# Prologue
## In Cahoots With The Robots

In the beginning, I was keen on the working title *In Cahoots With The Robots* for my book, but then, the more I remembered and the more I wrote, it occurred to me that, compared to other pop groups, we didn't fit into the pattern of a troupe of buddies at all. This was only a deeply concealed but longed-for ideal. Our electronic quartet was too diverse in personalities and family backgrounds. Although our fathers had been engineers, architects and opticians, they had all enjoyed very different social positions.

From the start, Ralf Hütter and Florian Schneider-Esleben had suited each other better. They had come from prosperous families where there had never been a lack of money or, in particular, of culture or education. They had elegant manners and had travelled widely in childhood. Karl Bartos and I, on the other hand, came from the so-called middle class. Of course, we had also been educated, particularly in relation to what is described as "emotional intelligence", although we also knew what it meant not to have any money sometimes, and what it was like if someone needed emotional support. On top of that, we were youthful and talented, and we stuck together for a long time because we had crucial things in common and because we respected each other so much as we were. Instinctively, each of us sensed that our special

1

relationship would be capable of producing great things in the future.

Two years ago I was trying to collate some unpublished photos from our early appearances for Tim Barr, writer for the British magazine *Future Music,* so for the first time in ages I opened my gold aluminium case, bought in 1975 in a store on New York's Fifth Avenue, to refresh my memories of the most electric years of my life. As I opened it I was hit by the concentrated aroma of those pioneering times, and I felt high. I leafed through the heaps of documents and photos, reading and falling into a state of analytical trance. Yes, there is a Kraftwerk smell for me, and it is delicately stored under the cultural category of "Thoughtful German". It is the condensed smell from the case that accompanied me to all of the hotel rooms during our years of tours and journeys. It smells of all classes of hotel room, of aeroplanes and kerosene, of a multicultural world, wonderful experiences and sobering prejudices dismissing us as privileged sound technicians from modern Düsseldorf. It is also the chemical smell of press photos, personal Polaroids, controversial newspaper articles from all over the world and the frequently torn films of my old, manually wound Bell & Howell eightmillimetre amateur movie camera. These relics were also surrounded by the technical odour of oxidised brass sticks that I'd had soldered for me right at the beginning of the '70s, and with which I had drummed for Kraftwerk thousands of times.

In 1997, the American journalist Dave Thompson had written a comprehensive, well-informed article for the US magazine *Goldmine* entitled "The Heart Of Teutonic Soul", focusing on my earlier group and my new music project, Yamo. We had talked enthusiastically on the telephone for half an evening, while I was sitting in my hotel room in New York. Dave encouraged me to write down my story. He said that there was an absolute need to explain why I had left Kraftwerk. Because this was the question that had most often been posed by every journalist and fan in the intervening years, I finally decided to make this report. I shall have to flashback to an earlier period, when the love of music and enjoyment of sound were awakened in me, so that my romantic heart and my "Teutonic soul" can be better understood.

We developed a new kind of music with Kraftwerk. At the beginning of the '70s, it took us to many corners of the world, completely unexpectedly. Without any preparation, we experienced the most unimaginable things and had beautiful, appalling and valuable life experiences. Jetting around the world, and our many personal encounters, sharpened my awareness of nature, people and ourselves. I realised that Düsseldorf was not the centre of the Earth, and discovered that I was a citizen of the world and was at home everywhere. However, I also enjoyed the feeling of being at home, the charm of our degree of latitude and of returning. Disappointingly, I was obliged to accept that travelling was not a comfortable experience for all of us, and after ten years I found that I was regarding my colleagues and myself from a more critical angle. Originally, slight doubts began to impinge upon events with Kraftwerk and what we were actually bringing to people. I began to mature, and at some point my thoughts no longer revolved around drumming, invention and how I got on with women.

While you are reading, you will notice that I often report more about my experiences on the boundary of our concerts and tours than about details of our everyday musical activities. In fact, it was the human encounters, the special events and wonderful meetings in a marvellous period of my life, that impressed me and now make me wallow in my memories. The settings of our synthesisers or technical details of our appearances and recordings have not stayed in my memory, and are not so very significant; that is skill and routine. Every profession involves such things, so please don't expect a book about VCOs, LFOs, oscillators or filter analyses. Mine deals much more with creativity, vigilance, helpfulness and consideration. It also includes loss, disappointment and betrayal.

We had the enormous luck of being able to reach people with our music and our visions and of being loved by them. I have learnt from many people, and I have written new accounts of their

3

stories, which sometimes became my own, for my current project, Yamo. Life educates, and the more someone has opened his or her awareness to its details and the changes in it, the more it is possible to draw from that precious treasure trove later.

I had known for a long time how it felt to be on stage. I had also experienced what it was like to be applauded. During my amateur period, I had been in many groups, and I had grown very fond of them, even if they were not particularly successful. They were all my bands, groups that I had founded. However, with Kraftwerk, the whole world stood open to me, and that was the thing – apart from my discoveries and my minimalist drumming – that most enchanted me through all of my years with the group. Human contacts in every nation, countless conversations and the flirtations that often emerged from them, the universal cultural worldview that I was able to form for myself without just getting it from books – all of these things gave me wonderful experiences which later, following my painful separation, also helped me to find a way to myself, to the love and sound of my new music. My time with Kraftwerk was one of the craziest and the most wonderful of all. We always tried to offer our fans something special. Today, modernity and independence are again my particular guiding stars. To echo Brian Wilson's words, "Don't forget that our music has always been made out of love for you."

# I

# Stages Of A Musical Life

"Anyone who swims with the current will reach the big music steamship; whoever swims against the current will perhaps reach the source."

*– Paul Schneider-Esleben, Florian's father*

"You're doing all right, lad."

*– Heribert Flür, my father, aged 85*

# 1 Serenity Supreme
## There Are No Accidents

DÜSSELDORF, 1 JANUARY 1999

What a magical number this New Year represents to us! For me, it's much more exciting than the next one – the one with so many noughts at the end of it – that is causing people to panic so much. On New Year's Eve, I had dressed up warmly and taken a long, thoughtful walk along the Rhine to the north of Düsseldorf in order to get a feeling for the approaching new age. In the late afternoon of New Year's Day, I was still lying in my warm bed, dozing comfortably, when I suddenly began to think about the meaning of life, of my life. It was not the first time that I had done this, but I have rarely seen with such clarity. I thought about the work on my new album with Yamo, which is dedicated solely to the subject of great merriment. I also remembered previous years, following my voluntary departure from Kraftwerk, some of which were not easy to deal with. Was it uncomfortable for me to cope? Had I only dealt with my life in general terms? Will I just put it behind me one way or another? Or do I enjoy dealing with this? What makes me happy? Many search for happiness in a binding partnership, sticking so closely to another person because life terrifies them so much that they always need someone to hold onto when they are living it.

Kraftwerk was also once a binding partnership for me, in which I felt supported and into which I also invested a lot of myself. But I would almost have lost sight of myself without even being aware of it if they hadn't made it hard for me to let go and to find my own balance for the future without using the band as a crutch. I can't describe what a feeling of relief this means to me today. I'm now working with independent young artists, and have been living alone for a long time, enjoying liberty and not allowing myself to be diverted from a sensitivity to life.

In the celebrated case of another man, such sensitivity to life tended to be stunted, and it was only after a near-death experience that he was able to arouse such feelings. You will certainly remember the dreadful tragedy of a Swiss Air flight in 1998. While this plane was travelling over the North Atlantic, near Halifax, in Canada, there was an electrical fire and smoke had started pouring into the cockpit during a night flight from New York to Paris. The pilots couldn't see anything, and they lost control of the aeroplane, which was full of passengers. The machine had fallen into the sea at great speed and from a great height. Two hundred and twentysix passengers died immediately, and they just lay on the sea bed, torn limb from limb. One man, however, had not died, and had instead been lying comfortably in the bed of his New York hotel, watching the early news tell him where he would have been lying at that point if he had flown with the plane. The Swiss tennis ace in question told a television reporter that he had already lost his match and had actually wanted to catch the next flight home, but his manager had persuaded him to do a bit of shopping with him. They hadn't wanted to book a return flight until immediately before their departure.

When he had understood how he had escaped death by a hair's breadth, his notion of his life had changed in seconds. He said that he had suddenly realised that he was still alive, and also recognised the feelings that he lacked. He had been constantly jetting around the world, always hunting for victory on the tennis courts, always wanting to be the best, the first and the fastest. That had been what made him feel alive, what he had believed he had needed. He had thought that this made him happy – along with a lot of money, which he earned and spent extravagantly, always greedy for coarser stimuli.

On that morning, it had suddenly become clear to him what it really meant to be alive. He began to yearn for the simplest things, and was happy that he could do something "normal" again. He had imagined that he had been sitting in the plane, and that the pilot had just announced the terrible news of the approaching disaster through the loudspeaker, and he realised just how much he would have fought, then, to cross the street one more time, and to hear everyday noises. Just to smell newly mown grass, or to watch a blue summer sky with white feathery clouds. To drink another cup of fresh coffee, and to take his beloved in his arms and smell the perfume of her hair. To hear the familiar noises of his house, which didn't otherwise mean anything to him, let alone the laughter of a child – his child would have been worth millions to him.

In shock, he explained that he had wanted to change his whole life from that day forward, and that "to always want to win" had suddenly become unimportant to him. He planned to lead a more modest life in the future, concentrating on what was really important, and enjoying the beauties of nature. He had also asked himself how often the moon would still rise for him. Ten times? Perhaps 100 times more? He wanted to enjoy his time now, to approach the freshly given privilege of life in a different way.

That man was really lucky that he was allowed to begin again from the beginning. I would like everyone who has lost the awareness of their lives to get it back – without such a drastic blow, of course. However, apparently some people need one before their dulled senses will become sensitive again.

Nevertheless, I am one of those who love the extremes of light and bright colours, although pastel tones and the twilight that refuses to leave the day and heralds the night have also always exhilarated and inspired me. The daily enjoyment of perception is the most important thing to me. The feeling of being alert, the delightful recognition that spreads in me again and again, is already worth my life on its own. Only pleasure can follow it, pleasure in life. I see with my feeling hand, I make friends with the winds, I sense the season early, listen to the day, prepare myself. How touching is an affectionate encounter! It produces the greatest joy of all. It's barely comprehensible luck that this function is renewed every day, constantly different and therefore new. Pleasure is never the same, and I can't understand how people are always complaining about boredom in their lives. Can't they see? Everyone in the doomed Swiss Air plane would have wished to stay a little while longer, and they certainly wouldn't have found it boring. Imagine someone sentenced to death, who has known for a long time when the end will be. Do you think that he will be bored with the rest of his life?

**"There are millions of people yearning for immortality who don't know what to do on a rainy Sunday afternoon."**
                                                    – *Maurice Chevalier*

But where is the sense in all of this, if I have to leave our lovely world so soon? What's it all about? Humanity, a special species, has attacked this planet like a natural catastrophe, and I'm afraid that this pest won't be here for much longer – it's behaving so irresponsibly, and in such a predatory way. This is perhaps a short guest performance, before something completely different occupies this beautiful blue globe swimming in space. Observed in wonder from a distance, it allows itself to be trampled by such strange creatures that give themselves their own names, can recognise each other and have such absurd characteristics as humour or even boredom. Creatures that have voices, with which they can laugh themselves to death. Animals that sing, play instruments and enjoy distorting their senses with music – one of the most incomprehensible things in the world – and that have fun making a right old noise from pure tomfoolery, doing something really useless.

9

For me, it's wonderful just to be here for a while, observing this adaptable creation and perceiving everything around me, a moment of light and noise in the darkness of space. It has also made me curious about what exists. Beauty, happiness and love are the things that keep us alive, which we need and which we must give. The perception of happiness, which I both give and receive, makes life worth living. I don't align myself with those who find life a burden and just get on with things, looking for happiness in acquiring tiresome property – I don't think of that at all. The pathetic desire to possess something is actually just a dull exhilaration. To what purpose do so many people strive so tensely, and yet still seem unsatisfied and sullen? I find it horrifying how few of my fellow creatures are happy simply with the pure feeling of existence.

I rejoice in my liveliness and my perceptions every day. Life is my luxury, imagination is my wealth, and I'm already in heaven now, in this life. We're here to enjoy life; and we're constantly breathing the atmosphere above us, which we're so eager to describe as our "blue heaven". What else are we waiting for, clinging to vague ideas of a paradise that's supposed to release us from the difficulties of dealing with life? Greedy humanity always wants more than life; it wants to get into paradise, its glittering supermarket of rewards for a life of hardship. It makes me want to laugh! They should have trading stamps to look forward to. Then they would be able to cope with their existence easier. The brief and privileged period of perception passes quickly, and many have not realised that divinity rests in their own creativity. People just have to discover and love themselves and take each other seriously. If they can do that, they will get on well with other people.

The last time I was coming back from the supermarket, four small boys, perhaps about eight years old, were walking in front of me. They were all the same height, and were carrying satchels on their backs. A handsome Turkish boy was walking a little way away and slightly behind the others. They whispered together for a while, and then the first one – who wore intellectual-looking

10

nickel-framed glasses – turned to the boy walking behind and asked him, "Have you got any money?"

With a fearful expression, raising his eyebrows obsequiously to his forehead, the dark-haired boy answered, "Yes, I have."

"Then you can come with us," said the first speaker generously.

The newly accepted companion then scrutinised his three dubious friends from the side, to see whether they all actually agreed. They weren't looking at him at all. I thought that it must really be worth a lot to the Turkish boy to be allowed to walk along with boys from his school. He wanted to belong, at least to all outward appearances. I was disgusted, unhappy and angry at the same time about what I had just seen, and was unable to stop myself speaking to the first one, because he was the ringleader. "Did I hear correctly what you just said to your friend? Does he have to pay money to ingratiate himself with you?"

"He isn't my friend at all," the young hooligan justified himself.

I was ready with my next question when the Turkish boy broke in, even defending the first boy. "I know him from my school. He doesn't do anything to me, but he isn't my friend either."

I was shaken by the fact that the feeling of belonging, of not being an outsider, was so important to the boy. He'd probably done everything because of that. I tried again: "And if he hadn't got any money, would he be allowed to go with you then?"

This time, the second boy answered: "We don't really care about him. He should do what he likes."

"But you don't actually leave him the option," I persisted. "You fleece him like robbers, and I think that's really rotten of you."

The three boys just laughed and shook their heads. They didn't want to understand, and they didn't see any injustice in their behaviour.

Why am I telling you about this encounter? Because it's a good example of early bullying, and in particular of money-making and discontent. The three boys had learned this from watching their parents, or from someone else, and had adopted it in their own behaviour. Morality and humane manners are gradually disappearing in our modern throw-away society. These days, almost everything – even our values, even love – is treated like rubbish. Unfortunately, I make similar observations relatively often, and I know that, even in the case of such young people, the roots of later dissatisfaction and excess are sprouting.

When I got home again, I began my daily housework, and I spent a long time thinking about the earlier events, which had saddened me. I thought about my own development as well. I've always been interested in people, and have supported them wherever I've been able. At the same time, I've also learned a lot from them. I've also supported myself. In the end, I'm only human, and I like doing things like that. I've never found it tiresome to look after myself. I wash my own clothes, clean my flat, groom myself carefully, and I like going shopping, where I often make such observations. I find cooking a relaxing and creative activity, which I can only recommend to those harassed by a world of appointments and schedules. It does me good to spoil myself, and I often cook for my friends, who always enjoy my cooking.

A short time ago, I was visited by Karl Bartos and Andy McCluskey from Orchestral Manoeuvres In The Dark. The evening became very cheerful, not least because of several bottles of dry Soave, and we messed about tipsily until early morning. Andy put pressure on me to make music again: "You're gonna be the Julio Iglesias of electronic music, I promise, Wolfgang." (He had discovered my romantic side.) But I wasn't interested in a career as a singer, and I certainly didn't want to be compared with the Latin crooner. At the time, Karl was working with Andy on the latter's new record, and was also quite happy again with his own band, Electric Music. Apart from that, he still also produces other artists in his studio.

At any rate, it's quite normal for me to demonstrate my happiness. At the same time, I express myself and communicate this happiness through the medium of music. At least, I try to do so, because I've gained so much from it during my life.

When my mother was still alive, she told me that once, when I was playing, I asked my five-year-old twin brother, "Winfried, are you actually happy that you exist?" She said that my brother thought about this for a long time, and then answered sagely: "Yes, Wolfgang, I am actually happy that I exist." At this, she said that I had agreed with him, saying, "Me too, actually." Even at an early age, it was important to me to know that those close to me were just as happy and contented. (Nevertheless, Winfried did work a hesitant "actually" into his answer; he was always a little more thoughtful and quieter than me.)

Winfried has dedicated his life to people and their welfare. Today, he is a doctor in Bonn, and is very popular with his patients. We can only thank our parents that they passed a lot of lucky genes onto us. When I die, my paradise will have passed, and then I shall be sad that I may no longer be able to give or experience happiness. It must be terrible not to feel colour, to taste light, to catch aromas, to stroke someone's skin and to enjoy voices or sounds.

DÜSSELDORF, 14 AUGUST 1999

It was about four o'clock and I was on my way from the station through the Graf-Adolf Straße, heading towards the Altstadt. Under my arm I had a small piece of plastic with which to repair the Perspex cover of the neon "Wolfgang" light which we used onstage. Suddenly, a small, modern, black town car swung illegally around and stopped at the pavement right next to me, braking sharply. The passenger window hummed down and the driver, a young woman with long, black hair and a friendly smile, leant across towards me and said, "Can you possibly tell me how I get to the Kunstakademie?"

While I attempted to explain the rather complicated route to this lovely girl, it suddenly occurred to me that the address was very near my destination. "I'm going the same way. If you're not afraid, you can take me with you, and I'll direct you straight to the door."

13

The girl quickly scrutinised me from head to toe and then threw the things lying on the passenger seat into the back. The door was opened, and I sat next to her in the small car. It seemed to be completely new, and was extremely well cared for, as was the young woman herself, whom I was then able to observe more closely. She was elegantly clothed, and looked more like a southern European, perhaps about 25 or 26. Slender brown arms emerged from the armholes of her black summer dress, and her manicured hands held the small steering wheel firmly.

As we drove off, she observed me closely with inquisitive side glances of her lovely eyes under spiritedly curved black brows. "What's that transparent material on your lap? It looks a bit like cartoon film, doesn't it?"

I was somewhat astonished. "How did you get that idea?"

"I'm studying film and video art," she said, "and we often use something like that to make cartoon films."

"No, no," I replied. "You're wrong there. I need it for something else." After several minutes of fast driving through the semi-darkness of the Rhine tunnel, which was full of afternoon traffic and to which I'd had to redirect her twice, she tried again: "But you are an artist, though?"

"You're not completely wrong," I confirmed. "I'm a composer and lyricist."

"I make a bit of music as well," she answered. "Would you like to hear it? I have a cassette with me."

By this time, I'd become inquisitive, and requested my impertinent chauffeuse to put her cassette into the player. A dreamy piece started playing in the style of the French *chanson*, but accompanied by electronic music. I'd never heard such a combination before and it was extremely interesting. I really liked her voice so I cheekily asked if she would like to sing with me some time.

"What sort of music do you make?" she wanted to know. "Is it electronic, too? And what's the name of your band?" I told her of my previous position in Kraftwerk and everything that I am doing with Yamo now, and she let out an amazed cry. "It's not possible! You? From Kraftwerk? I've loved your music since I was 17."

I can't deny that her enthusiasm was very flattering, and I confirmed her questions proudly. As soon as we emerged from the tunnel, the girl pulled the car over to the edge of the road and stopped. "Now, seriously, do you know what I threw into the back when you got in?"

"No! How am I supposed to know that?" I answered, amused.

"It's my university assignment." Her black eyes were flashing. "The subject of my paper is 'Coincidences That Do Not Exist'." I was flabbergasted, just as she was herself.

"You're in the right place with me," I explained to the amazed girl, "because I don't believe in coincidences either, but in radiant energy or a sense of mission." Thus started an inexhaustible theme for the rest of the journey.

It wasn't much further to the Kunstakademie, and we parted as friends, not forgetting to exchange addresses and to arrange a date for later – without radiant energy! – for her to make a vocal recording for my new album.

These sorts of everyday occurrences really make me happy, and show that people often sense an extremely special mutual attraction, if they are only ready and able to perceive it. She could have asked anyone else the way, but she asked me. Coincidence? Don't make me laugh. The height of happiness!

# 2 Khachaturian In Fever
## Playing Marbles, Rustling And Whispering

FRANKFURT AM MAIN, 17 JULY 1951
I began to be fascinated by everything that rings or resounds at the tender age of four. I tapped, knocked and patted every kind of material that came into my hands to find out the sound that it made. Nobody played a musical instrument in our house; we only sang under the Christmas tree when we were obliged to do so, and I remember with unease that this was always very forced.

I was born in 1947 in Frankfurt Am Main, a city that had been destroyed by bombing during the war. My parents were Hildegard and Heribert, and I was a twin, their third son. I enjoyed playing on the nearby bombsites with my brothers and the neighbours' children. There, it was possible to find all kinds of resonant objects. Of course, hideous and dangerous things also lay under the heaps of stone from the bombed houses in the Rubenstraße, which were overgrown with weeds and tall clumps of plants.

Sometimes the voyages of discovery into the deep, dark cellars were perilous, and we would go home covered in scrapes or ragged wounds on a regular basis. The climbs that we risked always frightened our parents but, because it was the period of reconstruction after the Second World War, there were hardly any toys and we had to devise our own games. However, there were no limits to our imaginations. The summers were always hot and we didn't need much. Everyone had just as little as everybody else, and for that reason there was nothing anyone had to be envious of. We didn't wear anything apart from sandals and the obligatory lederhosen, which were much too big and flapped around our thin bodies.

We often hung around the streets, where we would wait eagerly for the yellow ice cart, pulled by two horses, that supplied families with ice. For ten pfennigs the driver would skilfully strike measured pieces from metre-long sticks of ice and throw them into the tin bowl that we presented to him. Small, ice-cold splinters would fly glistening through the warm summer air and fall to the ground. They were our booty. We fought each other greedily for them and quickly sucked them away. The crunching and cracking of the heavy, crystalline bars had a tremendous fascination for me.

Father had been in the Luftwaffe during the war. He had been captured by the Americans, and had brought back swing records by Benny Goodman, Glenn Miller and Duke Ellington. At that time, Glenn Miller's 'In The Mood' was the hit that was heard constantly on AFN, the military radio station of the American occupiers. Father often played the fragile shellac discs, featuring the music that he had come to know during his "war adventure" (one of his own extended tours with his lads), on a cabinet gramophone in our flat in Sachsenhausen. Every time he did this, he would have to put a new steel needle into the guide slot in the heavy arm of the pick-up and screw it firmly into the pick-up's membrane. Then he would turn it with a crank handle on the side and pull the motor's spring mechanism to gain a few minutes of revolutions from the turntable, which was covered with a black velvet cloth. Opening two doors in the lower part of the wooden cupboard revealed a folded horn that released the music.

This expensive black music box was exciting for us, but we were strictly forbidden to fiddle with it. However, its music and the perfect clockwork mechanism fascinated us to such an extent that we immediately fell upon it as soon as our parents had left the flat and had forgotten to lock the living room in which the gramophone imposingly stood. Even if the room was locked, my twin brother and I skilfully let ourselves in with a skeleton key that we had made ourselves.

In the sideboard there was also a small bar. We would regularly have a nip of the sweet, creamy egg liqueur that was kept there, making up the level with milk. I couldn't get enough of it. Again and again I diluted the sweet concoction, until it looked quite pale and tasted completely weak. At some point, the trick was discovered and my father put me across his knee. I didn't make a sound. I was too proud to show my pain. I despised him for this cowardly act, which I'm sure he committed only because he wanted to play the strong man in front of his wife.

At an early age, I noticed that my father was a weak man who could not assert himself, especially with my mother. I also noticed that he didn't enjoy hitting me, that he did it for Hilde, who expected him to instil discipline in me. In any case, Mother wore the trousers in our family, and I can still see her before me in her elegant dresses or painting her fingernails. I would watch her secretly through the keyhole as she put on her sexy underwear, which I sometimes slipped on myself when she wasn't there. The scraps of silk felt wonderfully smooth and cool against my skin, and I would twirl enthusiastically in front of the mirror, observing myself from all angles.

We lived with our great-grandmother, on the second floor of her house at 6 Rubenstraße, and before we went to bed she would take us into her enormous room, which was packed with furniture. She would seat us at the large dining table, draped with a velvet cloth, and would read to us from *Grimm's Tales* using her enormous magnifying glass. At the same time, she would pull a cord to bring the ceiling lamp down low over the table so that the room became really dim. During this, the long fringe of the hanging lamp, knotted with glass beads, threw ghostly shadows and bizarre twinkling reflections onto the velvet cloth. The iron, coal-burning stove – on which my great-grandmother loved to stew apples – stood near the bay window. The whole room smelled of dried fruit and dried plums, which stood in rows on the sideboard, made into manikins with toothpicks. A square radio also stood there, and the alert old woman would often sit in front of this to listen to the news and the speeches of Konrad Adenauer, the first federal chancellor. She admired him beyond all measure. She was absolutely convinced that he was "the only sensible man in Germany". The atmosphere on these evenings was extremely sumptuous, and it made us receptive to the stories that she read to us. It's easy to imagine what will become of children who have the most beautiful and spine-chilling fairy stories read to them in such a comfortable environment. We couldn't have had better training for our imaginations.

Our father encouraged this education of the senses, and he was always photographing us and making short films of us. He was a member of a film club in Frankfurt that arranged regular competitions, in which he participated with friends and the whole family. These were always the most exciting times, when we were allowed to dress up. We felt like stars. I was hardly able to contain myself, and would often break into confused laughter because I didn't want it to end.

There was a lot of laughter in our family. My mother was a spirited person, full of *joie de vivre*, and she enjoyed entertaining friends and hosting parties with her husband. We children would lie in our beds at night listening to the rhythmic Latin American music, the samba, rumba, cha-cha-cha, mambo and foxtrot. I can still hear their lively rhythms.

Friday, our bath day, was always the most cheerful day. We would all sit in the bath at the same time and our father would scrub us. The water had to be heated laboriously by briquettes in a water heater beforehand. Washing was never done without some performance. Play-acting and performance were our favourite occupations.

In my mother's opinion, though, I dreamed and dawdled too often and too eagerly. I was always somewhere else with my

19

thoughts, and certainly not with "sensible" things, and she often had to call me back to reality harshly. Our grandmother, on the other hand, allowed us every freedom. I was able to sit at the piano and "play". It wasn't proper music, more like a violent, impetuous hammering on the compliant keys. My rhythmical din must have been a torment for Nana, because she would fly into her kitchen and drink a miniature bottle of champagne to ease her blood pressure.

I loved my great-grandmother most of all. She was always ready with wonderful, spine-chilling, beautiful stories for us. In the summer, I was sometimes allowed to spend my holidays at her little house in Filsen, a little Catholic place directly on the Rhine, opposite Boppard. The village surrounded the tiny church on the slope of the vineyards of the Rhineland Palatinate, squeezed in between the old B7 road on the bank of the Rhine and the tracks of the railway, which at that time was still running with hissing steam trains. The railway embankment gaped in the middle of this narrow area as if it had been cut by a knife. There was only one railway crossing, and if the signalman came out of his little house and put on his cap to crank down the barriers with a signal by hand, then nothing could be done for some time – Filsen was cut in half.

My pious great-grandmother had been friendly with the sexton of the church for a long time, and she always sent me to him to sound the bells at six o'clock in the evening. I really enjoyed doing this. I would pull on the thick, knotted rope long and rhythmically with my thin arms until I could hold fast to it and let myself be pulled up by the swing of the heavy, cast-iron bell. I hardly weighed anything, and I was no burden to the bell. Even then, the sexton praised me for my regular rhythm. "Boy," he would say, "you actually do that better than me." After this feat of strength, I would have to milk the sexton's goat in the stall that was built directly onto the church. Then I would proudly run down the dusty lanes to my great-grandmother's house, balancing the steaming milk in a porcelain cup filled to the brim. Often, however, only half of the contents of the cup would arrive. "The elixir of life for my old age," the clever old woman would mischievously explain to me.

In the evening we would often sit on the low wall of the old federal highway, on which hardly any cars still drove. It was at least 100 metres from the house, and we would watch the slow and ponderous passenger ships and the white Cologne-Düsseldorf paddle steamer chugging by, with tugs puffing deep in the water, pulling barges laden with cargo behind them on long steel hawsers. The nearer to us they passed, the greater our pleasure in the waves of their wake which swelled threateningly, slapping against the bank.

How I enjoyed myself with her then, and how I loved those intimate days in Filsen, when I had the dear old lady to myself for once. I would never have let her go, but several years later, at the age of 88, she was knocked over by a car when crossing the same road, breaking both legs. We all thought that she wouldn't come out of hospital but, after a few weeks, and hobbling bravely on a walking stick, she was discharged and drove home. We couldn't believe it. It was simply impossible to crush her, and with her robust constitution she lived to the age of 96. I hope I enjoy such a brilliant old age, as well as such a lively mind. Katharina was a real example of *joie de vivre* and strength.

The family moved from Frankfurt In Hessen to Deutsche Eck in Koblenz, where my father had taken up a better professional position as an optician. At this time, I became infected with music. An aunt had bought me a mouth organ, and this became my constant companion. The instrument was easy to learn, and because it was small I could always carry it with me in my trouser pocket. I often played short melodies, characterised by passionate melancholy, during Sunday walks with our parents along the banks of the Rhine to Braubach and Schloß Stolzenfels. At the age of eight, my twin brother seemed to like them particularly, prophesying, "You will become world famous one day, Wolfgang."

It was a treat for us if were allowed to listen to exciting radio plays. With the light in our room having already been put out, only the magical green glass pane of the station indicator would weakly illuminate the chest of drawers on which the radio stood. The darkness allowed our thoughts and our imaginative powers to develop as we heard the voices of the actors and the stories. This was more effective than television because we had to picture the figures, the landscapes and the events in our minds.

I was particularly fond of the dim light and the most delicate sounds at Saturday confessional at St Joseph's Catholic Church. On the other hand, it was always extremely shameful for me to betray my sins to the inquisitive chaplain in the intimate confessional. I often lied to him about the most lewd transgressions against the Christian catechism, so that pearls of sweat stood out on his forehead as he sat behind the carved wooden grille. We had the perfect relationship: he wanted these "filthy sins" confessed comprehensively while I wanted a long penalty. Ten Our Fathers and ten Hail Marys was the lowest penance that I was looking for. Then, contented, I would dart out of the confessional and look for an old woman on the women's side. When I found one, I would kneel quite near to her in the row and fold my hands, hardly able to reach above the top of the pew. I would close my eyes and concentrate completely on the sound of her whispering lips. Women said their rosaries – which were knotted with glass beads – extremely quietly. I would search for the quiet clicking of the beads and the whispering.

In the late-afternoon twilight of the church vault, and in the sight of the ruby-red eternal light on the high altar, I once saw a woman turn the tissue pages of her small, gold-edged prayer book. She did it so gently, delicately moistening her middle finger on the tip of her tongue, that the gentle rustling of the wafer-thin pages sent an appreciative shiver down my spine and gave me an erection. Again and again, I sought this enticing combination of clicking, rustling and quiet whispering. Every time, the same shiver would run down my young spine. I could abandon myself to this sinful pleasure of delicate listening again and again. I just couldn't get enough of it and I was therefore happy if I was allowed to make a long penance. Even today, I'm aroused by even the slightest whiff of the smell of incense.

At the age of ten, I discovered the wild world of transistors. My elder brother had brought home a small kit from his physics class and managed to put together a functioning radio with a crystal detector, diodes and other basic parts. You could receive radio waves with earphones, but I think only on medium or long wave. It crackled and rustled horribly, but you did get something. It was exciting to build your own small radio with so few components, and to hear real sounds that came from somewhere far away. I was bowled over by it and it really stimulated my imagination. As is always the case with siblings, I absolutely had to have my own "spy radio", as I called it.

Then, however, I discovered a comprehensive improvement on my brother's physics homework in the window display of a radio dealer on my way to school: a modern Japanese transistor radio. It even had a small built-in loudspeaker and a chrome telescopic aerial. I fell for this little box immediately. I remember clearly that it cost a little more than 10 DM, and that it was made of white Bakelite, with a tuning disc set behind a magnifying glass. An attractive-looking strap meant you could hold the thing in your hand and show it off when you were running around outside. It was so modern and it made me look good in front of my friends. I saved all of my pocket money for weeks (which at that time was 1.50 DM a week), and when I'd bought it I didn't let the thing go. It also had an earpiece, so I was able to sift through the stations in bed at night, hidden from my brothers. I liked listening to short wave the best because it brought foreign languages and new sounds from faraway places to me.

At the same time, I discovered that I really enjoyed music of all kinds. I had a secret spot, behind the gooseberry bushes in the furthest corner of my grandmother's large garden, where I would stay for hours on Sunday afternoons, turning the tuning dial and searching continually for strange noises. I was particularly taken by human voices.

23

I once had a cold and a high fever, and had to stay in bed while my brother went to school without me. From the radio loudspeaker in the children's room I heard Marke Saba caught up in the fever of Aram Khachaturian's 'Sabre Dance'. My burgeoning imagination painted pictures of the dervishes whirling through the Puszta and rattling their sabres. The piece moved something in me that was near my soul and I wanted the feeling to last forever. At my insistence, a record was found, and from then on I wore down my brothers' nerves by constantly playing the tempestuous, dramatic epic on the same Philips portable record player on which my older brother used to listen to hit records. But I liked Khachaturian's composition much better than the stupid, derivative rock 'n' roll of Peter Kraus that my brother was listening to.

Gregor had been bought a Telefunken tape recorder at an early age, and we soon began to produce radio plays, complete with sound effects. We collected everything that could be recorded with a microphone and performed our own invented stories in altered voices. My interest in sounds was growing constantly, and soon I wanted to play an instrument. First I picked the trumpet, but then I wanted to have a piano and later a guitar. Unfortunately, my rather conservative parents wouldn't entertain such "time wasting", especially since Father wasn't earning enough money at that time to be able to satisfy my constantly changing desire for different instruments.

# 3 From Beatnik To Mod
## My Generation

KOBLENZ, DÜSSELDORF, APRIL 1958

We moved from the romantic Deutsche Eck to the glass buildings of the state capital of Westphalia, north of the Rhine. Several years later, when I was attending one of the Düsseldorf secondary modern schools (separately from my twin brother), our English teacher, Frau Menzen, supported her boys' enthusiasm for music. She was an attractive blonde woman, who appeared quite happy to show off her sexy figure, so her enthusiasm was infectious. When she was questioning the class, she would sit up on her desk and cross her shapely legs, her tight skirt often riding dangerously high. I would wait impatiently for the rubbing sound of her nylons, which sent shivers down my spine.

Frau Menzen's erotic influence meant that we all became very good at English. We responded to her relaxed teaching and took note when she suggested forming a band to accompany the songs that we sang together in her lessons. When we sang, we were also supposed to practise correct English pronunciation at the same time. Gospel songs such as 'Swing Low, Sweet Chariot' and 'My Bonny Lies Over The Ocean' were popular English exercises. To accompany these, Rüdiger – a boy who sat next to me in class – would play a guitar, our class spokesman would rattle Father's rumba balls and I would play my mouth organ, which we amplified through a microphone and our old mono radio. The Bellows, my first group, had been born.

In this period, something else happened for the first time in my life. On a mild March evening in 1962, I heard the new sound of stereo. It was the most revolutionary discovery, and its ingenious sound engineers presented their sensational new medium to the world at the Berlin Radio Fair that same year. Through his earlier activity as an altar server at mass in our parish church of St Rochus, my older brother, Gregor, became friendly with the parish priest, who had bought the first portable record player from Dual. In the meeting room of his presbytery he played us stereo versions of Peter Ilitch Tchaikovsky's *Nutcracker Suite* and Bedrich Smetana's *Die Moldau* by candlelight.

This was a really moving experience. Today, it's hard to imagine how we had previously listened to everything in mono. But now it was suddenly possible to correctly locate the positions of the individual instruments of the orchestra in the panorama between two loudspeakers set up apart from each other. This technological musical demonstration was extremely enjoyable, and it has left a lasting impression on me, to the extent that I dedicated one of my favourite songs on my album *Time Pie* to the inventors of stereo sound reproduction.

My parents had a vegetable garden in Lohhausen, Düsseldorf. On one occasion, I was passing the gardens' meeting house and saw a guitar band rehearsing, clearly visible behind a large sheet of glass. The musicians were adults and they had proper amplifiers and a complete drum kit, and they were playing songs by The Spotniks and other guitar bands of the time. It sounded so perfect, so crisply electric, and the guitarist was playing with a great echo effect. I became jealous of how professionally they could play and when I discovered a skiffle band's rehearsal room with a real drum set in our school cellar, it was the final straw. The drums made such a noise and were so electrifying that I immediately wanted to become a drummer.

However, it was a long time before my strict father would allow myself and my twin brother to work in the brewery opposite our house during the summer holidays in order to earn a bit of money. Eventually, though, I was able to buy my first small drum kit, and as a 16-year-old boy I founded The Beathovens with friends from my class at school. We tried to copy The Beatles and the other English beat groups, which we heard constantly on the radio, and it became our Saturday ritual to meet at Rüdiger's house and listen to Radio Luxembourg's Top 20, broadcast on medium wave at four in the afternoon.

One miserable Saturday afternoon in November 1965, bored and frustrated in the living room of our rarely empty apartment, I heard a song on BFBS by The Who. At 16 years old and in the middle of puberty, I was masturbating in the hope of forcing some excitement from the grey day as I heard the lyrics stutter from the radio, constantly attempting the words "my g-g-g-generation". Not realising that the song would become the most significant teenage anthem of all time, I sprayed my sperm with liberating relief in an arc across my parents' fine rococo sofa, on which I was sitting with my trousers around my ankles, deeply moved by the song and moaning from youthful mischief. It was incomprehensible to me that stutterers were even allowed into the recording studios, let alone that their speaking exercises were broadcast, so this revolutionary song shattered everything that I had regarded as good pop music up until then.

While we were used to the pleasant singing of The Beatles' early works, here was a group roaring all of its youthful rage and frustration against a middle-class way of life, which would be unable to appreciate the semen-sticky upholstery of our furniture. I still had my twitching penis in my hand when I noticed the freshly besmirched sofa with satisfaction. I would have loved to have spoiled more of the furniture, since my parents seemed to dedicate more energy and financial resources to the living room than to encouraging the talents of their children. However, I had no juice left, and apart from this I feared being caught. Instead, the rest of

27

the afternoon proceeded less enjoyably, as I washed, brushed and dried the fine damask material of my parents' inherited sofa.

The explosive material of 'My Generation' did me good, and in particular the rebellious end of the song was like a revelation to me; I stored so much anger against my father, who never told me that he loved me, didn't stand by me and seemed to be trying to destroy my first love in an underhand way. If my "useless" music was being discussed at home he would only say, "Nothing will become of you." When The Who sang about the way in which kids are always put down by the older generations, they were speaking my language.

We bought the singles of the newest and most interesting songs that we heard on the radio and practised them in a small cellar in one of our classmates' houses. That was our kingdom. There we rehearsed, dreamed and smoked like crazy. In a short time, The Beathovens had developed into one of the best cover bands around. We played at wild school parties, in dubious clubs and at private parties all around the city. We diligently invested everything that we earned into our equipment, which we had bought in instalments from Jörgenson, a Düsseldorf music store.

Our Saturday performances at the British Army's youth club on the Rhine became a permanent fixture. The club was the favourite place for Düsseldorf youths to have a fling at the weekend. The low building inhabited by the British occupying forces lay in the middle of the Nordpark, on British territory, right next to their own Globe Cinema and the warehouse. The British children and the young locals had a meeting point there, where they could get to know each other and have a good time with music and dancing. Because we always played the most up-to-date beat music, The Beathovens quickly became the house band. Between the dances, couples could go directly outside into the park to cool down and neck. During the warm summer nights, mutual groping and petting in the bushy green spaces was very popular, but patrolling military policemen often disrupted couples with their powerful torches, driving half-naked people from the shrubs. I couldn't join in because I always had to drum, but I would have really liked to roll around in the bushes as well.

During the summer holidays in 1966 and 1967, we made a tour of the north coast in an ancient VW bus. One afternoon, while playing at a dancing competition in a beach café in the Baltic resort of Dahme, we chose our "Miss Beathoven", an androgynous Parisian with a sweet Courrèges hairdo. As fragile as the Eiffel Tower, she began flirting with me at once, very delicately in a typical French way. Inexperienced as I was, when she gave me "*lectures sexuelles*" my ears and everything else turned red. I had my first groupie! The flirtatious mademoiselle later followed me to Düsseldorf to introduce herself to my parents, which was very embarrassing. An adult woman in a sexy little Chanel costume, with fur cap and pointed patent pumps, she stood in the entrance hall of our apartment, asking for my hand in marriage in front of my family. I really wanted the Earth to swallow me up. She actually wanted to marry me, this luscious little lady! But me and marriage? She had to be joking!

Because none of us had a driving licence, my brother Gregor had to drive our "Flummi", which didn't have any functioning bumpers and bounced along the road like a ping-pong ball.

The highlight of my first band as a youth was our appearance as the support act at a concert in the Rheinhalle in Düsseldorf, playing with the German band The Lords and The Who, with a still-stuttering Roger Daltrey. By this time, a proper beat scene had developed in the city and the local newspapers were always reporting about us and our rival groups. We had bought orange corduroy jackets at the exclusive men's outfitters Seelbach especially for the occasion, and appeared elegantly dressed in white shirts and black ties. It was very important to us that the image of The Beathovens was not at all that of conventional rockers. At that time, The Who destroyed their equipment and their guitars after every show. However, on the afternoon of that concert, during rehearsals, I had discovered empty loudspeaker cases and

Marshall amplifiers next to the real ones. The final destruction was just a fake; everything was just show.

The Who's ultra-loud, anarchic performance shook my whole philosophy of obeying and not answering back or making a fuss, and gave me the courage to be angry myself. Undoubtedly, this early English punk band helped me to reject anything that I didn't agree with in the future. Every evening, The Who were only destroying empty boxes and cheap instruments that they had quickly swapped at the end of their show. At that time, I wouldn't have minded if they'd trashed their expensive loudspeakers and fine guitars, either; but even then I understood what they were destroying so brutally and symbolically, and it was a clear signal for me to start to follow my own musical path, even against the will of my parents. After the concert, the drummer of The Lords came into our dressing room and praised us admiringly. "Oh boy, do you have class!" We were blissfully happy.

In the following years, I founded the significantly wilder band Fruit with Klaus Gerber and Volker Langefeld. We'd had to disband the gentle Beathovens because Rüdiger, the guitarist, had fled the draft to Canada. With Fruit, we were the strongest competition for the even more chaotic Harakiri Whoom, whose singer (the son of an actor) was the still-unknown Marius Westernhagen. Harakiri also covered the songs of British and American bands. Marius was an excellent imitator of Rod Stewart and Steve Marriott, and I think that this is still easily detected today.

I didn't begin to develop my own songs until the end of the '60s, with my last amateur band, The Spirits Of Sound. The band comprised myself, the gifted guitarist Michael Rother and singer Wolfgang Riechmann, a charismatic and humorous musician who was later murdered, tragically just before his wonderful debut album, *Riechmann Wunderbar*, was released on Sky Records. It was the time of the hippies and fashion inspired by Twiggy, and as The Spirits we played alongside British stars such as Steve Marriott and The Small Faces, Humble Pie and Peter Frampton at the legendary Teenage Fair, a young people's event at the

Düsseldorf Trade Fair. The famous German film director Kurt Hoffman discovered us there and contracted us to work with Vivi Bach on *Ein Tag Ist Schöner Als Der Andere*, his least important and least successful film.

Drumming had become my whole life, and I was thrashing my drums as violently as Keith Moon. The angrier I was, the better I played drums, and when I was lovesick (as I always was at that age) I beat all my sadness into the expensive skins. I would often go home soaked in sweat and with bleeding hands after night-long sessions in clubs that were far too small and after smoking far too many cigarettes. I was extremely thin at that time, with hardly any reserves of fat, and during such nights I would regularly lose two or three kilos.

It was an extremely unhealthy period, but comradely nonetheless. My musician friends replaced my family, whom I felt increasingly misunderstood me, and from whom I was distancing myself more and more. They were unable to recognise my ambition as being something valuable and deserving of support. I became a rebel and achieved my aims mercilessly and often in a blind rage, much to the distress of my parents, who became increasingly unable to bring me up, awkward as I was. I had become difficult and uncomfortable. I refused everything that had to do with their values and their bourgeois attitudes. I didn't want to keep to their routines, and was totally unable to understand their exaggerated tidiness. I had to do everything differently, and provoked them constantly. I was a beatnik full of youthful strength, and I wanted to show it.

In midsummer I went around in a black roll-necked pullover, baggy black trousers and dark sunglasses, and on top of that sported a crop of hair that was growing longer all the time. I liked myself like that. I felt that this connected me to the English scene. Mother, of course, didn't like me dressing like that and distanced herself from me in public because she found me embarrassing.

When I was 21, I could no longer sleep in the same room as my brothers because it was growing more and more crowded. Two of us were 21 and my older brother was 25, and we still only had one room between us and no privacy. I couldn't handle this close co-existence and decided to move out.

I had arranged to meet my friends at six one Sunday morning in the spring of 1968. They waited punctually below on the street in our VW Bully while I dressed quietly and packed my few belongings. My brothers were still sleeping and I tried not to wake anyone, but my mother appeared in the hallway, wearing her dressing gown, and anxiously asked where I was going so early on a Sunday morning. She had a maternal premonition of a painful change for the family. We began to shout. When I told her that I had to go, she began to cry and tried to prevent me opening the front door. My brothers had woken up and didn't quite understand what was going on. My father stayed comfortably in bed, not wanting to know anything about my departure. He didn't take me seriously, in any case, and by this time I was only communicating with him by leaving notes. With tears in my eyes, I pushed my mother aside and did what I had to do to follow my own path.

Life then began to get really difficult. I moved into a small Heinrichstraße apartment that I had secretly rented and skimpily furnished with financial support from a woman banker with whom I was friendly. I was finally on my own, and very proud. However, I was unhappy there because I felt so misunderstood by my family and because I believed that I'd been forced into causing such sorrow for my dear mother. Still, I had my band and Brigitte, my first great love, and her family, who treated me with affection.

I would never have considered the armed forces, since I felt that I was a complete humanist, and so, as an alternative to military service, I began to perform community service in the medical laboratory of a diabetes clinic. At that time, it wasn't easy to be a conscientious objector, although the possibility for this had already been established in the Basic Law. There was a lengthy and degrading procedure with a strict, judicial test procedure in which my personal attitudes were called into question. When I had finally won my case, I had also won my first battle for my conscience and against Father and the omnipotence of an unpopular state, which had made me into a party injured by war. If my case had failed, I would have been sent to prison, in any case, for my conscience. I had already imagined that, and had factored it into my plans in advance.

Then, because I was freed from the responsibilities of active service, I enrolled on a course in interior design at the craft college, and I also spent some time engaged in practical training with an architect. He had advertised in the local paper for a young man who wanted to learn the trade by working his way up from the bottom. It was just the right thing for me, because I could earn some money towards the rent for my small pad.

I must confess that I didn't really enjoy studying. Actually, it was more the image of my parents' concern that their Wolfgang should become a good architect that spurred me on. I resigned from the interior design course after four semesters and concentrated completely on the practical course and The Spirits Of Sound. Uwe Fritsch, Ralf Ermisch, Michael Rother and our popular mentor and artistic adviser Rolf Kauffeld often visited me in my small apartment on the Heinrichstraße. The mother of Anita Pallenberg – the German girlfriend of Jimi Hendrix, whom we worshipped – lived in the same house. There together we discovered psychedelic rock, smoked dope and by candlelight we listened to the records of King Crimson, Santana, Jefferson Airplane, The Byrds and Emerson, Lake And Palmer, who were already using a synthesiser. However, The Spirits soon suffered a blow that would destroy the band, through the cruel poaching of our revered guitarist, Michael Rother.

# 4 *Kraftwerk On Mars?*
## *Kling Klang Melted?*

DÜSSELDORF, 15 FEBRUARY 1999
I was sitting with two visionary friends of Kraftwerk, who were telling me that they would regard the recording of a new Kraftwerk album with doubt. Martin and Markus, both from Düsseldorf, predicted that it could be a big disappointment. They said that, after fans all over the world had been waiting for a new sound for over twelve years, this wasn't so funny any more, and general expectations had been raised so high that hardly any musical satisfaction would be achieved.

In the meantime, Ralf and Florian were also getting on a bit, they reckoned, and as they grew older they were becoming contented and no longer inquiring, and an inquiring mind is vital for research. For these two, Kraftwerk was a band of astronauts, inventors and researchers of precise sound and romantic poetry, who flew them through the gloom of life into a "kling-klanging" galaxy so that they could be left to their own devices there. For my friends, "a mythical disappearance of the group would be best".

Martin imagined that we might be able to fly to Mars with the next space shuttle, as NASA had already invited us to do, to give the first interplanetary concert there. "On the way into space," he said, "the probe would be caught in the particle stream of an

Aurora Borealis and the link to the ship would be severed. Will they then have landed on the distant planet, or will Kraftwerk be drawn into dark space with the new sound of the veiled sphinx of the ice-cold Northern Lights, which has never yet been heard?" In this way, according to Markus and Martin, the myth of their beloved group could be best frozen and maintained for posterity in the future.

## COLOGNE, 17 FEBRUARY 1999

On the other hand, the intellectual Ralph and Robert from Cologne thought that one day Ralf and Florian would realise that they had worn out too many musicians. The humour of the themes and the lightness of the sounds would have disappeared, along with the inspiration of Karl and Wolfgang, their long-term colleagues, and these creators would go on a meditative pilgrimage. They believed that Florian would move through the world in his new guise as a technological preacher, and that Ralf would continue to dream of a fusion between man and machine. He would ride around the Earth on a racing bike and would be the first to climb Mount Everest with this mode of transport. Acknowledging that he could never become one with his machine, he would finally retire to the retreat of a Tibetan monastery. The "Fifth System" of Kraftwerk, the Kling Klang Reaktor, would meanwhile begin to live independently and develop passionate feelings. It would begin to melt down into a huge lump, incandescent with red-hot despair because of its inability to dispose of its sounds. The robots would break free from their corner and would have to give up futile love play. Angry that they hadn't been given sexual organs, they would switch off the Kling Klang Reaktor, but they would be in too much of a hurry and their stick-like arm and leg prostheses would get in their way. They would find the wrong switch because of their clumsiness and, tragically, would also destroy themselves. According to Ralph and Robert, the electronic melted lump would stand as a work of art in the Cologne Ludwig Museum, of all places, to remind all of those who have come too late.

I have always known it. Our friends have broad imaginations and a delightful sense of humour. People who possess these characteristics are attracted to each other like magnets. This applies both to fans and to musicians. If you look at it in this way, I couldn't have avoided joining Kraftwerk in 1973. Even if they had all been part of a criminal conspiracy, I wouldn't have been frightened away.

# 5 At The Invitation Of Ralf And Florian

DÜSSELDORF, 19 JULY 1973

In the hottest summer of the early '70s, I was visited by Ralf Hütter and Florian Schneider-Esleben in the architects' office, where I was completing my practical course in store building. Several months before the visit, The Spirits Of Sound had been disbanded after Michael Rother had been enticed away by a professional group. His new band was called Kraftwerk, and it was well respected in Düsseldorf.

My colleagues and myself, then 25 years old, had had a depressing time. We simply couldn't find a good guitarist, let alone one that could be compared to Michael. Of course, we were also envious of him for joining a professional group. When I'd started my course, it had been more out of a sense of pragmatism than from real interest in the architectural profession. Urged by my parents, I'd successfully completed a cabinet-maker's apprenticeship after leaving school, but I'd only completed the four semesters of the interior design course, and then only half-heartedly.

After The Spirits Of Sound had been disbanded, I felt deserted and unhappy, uncertain of my musical future. I had even sold my fantastic drum kit. While I sat at the drawing board, unenthusiastically drafting ground plans and wall views of large department stores, again and again my thoughts returned to music. My memories of my previous bands wouldn't give me any peace. They had been my life and my love. I'd felt such freedom when we had been in the rusty VW bus at weekends, making appearances in clubs and schools. I missed it so much. It was the opposite of what I had experienced in my unartistic family.

I only had a vague idea of Michael's new group. I had once been to one of their gigs at the Clara Schumann Gymnasium in Düsseldorf-Golzheim. On that occasion there had just been a lot of noise, and their performance had sounded like Stukka air raids – they obviously enjoyed imitating the sounds of war. It certainly wasn't music, and I was horrified. Why was Michael getting involved in something like this? As I later learned, this was experimental music, but I can still remember one song that had some sort of a structure. It was called 'Ruck-Zuck' and, now and again, it was even played on the radio. The interesting thing about it was that Florian played rhythmical and accentuated transverse flute on it. There was no singing, but the song had another distinctive feature because the drumming of Klaus Dinger sounded so stoical and mechanical. Later, the recording companies and the media would stupidly call it "krautrock".

So now these two gentlemen were suddenly standing in my office, hemming and hawing a little. They began by complimenting me. It seems that they had previously seen me perform, and had heard me playing drums with my band in a club in Mönchengladbach. The club had been called Budike, and it was an unusual venue because it hosted performances from amateur bands. The Spirits Of Sound had covered radio hits fairly perfectly there, and it had been the best training on our instruments that we could have had. Sometimes we were even paid, although we didn't actually need much, because most of us were still living with our parents. But Ralf and Florian had heard me there and thought that I was "a good drummer". They said that my timing was really good and asked me whether I felt like going to their rehearsal room some time to do a session with them. That was a real surprise to me, because I really couldn't imagine how I could fit in with their music, and I thought of Michael; but the temptation of making music again and the comfortable feeling of their flattering remarks left me no other choice than to give them my cautious assent.

This band, which took their unusual name from an energy company, already had a proper star aura. Apart from this, I have always been inquisitive, and I wanted to see their rehearsal room, so we arranged to meet on the following evening in the Mata Hari, a modern bistro in a passage in the old part of Düsseldorf which was famous for its unconventional clientèle.

Ralf and I liked such "soft" venues. All kinds of people from the world of showbusiness met there: the most kind-hearted entertainers, disco queens, people from the fashion world, and naturally, if the IGEDO trade fair was there, often some of the most beautiful models in the world were as well. Above all, it was also a meeting place for the crooks of the old town, the gamblers and the gangsters.

When I entered the Mata Hari at the arranged time, Ralf and Florian were already sitting on an upholstered bench at a small table in a corner of the room, where they had a good view of people coming and going. People there liked showing themselves off and observing other people. Bright lighting from many coloured neon lights and advertising signs gave the establishment a kitschy atmosphere, in which everyone could enjoy a dandified entrance.

Ralf was sitting on the bench with his legs tightly crossed. With his pale complexion he appeared very doll-like, and although his grin was cautious he was enjoying the situation. With his insurance salesman's framed glasses straight from the '50s and his shoulder-length hair, he looked more like a character from the classic film *Psycho*. Ralf's skin-tight, black leather trousers were legendary. I could see that he'd been impressed by the style of Jim Morrison of The Doors. I learned that he always wore pointed, winkle-picker ankle-boots, like The Beatles, and that he had several pairs of these. At any rate, I almost always saw him wearing only this type of footwear, apart from his white moccasins. (Later, when we

39

were on tour, he would touch these up with white shoe colouring instead of cleaning them.) I also noticed his transparent nail varnish. He made a quite a feminine impression on me, and I liked that because I like men with feminine attitudes.

On the other hand, Florian had a preference for German peasant fashion, wearing a loden jacket, a cotton shirt with checked pattern, flannel trousers and an elegant neckerchief. He could have been an actor from a sentimental regional German film. Both of them seemed extremely unusual to me, because this was the outgoing hippie period, with a lot of romanticism and even more colourful dress. A lot of people could be seen running around wearing wide baggy trousers with sewn-in, crushed folds.

For myself, I favoured dungarees and white silk shirts for everyday clothes, platform shoes above all. How I loved this new fashion, which made me taller! Those shoes increased my height by at least two centimetres. Previously, at 172cm, I had felt that I was definitely too short. For this reason, I clung for so long to these platformed soles, which I sometimes sprayed with green metallic car paint. I wanted to make an impression with my appearance. I absolutely wanted to be *in*. What else could have reinforced my self-confidence? I'd even grown a moustache, *à la* D'Artagnan of the Musketeers.

We were as different in appearance as we were in our internal attitudes and family backgrounds, when we met on this warm, musically historical summer evening, none of us quite knowing how we should proceed. It was after five o'clock, as I didn't get out of work until that time. Ralf had ordered a whisky and coke, Florian was drinking bitter lemon and I had a coke with a dash of lemon juice, which is still my favourite drink on hot days today. At 25 I wasn't interested in alcohol at all, but I liked smoking cigarettes, as both of them observed with raised eyebrows, although they refrained from comment. We chatted a little about this and that and everything that we'd done in the last few years. The conversation was more of an ice-breaking affair, and our meeting was rather embarrassing and awkward. Ralf suggested that we should just drive over to their rehearsal room. "We'll just see what we can do there, *ahm*." He had an unusual way of clearing his throat, as if he was uncertain or embarrassed by something.

Ralf and Florian paid for our drinks and went through the passage to the swinging door to the Hunsrückenstraße. Through the window of a fashion boutique called Superstar For Men, they greeted several effeminate-looking salesmen who were dressed in leather and who waved back with incredibly vigorous gestures.

Ralf owned an old, battered and pale-grey VW Beetle, which looked like an official local government vehicle. The seats were covered in moulded grey artificial leather that smelled sour. We drove to Stresemannplatz by way of the Kasernenstraße, and then turned left into the Graf-Adolf Straße. We drove on almost as far as the main station, then right into the Mitropstraße. It was my first visit to the Kraftwerk studio.

Ralf was a very careful and confident driver. He didn't need a car to look swanky and show off. His driving was very restrained and courteous, and I greatly admired his attitude in traffic.

We stopped in front of a house clad in yellow tiles and with a large rolling door, an ugly building from the '50s with many similar-sized windows. It was a typical office building, such as had been built everywhere in German cities after the War, featuring functional architecture without any particular individuality, apart from the ugly tiled façade. Florian, who had been sitting in the passenger seat, unlocked the electric lock at the side of the door with a BKS key. The door began to move with a loud, metallic sound. (I've heard that sound so often that it is still perfectly stored in my memory today.) The door was constructed of horizontal ribs that were wound around a roll by means of an electric motor. When the door was half open, Ralf drove the VW into a large enclosed courtyard behind the house. Florian immediately locked the door behind us and the door came down automatically.

The courtyard was just as ugly as the rest of the building. Everything was painted dark brown. I hated dark brown. Brown mixed with orange and olive green was the most unaesthetic combination of the '70s. On the right there was a wooden loading stage that was used by the HGVs of the electrical installation company which had its offices on the upper floor. There were also the storerooms of other companies on the ground floor and in the basement.

We walked up the ramp through an open doorway and stood in front of a cheap wooden door. After it was opened, we walked through a small anteroom full of junk and then through another door that appeared to be just as amateurish. This door wasn't locked because we found ourselves in the studio itself, a large room about 60 metres long and four and a half metres high. The ceiling was a transverse-running vault of bricks, which had been thinly plastered so that the original structure was still visible. Egg cartons were stuck to parts of the bare brick walls, attached there in the hope of making the place look like a studio and to achieve some sound insulation.

There was also a window to the left of the door, but it was closed and crudely blocked by a heavy, enclosed box made of wooden boards, with thick dark brown felt stuck all around it. The box had the inner dimensions of the height of the window and was attached to a hinge that was fixed onto the side wall. In this way it was possible to swivel the box into the hollow and press it firmly into place. The felt band was extremely good insulation. The device simply but effectively insulated the studio from outside noise, and this was absolutely essential, as I later experienced for myself.

We stood on a smooth concrete floor, which showed enormous cracks in some places. Florian switched on a naked ceiling light, which he immediately augmented with multicoloured illumination – two neon signs in light-blue neon letters stood on the floor forming the first names of the two musicians. Florian also switched on several other coloured neon tubes that were lying in the corners on the floor, which bathed the walls in cold, bright light. There was also a brass living room standard lamp with a swan neck, coloured paper cones and a plastic pineapple. Lamps like that were familiar to me from my parents' apartment. They were the dust collectors of the '50s, and belonged with the standard three-piece suite. However, I've never liked these lamps, and its ironic presence was a mockery of middle-class existence.

Florian noticed my strange mood and attempted to introduce some friendliness with pleasant words and jokes. I had the feeling that he liked me a lot, while Ralf seemed to be distancing himself from me. It seemed that there were two workstations for the musicians. I recognised this from the arrangement of the keyboard instruments, which were new to me because I came from a guitar band. Ralf had positioned himself to the left of the room and Florian had grouped his devices to the right. This wouldn't change in the years to come.

Hesitantly, they each went to their instruments, flicked several switches and turned on a lot of lights. This looked exciting because it had something electric about it. The first keys that they pressed produced sounds that my ears had never heard before. I'd had no idea that they used a synthesiser. It was simply fantastic that these innovative instruments could produce such brilliant effects with so few tones. The sound of the synthesiser ranged between velvety rich and mercilessly hard. I was astonished. The entire set-up looked more like a laboratory set up especially for experiments on sympathetic ears.

Then, full of pride, Ralf showed me his synthesiser. It was a Minimoog, at that time as expensive as a new VW, which was a fortune for him. He also played a Farfisa organ, and an old Hammond B3 stood in the corner behind him, sawed through in the middle so that he could transport it to gigs.

Florian's "witch's kitchen" was more difficult to understand. It had a number of remarkable effects machines, a small console, a band echo with the famous magical eye and a brand-new ARP synthesiser, which didn't have any mechanical keys in the usual sense but instead had only key symbols printed onto it, which closed a contact when pressed. He also used one of his transverse flutes, which he amplified through a Shure microphone and distorted with wonderful echoes. There was also an oscilloscope standing on top of his box which reproduced the optical frequency image of the sounds played on a green screen. It looked very modern and technical.

What was I supposed to do there, though? There was actually no proper drum kit, although they had both offered me the use of one. There was only a small miniature drum kit for children or really small people standing at the back of the room to the left, in the windowless corner. It comprised a wobbly bass drum, a snare drum with a terribly worn skin and a tom-tom which hung miserably on the side and sounded dreadful. It was simply intolerable. Nevertheless, I did my best to take a position on the fairly professional drummer's seat behind the set. Then I started drumming, and attempted to play a rhythm supporting the sounds of the pair in my own way.

Ralf and Florian didn't show any reaction. There was no feeling that I was at a session that evening. With my previous bands, we had always learned specific songs completely, but with Ralf and Florian we had to find some in the first place. This was new to me. We finished after a good two hours, and Ralf drove me back to my place in his VW. He was always glad to take me home; he had a lot of time, and used every opportunity to be among fellow musicians. To drive a friend home was company for him, and he really enjoyed it.

However, by the time I arrived home I was actually feeling extremely frustrated by the whole evening and about encountering a kind of music that couldn't have been more alien to me. I hadn't warmed to anything. Later, back at the office, I soon put the episode out of my mind. Instead – usually in the evenings – I hung around Düsseldorf's old town. To arouse the interest of girls, I tried to strike poses in my favourite bars, the Uel, the Golden Einhorn and the Ratinger Hof, which still had thick carpets on the tables like as Dutch coffee shops. I was very shy, but I sometimes managed to attract some attention. I usually fascinated very strong women, and this satisfied my vanity. I wanted to flirt rather than have a firm relationship.

One afternoon, there was a knock on the door of the office, where I was sitting at a large floorplan. It was Ralf and Florian: "Hello, Wolfgang. We thought that was really good with you in the rehearsal room last time. Would you like to meet up again?" I was floored. I hadn't counted on a second meeting, because our first had been a couple of months ago and I had not got in touch with them, nor they with me. I thought the matter was over and done with.

Then Ralph confessed, "We have a gig on television next week, on ZDF's cultural magazine programme *Aspekte*." He went on to say that they had to practise at least three pieces that they wanted to present there. "It would be brilliant if you would join us. There will also be money, and we're flying to Berlin next week. We've booked a hotel, and we'll go out in the evening." I couldn't understand what they had found so impressive about our session – I hadn't even played properly. Ralf's offer gave me the impression that they were pretty pushed for time.

I couldn't shake off the thought that they hadn't been able to find a different drummer and, in any case, I was unsure what I should do. On one hand the offer to play in the already-famous avant-garde band, to appear on television and just to get out of this city was attractive – after all, I hadn't seen much of the world yet. But on the other hand, the music of this band, which I hadn't founded, didn't appeal to me much. Nevertheless, I cast my doubts aside. To get out onto the stage – that was what appealed to me! To be on the road and to make music. We would soon have a chance to organise ourselves and get used to each other. I saw a chance and took it. I've often made intuitive decisions in my life and not regretted it.

When I asked about Michael Rother, whom I thought to be still in the group, I received the disappointing answer from Ralf that he was no longer with them. He had been unable to fit into their music, and so now he was planning to found his own band with

45

Klaus Dinger. If this was true, it seemed quite brave to me because I had no idea how Michael would manage that. I was sad that he was no longer with the band, and that I wouldn't meet any of my old colleagues again, but in some way I sensed that this chapter had closed. I decided to throw my lot in with this up-and-coming group. I wanted to drum for all I was worth.

However, first we had to rehearse. The pieces that the two members of Kraftwerk wanted to present were already written. The compositions 'Ruck-Zuck', 'Heimatklänge' and 'Tanzmusik' had already been released in Germany on their first discs, so we wanted to practise these pieces at another meeting.

The pair also filled me in on their previous attempts to reinforce the band with other artists in order to have a greater presence on the stage. They told me about their appearances with Thomas Lohmann, a jazz drummer who was well known at that time, and how, after him, they made an attempt to get on with Klaus Dinger. This must have been a trial for them because both drummers had strong personalities and both regarded their drums as solo instruments – Klaus Dinger formed his own band, Neu!, with Michael Rother for this very reason. It's the eternal dilemma of percussionists in many bands that I've seen, who like to see themselves as dominant artists and therefore play these wearing, extravagant drum solos during their appearances. More often than not, the other members of the band slip offstage at this point, only to come back and take over after the seemingly interminable banging has finished.

That has never been my style – I wasn't trained enough, for a start. My strengths were my simplicity and my ability to empathise. I knew this, and people told me so as well. Fortunately, at the time, Kraftwerk's music was already very minimalistic and a complicated drum part would have dominated it too much.

Back in the studio, I was able to take a closer look at the remarkable equipment and to hear it as well. There was a quite splendid-sounding bass loudspeaker which stood behind Ralf, one of their own constructions, fashioned from plywood and built like an enormous horn, more familiar as the shape of treble loudspeakers. This one had been built according to a blueprint and was as big as a cupboard and very loud. It produced amazing power, which didn't roll off properly until you were a few metres away, producing comfortable feelings in the stomach.

On top of it was a medium-sounding horn made from solid cast aluminium. Someone had covered it in gold leaf, and this speaker could rip up a drum skin if one went too close to it and the music was playing too loudly. It looked impressive. I was unable to judge whether the bass horn had been put together according to the rules of acoustics. At any rate, I remember that there were creaks and roars within this enormous box.

In the case of Florian, who was constantly busy with his devices, I noticed that violins and a Hawaiian guitar also lay in his corner, so it seemed that he was acquainted with other instruments, although I can't remember that he ever played them in my presence. These instruments belonged to an earlier phase of their musical experimentation. At that time, as Ralf told me, they had called themselves Organisation and had often played with non-musicians.

This time rehearsals proceeded slowly, in an extremely relaxed way. I tried to elicit a reasonable sound from the fragments of the drum kit, but it was humiliating to have to sit at this child's kit and impersonate a real musician. I yearned for a proper drum kit, but I didn't have the courage to ask them whether they would buy me one. I didn't have any money for one myself; I couldn't afford a new kit with the little money I was earning from my architect's course, so I was at least hoping that the opportunity to own a good drum machine would arise one day.

# 6 Kraftwerk With New Percussion

DÜSSELDORF, 7 SEPTEMBER 1973

Something exciting happened during the rehearsal this evening that was completely new to me and would have a decisive influence on the band's musical future, as well as that of other electronic bands. One evening, during a break during our rehearsals for our appearance on ZDF in October, in a corner of the rehearsal room I discovered a little box adorned with several keys that described various rhythms: Foxtrot, Waltz, Bossa Nova, Beat 1 and a really fantastic Beat 2. There was also a volume wheel and a tempo control.

It was a small beat box that Florian had bought in a shop. Because he and Florian had so often had problems with drummers before, he had been unable to pass by a device like this, which was probably an accessory for organists. I asked Florian to connect the box to a loudspeaker so that I could hear how it sounded. The fixed settings of the styles sounded artificial and quite electronic, but there were some keys on the upper side of the casing that each triggered a single impulse of a sound, and these were what interested me. Like a proper drum kit, there was a bass drum, a snare, tom toms, crash and ride cymbals, claves and a hi-hat. These sounds, triggered individually by the keys, had a really

48

naturalistic sound, and the bass drum sounded particularly good – above Ralf's plump bass horn, it was indescribably rich and dry, ringing out in a wonderfully leathery way. If I pressed the key repeatedly, I thought that, with a little practice, I'd be able to play my own rhythms with my fingertips. Although it wasn't a very comfortable device to play, it had an electrifying sound, and it was quite advanced for the time.

Florian and I were deeply enthusiastic, and that evening we played the drums totally live, without the pre-programmed rhythms. How could we arrange things so I could play it more comfortably, perhaps like a proper drum kit? After a lot of toing and froing, it occurred to us that we could detach the contact cables leading to the small keys and link them to other contacts. Ultimately, they were only interrupted contacts that triggered a new contact if reconnected, so all we needed to do was to solder a metallic object to both sides. If these objects were then brought together, the same function would be created as that of the keys. I had to find out how these two metal parts could be fashioned so that they could be played by a drummer in a controlled, regular way to produce a beat.

It didn't take me long to find out that the device would have to be similar to a drum. You'd hold a stick in your hand and hit the flat surface. The stick would have to be from a conducting metal, such as copper, and the flat surface would have to be made from a conductor, too. The plate would have to be rounded in shape, like a drum skin, and an individual disk would have to be provided for each sound. The stick would be connected to a cable carrying low-voltage current, and you could easily rig up another stick via a second cable, giving you two drumsticks, just like a genuine drum. Likewise, you'd be able to strike all the available sounds on different surfaces.

By this time, we were hugely enthusiastic and were hoping that everything would work out as we had conceived it. At any rate, Florian was really pleased that someone else besides him liked doing finicky work. I think that he hadn't expected this from a

49

drummer, and he certainly didn't think that I would later play the whole thing in public, but we were united on this point.

Another significant encounter took place at around this time. One evening, I met a good friend of Ralf and Florian's in the fashionable Zur Uel bar, which is still on Ratinger Straße. He and Ralf were playing pinball. Both men were wearing tight, shiny, leather trousers. Ralf's were black and his friend's were cream. I went over and said hello. They seemed rather hesitant and conspiratorial, almost shy.

Ralf made the introductions. "This is Emil. He's a painter and he also contributes to our lyrics. He's even played guitar at some of our appearances." This Emil Schult was a very self-conscious, good-looking lad with brown curls and soft, blue-grey eyes. He reminded me very much of an actor in a Federico Fellini film, and I liked him at once. Although we didn't talk much, we understood each other immediately. As always, I drank Coca Cola; I still hadn't developed a taste for the dark beer of Düsseldorf.

After a while, the pair invited me to go with them to Emil's flat in the Berger Allee. Ralf said that he'd once lived there for a while, too, but that he'd then moved back into his parents' house. The flat wasn't far away. It lay at the edge of the old town, where it was romantic and quiet, in a building from the end of the 19th century. The whole terrace consisted of these ornate and spacious residential houses, which had been built initially by prosperous merchants from Düsseldorf.

There were no houses on the other side of the road because there was a low-lying pond there called the Spee'sche Graben. The southern gate of the city must have stood here when Napoleon entered Düsseldorf with his troops. Today the city museum stands on the site, surrounded by large lime, maple and acacia trees. Old gas lights cast their gentle light onto the line of houses and I noticed that number 9, in particular, was covered all over with fat spiders and a thick, gossamer-like material. This was certainly because of the warm, midge-ridden summer. I actually felt a bit disgusted at the sight of it.

Emil opened the ornate oak door at 9 Berger Allee. He had the only ground-floor flat, and the rooms were enormous; I had never seen such spaciousness. The ceilings were very high and decorated with stucco art nouveau ornaments. The floor was laid throughout with zigzag parquet. It creaked like in an old castle, so I asked for a pair of felt slippers, suppressing a smile.

The first room was a proper hall, in which Emil had arranged his possessions. A large double door inlaid with decorated glass stood wide open, revealing a view into another even larger room. There wasn't a lot of furniture in it, but I detected the smell of oil paint and saw several portraits of pretty girls and a self-portrait of Emil holding a guitar on the walls. Urban science-fiction landscapes painted in oils also hung on the walls, under large glass cupolas, and these interested me particularly. There was also a huge Alpine panorama standing there, leaning on a simple wooden table, obviously his current work in progress. Gas bottles, airbrushes and a draughtsman's table piled with sketches stood in the recess of a window which boasted a view of the pool opposite. The artist's sleeping place was provided by a rather crudely carved wooden bed, propped up on short stilts and decked with a foam rubber mattress. In every corner of the ceiling, Emil had painted pale watercoloured stucco portraits of girls, and everything looked very sensual. Then again, all he had in the other room was an old television set and a huge couch covered with a fluffy tiger-skin throw. We sat down on it and chatted, but conversation made me feel self-conscious again.

Later, while I was looking more closely at the other rooms, Ralf and Emil discussed another picture, on which I recognised a hilly landscape with roads and electricity pylons. You could really make voyages of discovery in this flat! I had no idea that they were talking about the commission of the subsequently famous cover of the *Autobahn* LP.

I discovered yet another room in the rear of the flat. From there, I gazed through big sliding windows across an empty space down to the Rhine. What a lovely room! In the distance, I could hear the humming engines of the ships on the river. I particularly liked that. It reminded me of my childhood. We had lived near the River Main after my birth in Frankfurt, and the noises of the ships there had always soothed me when I went to bed in the evening. Even later, when we were living in Koblenz for a few years, our house was very near the Rhine. Noises like that are buried deep in my memory, and I shall find this sort of atmosphere comfortable for the rest of my life.

Ralf had lived in the same room about a year previously, when he was still studying architecture in Aachen. Now the room was empty, however, and they were joking that I could move in. I didn't believe it, and thought that the pair of them were just fooling around. Later in the evening, we returned to the subject of the room, and Ralf and Emil said that they thought it would be great if I moved in. Inside I was trembling with happiness.

We also talked about our forthcoming television appearance, which was something completely new to me. What we were going to wear and how we should present ourselves was very important to us. The thought that I was supposed to appear before the cameras with a child's drum kit didn't please me at all, however, and over the next few days I brooded about how I could improve the situation.

I was able to move my few belongings into Emil's flat quite quickly, and it suited me to pay much less rent than I had been. Ralf and Florian had rented the large flat very cheaply from the Mannesmann company two years previously, and so my share of the rent was only 220 DM, including electricity and heating. That was good for me because I wasn't earning much on my practical course. I made myself at home as well as I could with my meagre belongings. Emil lived at the front and I lived at the back. I often visited his room and watched him painting and spraying. Women also often visited him, but then his doors were always closed. He was painting them.

A long corridor separated the flat into two halves, and we often met in the large kitchen in the back half. This room was our communications centre. We both prepared our meals there, and each of us soon had his own fridge and food supply. We often went shopping together in the nearby weekly market at Karlplatz, in the heart of the old town. On one of the first evenings after I'd moved in, Emil provided a rabbit, which he cooked delicately. His cooking tasted good, even if it was sometimes unusual. As we were making ourselves comfortable on the parquet floor to enjoy the rabbit (we even lit candles – very romantic!), the doorbell rang and Barbara entered.

At that time, Barbara Niemöller was Florian's girlfriend, although she obviously liked Emil a lot. She was a quiet girl and was very delicate, almost spiritual. She appeared almost translucent, with her pale skin and pale blue eyes. Her thin body seemed to sway as she walked. She wasn't a very lively person, though, and was absolutely androgynous. When she talked, she used only a few quiet words. Nevertheless, this slight woman perfectly suited the gentle young man who was becoming like a new family to me.

In the basement, which was reached from the hall through a wooden stairway, there were two more rooms, one behind the other. They had heating and high windows to allow in daylight and the floors were made of brittle terrazzo castings. Previously, these would have been the domestic offices of the master and mistress who had lived in the house. There I was able to potter about on my own, and I loved it. I have always enjoyed building things from stuff that I've found lying around, and since I still had the tools from my cabinet-making apprenticeship I was able to set up my own workshop down in the basement.

I began to build the base that would take the metal discs for the electronic percussion kit. I had a wooden board sawn for me at a timber yard near the market that we used. It was 3cm thick and about 40cm by 50cm. Onto this I stuck blue-grey marbled celluloid that had been given to me by Florian's sister, Claudia, who was studying architecture and had picked it up at an old plastic factory near Moers that sold the thin, sparkling foil in every imaginable pattern. Unfortunately, the factory had to close after it became illegal to sell celluloid because of tis highly flammable and explosive nature. In any case, Florian's sister, who made costume jewellery from it, had given me a cover to my specifications, measuring 120cm by 60cm. The colourful plastic, which was only half a millimetre thick, looked great on the base, and I also stuck it onto the edges. The corners had been smoothed with a file, and the board looked as if it had been cast in one piece.

Emil was just as enthusiastic about such fiddly work; he was often down with me in the workshop, watching me. I was quickly declared an equal, although I soon learned that if Emil made something, it didn't look to good afterwards – more like a piece of handicraft. He didn't have enough patience to get a perfect result with hard work. He was a painter and an artist. His strength lay in inspiration and innovation, but I was better suited to practical application. For this reason, we often quarrelled, as friends do. Each person wants to be the best and to do things perfectly and be praised constantly. Even so, these disputes were always friendly, and they were never particularly heated. Emil, after all, is Libran. Just try to have a serious argument with a Libran!

At any rate, he had a great idea for how we could make the metal discs for the contacts of the drumpads. During our walks around the neighbourhood, Emil had discovered a large scrapyard very near the docks that was full of coloured metal. We arranged to meet up one morning to have a look around to see if we could find something usable.

This, it turned out, was a really good idea. Metal industrial waste was stored in the scrapyard and pressed together so that it could be melted down again later. There were assorted heaps of copper sheeting, brass forms, aluminium waste and stainless-steel parts, and the friendly site guard allowed us to take whatever we could use.

It wasn't long before we found a mountain of round pieces of sheet metal in all sizes. Initially, we decided on the ones punched out of copper, because we thought that they would best conduct the low-voltage current flowing within the electric system of the beat box. We packed up a selection of round discs, ranging from only six to ten centimetres in diameter and about a millimetre thick, and the kindly scrap dealer gave them to us. They weren't worth much, really.

Back at home, I drilled two small holes near the rim of each disc and fastened them to the upper side of my shining board with small, similarly coloured screws. In this way, there were three discs with a diameter of ten centimetres in the upper row. Another three discs with a diameter of ten centimetres were screwed in a second row below it, and these were intended for more important sounds. A third row, fastened to the lower edge of the playing board with four more discs, was intended for less important sounds. I had previously soldered a thin cable to one of the fixing screws and pulled it backwards through a hole to the back of the board. I now had ten thin cables there. I soldered them to a strip plug, which had two more connections for the drumsticks.

The sticks were a problem in themselves. In fact, those that I had found in a hobby shop were too thin and had bent much too quickly when I hit the discs with them, and the copper was also too soft. After experimenting with other materials, I achieved the best result with brass tubes. These conducted electricity equally well, but they had to be thicker because they were hollow. I soldered the front opening closed, so that the tubing was a bit heavier there, and fixed the flexible power cable behind it. The connection to the board had been rigged up from cheap banana plugs.

I had no idea whether the thing would work. In order that it was possible to set up the board at some distance from the beat box, I made a length of multicore, about one and a half metres long, with the heavy plug at the end that was to lead to the electronic box, and a drum stand that I bought from a music shop and customised slightly served as a support. After that, it was possible to position the percussion board in front of me and adjust its height. The angle was also variable, thanks to the adjusting head in the stand. It looked great. Just wonderful!

That same day, I took this unique instrument into the studio and showed it off to my new colleagues. They were impressed but by the way it looked. When it was finally attached to the system, we could hear that our drumpad – as we later called it – functioned outstandingly. We had a completely new instrument. We knew at once that it was a breakthrough. It was so easy to play. It was simply incredible how fast and easily the drumpads sounded if they were touched with one of the metal drumsticks. Of course, the volume couldn't be raised dynamically; it was only possible to hear the simple sound of each disc, according to its preset volume. *Ping-pang-zakk-boing-boom-tschak!*

Kraftwerk were now equipped with a new percussion kit. Now I could play percussion standing up quite simply, with minimum effort. Florian was so impressed that he kept pushing me away from the board to hammer on it himself. He had such fun! We argued about who could play with the box, but of course I always won in the end, because I was the drummer. Ralf was also pleased with the new device, and it was the beginning of our striving towards technical innovation.

We had a totally unique instrument, but we didn't think about this at all. Any other person would have registered a patent on it at once, but we were much too artistic, much too unworldly, to consider commercial possibilities. The children's drum kit, which was still standing about in the studio, was never used again from that point on, and I was no longer worried about our appearance on *Aspekte*. With our new addition, I was really looking forward to it.

# 7 *A Novelty On The Culture Channel*

BERLIN, OCTOBER 1973
We flew to Berlin, with our electronic drum board, on a British Airways plane. It was the first time that I had travelled by plane, and I felt very uncomfortable during the flight. I'm not an over-anxious type of man, but I was asking myself during the flight if we weren't provoking nature too much with this most unnatural means of locomotion. You always sit on large quantities of fuel, and you allow yourself to be shot to the edge of the stratosphere by jet engines. You're sitting in excruciatingly restricting seats in the artificial climate of a fragile pressure chamber with a thin aluminium skin. It's very uncomfortable for both the ears and the blood pressure. I'll never understand people who like this torture. Then there are the hot exhaust gases that jets blow into the atmosphere. Give me the train any day. You can stroll around and eat a good meal in the restaurant car. You can sit comfortably in wide seats while the view outside alternates between green landscapes, modern cities, romantic villages and glittering industrial plants. On a train you can see and experience something. The journey lasts longer, but I've always liked things to last longer. I've never really ever been in a hurry. Even as a child, dreaming and dawdling were my favourite occupations.

Anyway, we landed in Tempelhof Airport in one piece. Glad to stand on *terra firma* again, I was overcome by the size of the city, which was at that time still isolated from West Germany. It was something really different from glassy Düsseldorf. I had my first taste of what it meant to be on the road with Kraftwerk in the metropolises of the world.

Matters proceeded with unexpected professionalism in the television studios of ZDF. Our few bits of equipment were quickly set up, and we were really very excited. We played 'Tanzmusik' live in front of the cameramen, who were very impressed by the remarkable electronic device I was playing which we had built ourselves and had a lot of cables hanging out of the back. When I looked back on the long-lost videotape of the ZDF performance many years later, I realised that we actually seemed rather grotesque during this appearance. From today's perspective, our presentation was rather intense and uncertain.

The most spectacular aspect of the gig was my innovative style of drumming. Here I was clearly the star, and the cameramen directed their huge lenses onto the amazing rhythm board I was playing. The Minimoog synth still looked like an organ fitted with a normal keyboard, and Florian's transverse flute also had nothing spectacular about it. Looking back today, the fact that I actually had the nerve to appear before the cameras with such an amateurishly assembled construction suggests that I've always had a large slice of craziness in me. After this success we became more and more enthusiastic about the electronic production and presentation of our music and continued to develop in this direction. Without this initial small step, we certainly never would have taken a leading role in the development of electronic pop music.

Berlin offered us many opportunities to enjoy its nightlife, so after the programme we didn't travel back to our hotel straightaway but instead strolled through Berlin, ate at the Café Kranzler on the Kudamm and wandered through bars and discotheques all night. We were very inquisitive about new experiences in the subculture, but as the first light of day arrived we grew bone tired. I can still remember travelling back to the airport in a taxi at 6.30am, completely exhausted. It was raining and the weather had grown cold – not a productive combination for over-tired artists.

When we were finally sat on the aeroplane (on one of the first flights that morning), the captain arrived. He was wearing his wet raincoat and seemed grumpy because of the early hour. As he negotiated the narrow gangway, he juggled a steaming cup of coffee with his briefcase before disappearing into the cockpit. His appearance wasn't particularly reassuring. Hardly any passengers were on this flight to the West, apart from a few businesspeople and us worn-out Kraftwerkers.

It wasn't a good day for flying at all. In fact, after we'd left Berlin some way behind, the aeroplane began to tremble and shake dreadfully. Violent gusts of wind caused the plane to make such terribly irregular movements that suddenly several of the ceiling panels crashed into the gangway, exposing the hydraulic pipes and cable conduits. It was a terrifying experience. I thought that it was the end for us, and I saw similar emotions in the horrified faces of the other passengers. From one of the back rows, I heard another shocked passenger call out, "Always this shitty English disease!" I already knew this slogan, which had actually been coined for a model of British car which fell apart. (We later had to fly with that airline again, from Bombay to Düsseldorf. Thankfully, everything went well on that journey.)

When we got back home in the late afternoon, I fell straight into bed, dog tired. I was absolutely worn out, but happy and proud. Something had clicked within me. I knew instinctively that the business with Kraftwerk belonged to the future, and that the sweaty drummer of the English beat era belonged to the past.

# 8  Röder

From the local gigs that we played and from our television appearance in Berlin, it had become clear to us that, as a trio, the band was too small to make a respectable sound on the stage, and so we decided to augment the line-up with an additional member. A few days later, this person stood in the studio in the guise of a young Messiah. God knows where Florian kept conjuring these people up from, but he had picked him up somewhere and now we were supposed to get to know each other and get on with each other.

This was not at all easy for me at first, because I already had problems with his appearance. His name was Klaus Röder, and he came from the Neuss area, 15 minutes' drive from Düsseldorf. In absolute contrast to me, Klaus was a real hippie. I had previously only dressed myself in hippie fashion, but Klaus lived quite independently, and had this spiritual look about him. He wore his hair down to his bottom and he went around in open sandals and bare feet in all weathers. He played guitar and a violin, which he'd made himself. It looked like a whitish grey lump and was electrically amplified. It was actually the reason why Florian had brought its owner with him. In any case, Röder was a really

60

unusual person, who proved to be absolutely charming. He even played violin on several recordings on the *Autobahn* LP (although these weren't used in the final mix), and he was photographed for our first publicity shots.

The photographs for the back of the cover for *Autobahn* had a particularly special history. For the front cover, Ralf and Florian had planned that the whole band should sit on the back seat of the Mercedes as it travelled on the autobahn. On an early pressing, our faces can be seen in the rear mirror above the dashboard. Because they were still uncertain whether I would stay with the group, they gave Emil the chance to sit in the car with the rest of the band and be photographed on the cover in the same way, as the artist. He was obviously very pleased about this, but when it became clear that I was staying as a permanent band member he was unceremoniously commissioned to cut out his own head from the finished photograph for the back cover and to splice the photograph of my head onto his body. It had to be a montage because there wasn't enough time for a new photograph. This must have been very painful for poor Emil, but he held no sway over decisions made by Ralf and Florian. If we spent evenings in the studio, working on pieces for the album, he was often there listening to give his opinion on the songs. The car sounds on 'Autobahn' were been recorded on the mobile equipment of the band's former co-producer, Conny Plank, and mixed into the song in his new studio in Neunkirchen.

Around this time I noticed that Ralf and Florian weren't getting on as well as they'd hoped with Klaus. He often didn't attend band meetings, and he was soon thrown out.

# 9  The Electric Quartet

DÜSSELDORF, JANUARY 1974

We'd parted from Klaus Röder because, with his long hair and beard, he no longer fitted with our new image, and our kind of pop music was no longer his thing. Ralf and Florian had chosen an austere, extremely German image for Kraftwerk, which Röder didn't fit into. When I joined the band, I still had a hippie hairstyle and a moustache myself, and even Ralf still had shoulder-length hair at the beginning of the '70s. That may have been appropriate during their musical experimentation with Organisation and the *Kraftwerk I* and *II* albums, but I clearly remember that, at the time of *Autobahn*, we adopted the "German" image at Florian's suggestion, based on his love of the fashions of the '50s. It was like The Beach Boys, who represented an American prototype with their "All-American Dream". I approved of it at once. I can still remember having our hair cut and buying suits in town. Ralf and Florian bought suits from a Düsseldorf bespoke tailor, but even so they also paid for our off-the-peg suits because they were work clothes, as it were. We just wanted to stop being compared with the English pop scene or with bluejeans-clad American rock bands.

In any case, musically speaking, this was no longer possible.

We wanted to show that there was also modern, stylistically independent popular music in Germany, rooted in our own culture. This music had been devised by Ralf and Florian. With the rest of us, they were developing an intellectual and, at the same time, entertaining musical concept based on our romantic folk melodies, but combined with modern scientific and technical themes, contemporary instruments and a selfconfident, autonomous presentation. I was growing to understand what they wanted, and was pleased to be allowed to perform this music with them.

However, we still had too few personnel onstage, particularly for this type of presentation. Florian asked a professor he knew from the conservatoire for advice and he led us to his student, Karl Bartos. A highly talented musician, Bartos had learnt to play drums, piano and vibraphone at the Düsseldorf Institute and was just about to take his music exams.

When Florian brought him to the studio one day, Karl still looked very much like a student, with a duffel coat, trainers, jeans and a dark-red sweater, which he wore constantly. He was also several years younger than us, but I noticed at once that he was confident and self-assertive. At first he played his conventional vibraphone, which was then his favourite instrument. We even lugged it around for our first American tour, but Karl had also intended to play drums. He was a trained concert drummer and could play rhythms that I was unable to play myself. He was a colossal acquisition for us, in any case, and at the beginning I was sometimes afraid that he might be able to replace me. However, it soon became apparent that these thoughts were unjustified, because I had become important for other reasons.

I soon built up a good relationship with Karl, whose family background was similar to my own. From that point we both had the same status, even though I'd been a member of the band for two years longer. We were permanent guest musicians in the most intellectual and electronic pop band of all time. I later built an electronic percussion set for Karl out of a rhythm box and another percussion pad. The principle was just the same, although the sounds from his box were different. These were converted to rhythmic sounds, and individual sounds were triggered with sticks resembling knitting needles. We commissioned new autograph cards from an old portrait photographer in the Blumenstraße, and on these cards the image of Kraftwerk that would remain unchanged for the next 16 years – the most creative period of the band – was seen for the first time.

One day, two more rooms became free in the rear extension of our flat in the Berger Allee. Until that point, a Greek man called Platon Kostic had lived there, a friend of Ralf's from his student days. Like me, both had studied architecture, but unlike Ralf and me, Platon had taken his examinations, and was now going back to Greece with his German girlfriend. As a result, his two rooms became free, and so we offered them to Karl, who leapt at the chance of moving out of his scruffy attic in the Oberkassel district. Our new colleague was now living at 9 Berger Allee, and that suited everyone.

# 10 *America Endless*
## *Too Fast On Broadway*

DÜSSELDORF, 9 MARCH 1975
Karl had his work cut out for him with his music studies, and he often had little time to rehearse with us. However, this didn't matter too much. *Autobahn* was the last album that we had to submit to Philips in order to honour our recording contract. Now we had to wait and see how the media and the public would accept the work.

Meanwhile, we were enjoying life. I still liked walking in the surrounding countryside with Emil and I was even able to buy a red Opel Kadett, which made it easy for us to drive to the beautiful region of the Lower Rhine. Emil showed me the town of Kevelaer – the place of pilgrimage in which he was born – and took me around its flat, rural surroundings. We both loved making excursions into the countryside and a wonderful relationship developed between us.

In the meantime, we also had mutual friends of both sexes from different circles. At the time, Emil was still an art teacher at the Düsseldorf Rethel Gymnasium, and his pupils often visited him in the Berger Allee. On those occasions we would meet in our large communal kitchen for coffee and home-made cake. We had a real long-term relationship, even if I sometimes pinched pretty girls from him. He would bring them from somewhere and I would then entice them into my room and "coach" them. Emil never bore grudges. He was always an impressive and generous person, and I've never met anyone else like him in my life.

There was always something going on in our flat, particularly now that Karl was also living with us, and we were never bored. We held parties as often as possible, and it became obligatory to steal women. There was a battle every time we cleaned up the kitchen, and when the monthly telephone bill arrived war broke out. It was a wonderful time.

One day, Ralf and Florian rang us up and invited us to a café in another area to discuss things. They were very secretive and didn't want to give any reasons on the phone. We drove out to the country in Ralf's grey VW. In the spring of 1975, the weather was already warm and so we sat outside. Ralf cleared his throat in his familiar way and said, "What do you think of America, you lot?" We had no idea what he meant by this. He continued: "Our single is in the charts in the USA and is moving up fast. It's just reached Number Five so we've been given a great offer to tour all over the States."

We were flabbergasted. Madness! Crazy! Us in *America*? It was unbelievable. What had we done? How could this have happened so quickly? Elated, we considered how we should present ourselves in that huge country, birthplace of sweating guitar rock. Of course we wanted to go! Crazy ideas began to fly back and forth between us, and this continued during the journey home. Talk about exciting! The tour was scheduled to start in April. According to Mouse Ltd's Ira Blacker, an initial schedule of 21 concerts had been planned, and we prepared to spend a whole month in America.

However, things turned out a little differently. Our flight from Düsseldorf to New York was booked for the beginning of April. We were all very excited, and we'd already bought all of the equipment and cases we'd need for the journey. On the morning of our departure, Florian, Ralf and his sister, Anke, turned up at the Berger Allee and we chatted, trying to decide if we'd forgotten anything. We'd already sent on the few instruments that we then possessed, and we were more concerned about the suits that we were taking with us, whether we had packed all our passports and whether they were still valid. Did we all have our visas? Ralf's sister drove some of us to the airport in her brother's VW, while the others followed in a taxi.

When the cab turned up, I quickly ran back out into the street to park my car in a secure space that didn't charge for parking. It was high time to go to the airport, and we were very nervous because this would be our first flight over the Atlantic. After parking my car, I slammed the driver's door shut and, at the same moment, felt a hammer-like blow on my left thumb. It was so painful that my knees buckled. Pale from the agony, I didn't want to believe what I saw. My thumb was jammed in between the bodywork and the door frame. It must have been squashed flat to fit between them! I cried out in pain, and Emil and Florian came running over at once and tore open the door. How on Earth did I come to have my thumb stuck there? It must have been nerves and all that frantic rushing around that morning.

I stood there in the middle of the Berger Allee, my thumb growing scarlet and swelling hugely. I suppose that I should have gone to see a doctor at once, but there wasn't any time. My friends took my arms and dragged me to the taxi. I threw myself into the back seat, almost in tears, and we left for the airport. The throbbing in my thumb was overwhelming. As the others carried the luggage, I was scarcely aware of my surroundings and just trudged along behind them.

It was an age before we were able to take our seats in the Pan Am jumbo. Emil took care of me immediately, and spoke to the stewardess. Without turning a hair, she said that the best thing for me would be iced water. Yes! That was just what I needed. She must have had first-aid training. I remembered then that cold is good for bruises – at least, for normal bruises.

The stewardess brought me a glass of water full of ice cubes from the kitchen. I put my thumb in it, and within a few seconds the pain had vanished. Soon, though, it was replaced by a new, if less serious, pain. In fact, the icy cold was also painful. I had a choice of discomfort: it was a roller-coaster of pain. Again and again, through that excruciating nine-hour flight, I had to put my battered thumb into iced water and take it promptly out again so that it didn't freeze, so I had my hands full. I couldn't even think of sleep. The others were touchingly concerned, and did their best to console me. Emil helped me to eat while someone else fetched fresh ice cubes from the kitchen when the old ones had melted. I had never imagined that the beginning of our American tour would be so dramatic.

Eventually, the flight was over and the plane landed in New York in the late afternoon. We obediently went through the elaborate immigration process and entered the country as tourists, and so we quickly gained the American Consulate's permission to enter under the terms of a working visit without any further complications. We were greeted in the hall of Kennedy Airport by the fat manager Ira Blacker, who took us into town in an incredibly long, black stretch limousine, driven by an equally tall black chauffeur.

Everything that I could see on the journey into the city was large, long and high. It was already beginning to get dark outside, and the highways were crowded with cars bursting with chrome and with the long, phallic hoods typical of the '70s. The journey lasted for what seemed like hours. Without my glass of iced water, the painful throbbing in my thumb grew worse. By now I had been plagued with it for more than twelve hours. Mr Blacker promised that he would take me to see a doctor immediately, as soon as we were at the hotel.

Karl, Emil and I had been booked into the Goreham Hotel on 55th Street, while Ralf and Florian were staying nearby in the more upmarket Mayflower Hotel on Central Park West. We didn't become properly aware of our new environment until shortly after I had made things comfortable for myself and Karl in our room.

On bringing up our bags and opening the door for us, the bellhop had also switched on the lights and the fans everywhere, and as soon as he'd gone I switched them off again because it was cold outside. It was apparently the hotel's custom to switch everything on in order to demonstrate the comforts available in its rooms.

I glanced through the sliding window into the depths of the ravine of the street, and saw that we were on the 27th floor, at least. The people and the cars looked like nothing more than small, moving points. A barrage of street noise and police sirens – which I had previously only known from American crime novels – penetrated our room. Things suddenly seemed real. I felt like an American.

I liked the view of New York at night and of the surrounding buildings with their old-fashioned, wooden water tanks and the enormous neon advertisements, although I didn't find it very modern. Things were so different to the way they were at home, though, and the town was seething with energy and light in spite of the late hour.

The bellhop didn't want to leave, and hung around the room with an expectant look on his face until we tipped him a few dollars. One green note looked just like another to us, and we must have given him a rather lavish sum, as the young man thanked us extravagantly and over the next few days fulfilled our requirements without us having to utter a word.

Soon, our colleagues came over and joined us. As they knocked, I realised from the many bars and locks on the door to the apartment that the area in which we were staying was probably not the safest. Ralf introduced to us Henry Israel, an employee of Ira Blacker who was to be our tour manager in the USA. Henry, a good-looking young man with a black three-day beard and twinkling dark eyes, wanted to drive with me to a hospital where he knew there was an emergency service at night so that I could have my thumb looked at.

When we arrived at the hospital, I was struck by the disorder of the place. It was completely different to a German clinic. Perhaps it was only a simple emergency station, used to coping with freaky cases. I must confess that I didn't have much confidence in the staff. After we had waited for a short time, a doctor ushered Henry and me into his treatment room. He examined my poor thumb closely and was very surprised that I had stood the pain for so long. I described my clumsiness with the car and the ice-cube treatment during the flight, and he was pleased with the stewardess' quick thinking. After he had taken an X-ray and confirmed that there was no fracture, he told me that I had a bad haematoma under the thumbnail. The pain came from the pressure of the accumulated blood that couldn't be distributed because of the thumbnail. The doctor then took a paperclip, unbent it and heated one end over a Bunsen burner until it was red hot and then bored a small hole in the middle of my fingernail with it. The blood flowed out immediately, and the pressure in my thumb decreased at once. I could have hugged him. How cleverly, how painlessly and how quickly he had helped me! I also thought to myself that, if I'd known what to do, I would have done it myself on the plane. At any rate, I felt considerably relieved as I packed a small dressing onto my thumb and travelled back to the Goreham with Mr Israel by taxi. Now I too could finally enjoy our visit and look forward to the tour.

The following morning, we were picked up again and driven to breakfast together at the Rumpelmayr, one of the most well-known cafés in the city, directly next to Central Park. There they served the best cheesecake, the creamiest cream cakes and the finest Macedonian salad that I had ever eaten. Later, I lost no opportunity to have breakfast there if we were ever in town. I noticed that they even skinned and depipped the pieces of orange and grapefruit in the fruit salad. It was a very comfortable place for a *bon vivante*.

We still had two days in which to get used to the change in time zones and the climate, which was cold, and so that afternoon we rehearsed for a short time in a hired studio. On the following afternoon, we were photographed by Maurice Seymour, the famous New York celebrity photographer. Three years later, this black-and-white shot became the cover for the German release of our album *Trans Europe Express*.

We attended a small party at the reception of Famous Music, Florian's music publisher, who had offices in one of the many skyscrapers in Brooklyn and where the staff looked at us as if we were extraterrestrials. A female employee that I liked immediately was sitting at the large conference table. She was an extremely individual young woman who looked very Indian, with long black hair, sharp and regular features, lively, almond-shaped eyes and dark skin. Later, she was introduced to me as Anne Gardner, the boss's right-hand woman, and apparently she liked me. She had planned a picnic in the open air for the following day, which I filmed with my father's old super-eight camera. A few rugs and a few packets of sandwiches, cakes, coffee and doughnuts were quickly organised, and we played frisbee in the still-cool but sunny Central Park. We were only fooling around on this cold April day, but I was growing to like Anne more and more. I had never seen such a beautiful woman before. My feelings toward her were growing quickly, and her beauty was making me unsure and crazy. Soon I was thinking only about her. She had glanced at me several times in a frank, unambiguous way, but I still had to wait for an opportunity to follow up on this.

One of our first concerts took place on 3 April 1975 in Rochester Town, to the north of New York State, and it proceeded in a totally unspectacular way and went unnoticed by the press. This was part of the plan, because we had to warm up first. The venue in Rochester was a rather uncomfortable, cold hall, and the audience really didn't know how to take us. I would be inclined to think that they hadn't heard our music on the radio there. I can't remember any highlights, apart from the fact that an icy blizzard was sweeping over the country during our performance and that later, when we left the hall, we looked onto a white winter landscape before us in dismay. A cold snap of this severity was just as alien to us as our cool storm of electrons was to the youths

71

of Rochester. The town's small airport had been closed, and on the following day we and our manager, Henry, had to risk skidding through snowed-up highways back to New York in a rented estate car. In New York, the streets were finally free from snow, although it was still bitterly cold.

We were lucky to have brought our winter coats and woollen jackets to America. I'll never forget the image of Ralf in his black coat and fur collar, looking more like an industrialist or a banker. He kept his leather attaché case with him all the time, and looked very conservative in his old-fashioned, horn-rimmed glasses, not at all like a pop star. In contrast, Florian wrapped himself in a long, beige, camel-hair coat, which looked absolutely appropriate for the '70s and which could have belonged to a Mafia don – the gangsters in the films of Scorsese always had fashionable coats with wide lapels like his. Florian also constantly wore thin, dangerous-looking sunglasses.

I, on the other hand, was much more colourful. Before the journey, I'd bought a gaudy, three-quarter-length woollen jacket with large checks and buttons, just like those worn by lumberjacks in Canada. I also wore my hair even longer than the others, and I wound a soft, bright-red woollen scarf around my neck. Karl, meanwhile, doggedly wore his dark-brown duffel coat. The wearing of once-white jeans and trainers was almost an artistic philosophy for him.

We stayed in New York for the next few days, spending our time windowshopping and rehearsing in the afternoons. Ralf had brought a special device with him, the Vaco Orchestron, a further development of the Mellotron, which was still quite new on the market. With this gadget, it was possible to reproduce samples of instruments and choirs by means of thin cellophane discs, on which optical sound lines were printed. The gossamer-thin, transparent discs were as big as seven-inch singles, and like them had a hole in the middle. However, optical sound lines don't run in a spiral from the outside to the inside like records do; instead, they form individual, enclosed rings. On the Orchestron, each ring created an individual voice or tone pitch. It was possible to play them through polyphonically, by means of a normal keyboard, because all of the rings were simultaneously touched by a row of photo-electric cells. The sound was fantastic. The device worked really well, and was really a great find.

During this tour, Ralf was already using the Orchestron in our songs. The choir and string voices were the most fascinating, their droning and melancholy quality caused by the unstable drive across rubber bands, resulting in variations in synchronism. However, this didn't detract from their charm in the least. On the contrary, the slight wobble was a particular characteristic of the instrument, which was housed in a huge, heavy wooden box. Later, it was replaced by a two-handed model equipped with two drives, so that we could play different instruments or choirs at the same time.

One evening, Ralf and Florian – who were always attending business appointments without us in the daytime – came to our hotel. As usual, we had arranged to meet for a meal, and we drove together to an elegant restaurant with our manager in our mile-long limousine, driven by the huge chauffeur. Ralf and Florian proudly showed us the new wristwatches that their music publishers had bought for them that afternoon in an expensive jeweller's shop as a bonus for sales of the record, which had so far sold 450,000 units. Ralf happily told us that they'd been able to choose the watches themselves. His was an elegant watch, manufactured completely from gold, which told the wearer what the time was anywhere in the world. The dial represented the globe and was divided into time zones by vertical lines, and the continents were picked out in different shades of gold. A small aeroplane formed the tip of the large second hand, which ticked regularly around the Earth. It was a quite beautiful and certainly a very expensive work of art.

In contrast, Florian had decided on a heavy Rolex watch, a showy piece of techno platinum with a heavy winder and large buttons, with which it could be used as a stopwatch. The choices of both the musicians spoke for themselves. Ralf and Florian were as different in their tastes as they were in their musical talents, but this fact served to forge their creative unity.

However, I felt deeply hurt that they were separating themselves from us and showing their valuable gifts to us like this, and this wasn't the first time that their behaviour had forced me to think about our relationship. It wasn't always easy for Ralf and Florian to associate with their friends. I felt that they hadn't considered our feelings, but this wasn't intended maliciously; maybe it was just a lack of empathy. It was because of our different family backgrounds.

At any rate, everything in New York was so excitingly new and positive that I quickly pushed such minor worries aside. The first of our larger concerts was to take place on 5 April, following two warm-up gigs. We were scheduled to play in the Beacon Theater on Broadway, and when we left our hotels and walked to the venue in the afternoon, we were pleasantly surprised. The Beacon was a well-maintained, elegant art deco theatre, and we learned that it had been under a preservation order for many years. With several rows of balconies, it must have had about 2,000 seats. All of the ornamentation was gold coloured, and the seats had been upholstered in purple velvet. To a certain extent, it reminded me of the Olympia in Paris, where we had already made a minor appearance in the previous year and which was also reddish and plush. Here, however, everything was much larger and much more luxurious. This was, after all, America, where everything was larger and more expensive. On the artistically designed façade outside, an enormous neon light with our names and those of our two support groups – Greenslade and Michael Quatro – attracted the attention of the public to the evening's unusual musical event.

We quickly set up our equipment, helped by the stage assistants. We didn't have much, in any case. We only had the two synthesisers, a Farfisa organ, our two new electronic drums, Karl's vibraphone and Florian's electronic flute. Our loudspeaker boxes – which could be stacked inside each other – were also placed behind us on the stage so that we could hear ourselves.

These boxes had an unusual characteristic. I had built them three years previously from veneered wood board and plywood offcuts, following a German plan, and they were called bass slides. They worked by means of a deep-tone loudspeaker in the upper part of the box broadcasting its waves forward. The frequencies broadcast backwards weren't dampened by the usual insulated bass box, as they would have been in a normal bass loudspeaker, but were instead conducted into a lower part of the box through a folded horn and emitted from the front via an exit slide. The effect was immense. The deep tones that emerged below were amplified many times and had this wonderful sub-bass that could turn your stomach over.

All of our equipment differed in its construction in that the walls of the boxes in which the devices were housed had two thicknesses. The lower sections with the exit slides could be removed by means of quick-acting fastenings and stacked inside each other for transportation. This saved on a lot of space, although we weren't able to use these fine speakers for long because they weren't up to the rough handling of a tour in the long term. The boxes were smashed very early on in the tour, and we had to leave the debris behind somewhere in the States.

We also brought along with us boxes with coloured neon tubes, which I had built in the previous years to form a light show, and we put these behind us on the floor of the stage. These blue neon signs spelled out our first names, and we had one each, placed directly on the floor in front of us during gigs. Emil had stretched out a large screen, onto which he projected several of his beautiful slides to accompany our songs during the show. It actually worked very well, but they were fairly dim because our projector had a rather feeble lamp, and video projectors still weren't available at that time.

The evening drew near, and we wanted to get through our baptism of fire in the most famous metropolis of the western world. All of the 2,000 seats in the theatre had been sold. Our hit 'Autobahn', which was constantly played on the radio, was the best advertisement for our concert. Late that evening, after the support acts (both of them guitar bands) had completed their unspectacular performances, the four of us walked onto the stage. As we began our minimalist show, utter silence reigned in the theatre. The audience were fascinated, probably even shocked by our meticulous appearance, all suits and ties and merciless formality. They'd never seen or heard anything like us.

The exotic sounds naturally had their usual effect. The heavy, deep synthesisers were completely alien to the audience. Although synthesisers had been discovered and were manufactured in America, they had only played a subordinate role in pop music until that point, although bands such as Emerson, Lake And Palmer had already used them, and other musicians had recorded riffs with them in their songs, but the instrument was completely new to Americans in the way that we used it for all of our music, with such complexity and consistency. It can't be ignored – we were light years ahead with our work. When Ralf panned the thunderous sounds from left to right and back again over the whole stereo width of the stage during 'Autobahn', all I could see were open mouths and bewildered faces with wide-open eyes. That song was our battering ram.

Because we didn't have many songs, we played the few that we did have very slowly. We played pieces from the albums *Ralf And Florian* and *Autobahn* as if they were mountains of tones. We played titles such as 'Mitternacht', 'Tanzmusik' and 'Kometenmelodie' for almost twice as long as their recorded versions, and we stretched 'Autobahn' to a cool 23 minutes, while Karl and I beat our electronic percussion boards like madmen. We managed to achieve a respectable length for our show, but even the protracted tuning and recalibration of the synthesisers between the songs was so interesting to the audience that our mini repertoire wasn't a problem.

The following day, *The New York Times* wrote that the audience had left our concert as reverently as if they were leaving a church. Even the German teen magazine *Bravo* had flown over to see our triumphant concert, and dedicated an article to us with the same title as the following chapter.

# 11 *Krautrock Is Top*
## *Kraftwerk Electrifies America*

Everything was amplified through a mixing desk and a tower of
amps, which our manager, Ira Blacker, had rented in the States
and which a sound company would reconstruct in whichever city
at which we were appearing. These people had to travel with us
throughout the following weeks. The gig at the Beacon had been
a great success, and a great opener for the whole tour, although
New Yorkers didn't quite understand what we children of post-
war Germany actually wanted to express with our music. But
we were already very proud to have dazzled an audience on the
worldfamous Broadway with our futuristic and minimalistic
presentation.

The following concerts didn't always fit perfectly into the
framework of the tour plan that Ira had drawn up. His tour poster
clearly showed that we were "taking offers now for May", and
he was looking for additional promoters in other cities. He had
obviously planned with Ralf and Florian to do this; the pair had
already given us advance notice in Düsseldorf that the tour might
last longer than the planned 21 appearances. In 1975, the words
"Kraftwerk – Die Menschmaschine" ("Man Machine") were
already appearing in thick letters on the US tour poster. On Ralf's

instructions, Ira Blacker had got his graphic artists to depict what we eventually wanted to become: a musical and philosophical human machine. The design of this early poster already displays Fritz Lang's global city, Metropolis, which would become one of our later themes.

Gradually, the concerts in the States that had been publicised proceeded more and more smoothly. I never would have imagined America to be so diverse. We were often in regions that seemed like northern or central Europe, and then we would travel through parts that seemed thoroughly southern, with little vegetation and a dry climate. We escaped death in a snowstorm in the high north only to protect ourselves from the sun in San Diego or Hollywood on the west coast and in Florida a short time later. Our tour grew longer and longer as Ira Blacker received more and more offers of concerts from arrangers throughout the country, and he had his hands full fitting the new dates into a practical and economical timetable.

We even played in smaller places, such as Little Rock, Arkansas, the home town of Bill Clinton, which back in 1975 hadn't yet become famous. We also appeared in Dallas, where John F Kennedy had been assassinated. It was very sultry there, and we saw hordes of cockroaches boiling out of the drains in the pavement. It was disgusting. We also played in Florida, in the jazz city of New Orleans, and even in rundown rock dumps in small towns in the Midwest which didn't look at all safe.

Sometimes, Henry Israel wouldn't let us perform unless he'd been given the entire fee from ticket sales in advance, before the performance. He'd had a lot of experience in dealing with promoters because he'd been accompanying bands on their tours for years. He knew exactly who was to be trusted and who you had to demand the money from first. Sometimes, he even had to hire bodyguards to guard his money chest during our concerts. There was nothing that he hadn't already experienced in that country, where guns are always ready to be drawn. Meanwhile, Karl and I received a fixed monthly wage from Ralf and Florian.

We didn't worry about money, because we trusted each other and never negotiated any contracts among ourselves. Ralf and Florian had already paid us for the tour in advance, back in Düsseldorf. It was enough to live on; we didn't need much.

I bought myself a map of North America in a newsagent's at one of the tiny airports we visited, and from then on I drew a line from one town to the next on the flight there. The way that the tour was stretching across the continent had become so confusing that I desperately needed a reminder of the route for future reference. The map soon became criss-crossed with lines. After we had played the original 21 concerts that had been planned, things became wilder and wilder as we played the new bookings. In the end, we performed twice as many concerts.

Meanwhile, the first headlines about us appeared in the dailies and picture papers in Germany. My mother collected everything that she found to read about Kraftwerk. Headlines appeared such as:

*German Pop Autobahn Conquers America*
*Kraftwerk* – Sie Fahrn, Fahrn, Fahrn *To The Top Of The World*
*The New Conquerors Of America*
*Kraftwerk Electrifies America*

Yes! We liked that. Until that point, the German media had habitually greeted us with pitying but uncomprehending smiles. They had seen us as sound-crazed buttonpushers, or monotonous robots.

We often had days off between flights and concerts, and we would use these to attend to private business. I sometimes wrote to my parents, telling them proudly about our experiences in the States. Somehow, I was still searching for the recognition of my success from my father, who had so little regard for my subversive musical life. I often went swimming, if the hotel had a swimming pool, or I looked at that day's town.

I once flew back from Memphis to New York with Emil, Florian and Ralf. We had played a concert back in the town of Elvis Presley's birth, and Karl desperately wanted to stay there for the following free days because he had fallen in love with a beautiful black girl who lived there. He had met her in a disco and had arranged a secret assignation with her. We were a little worried about the depths of our friend's passion, and it would have been better for him not to appear in public with the girl, because she was the girlfriend of a famous blues/funk musician. Henry Israel had warned Karl about the guitarist's violent tendencies, but Karl didn't want to listen; he was too passionate about the girl, who also liked him and taught him to dance the bump in the disco. I think that Karl was hoping to learn a lot more from her... The rest of us flew back to New York with the telephone number of his hotel and mixed feelings, but I had arranged with him that we would telephone each other at least once a day to swap erotic news.

New York had become cold and rainy. I had my room all to myself over the next few days because Ralf and Florian were also constantly on the road, and I began to enjoy some privacy again. Somehow, I had the feeling that they were quite consciously keeping their distance from the "gang", so I undertook several excursions into the busy city alone, wandering through the ravines of the streets for hours.

One afternoon, I reached an area that didn't look at all like the big city. The houses were much smaller and more decrepit, the streets were dirtier, the people (mostly black) looked poorer and the prices in the shop windows were lower, which suited me, because I was in a mood for shopping. Eventually, I found a shoe shop that had just the kind of short boots in the window that I was thinking of buying. While I was pressing my nose to the window, two black men suddenly asked me if I was interested in buying some leather boots. They murmured something about a "discount" and a "proper offer". One was wearing a long, reddish leather coat with wide lapels, while the other wore a fringed leather jacket and a leather slouch hat with a huge brim. I thought that they were both employees of the shop, hoping to tempt me in as a customer, so I answered in the affirmative. My English wasn't perfect, but I thought I understood that they had better offers a few houses away, so I gathered then that they didn't actually belong to the shop. However, I was naïve enough to follow them, and they were professional enough to deceive me. They walked suspiciously close to me, one to the right and the other to the left. I didn't feel at all comfortable being sandwiched like that.

I remembered a similarly uncomfortable experience in a Paris flea market, and my sixth sense told me that I had to get away at once. Then one of them asked me how much I wanted to spend and how much money I had on me, and I immediately knew that they were after my money. They stopped at the entrance to a house and tried to push me into it, but I got away from them and ran in the other direction as fast as I could until I could run no more, and took refuge in a coffee shop full of people. Gasping for breath, I ordered a doughnut and a Sprite at the bar. For once I'd had quite enough of shopping, and I continued to watch the entrance to the bar anxiously in case I'd been followed.

For the next few days, I only walked in safe areas near my hotel, and I later bought some shoes on Broadway. They weren't actually boots but white shoes with a lot of stitching, like the spats worn in the States at the time of *The Great Gatsby*. Anyway, these shoes weren't on special offer; they were very expensive.

That same day, I also bought a Polaroid camera in one of the many electrical goods shops around Times Square. The camera was a hit, because it was as small as a paperback when it was folded together flat. I began to take photographs like crazy, and that cost money because the films were very expensive, but I had a new hobby, and could use the new camera alongside the small eight-millimetre Bell & Howell movie camera that my father had given me for the journey. Filming with that was quite impractical on the road, because I always had to thread the film awkwardly in some dark corner and then take it out and turn it around after four and a half minutes, just for four and a half minutes of film.

82

That was troublesome, but in spite of that, I put up with it through all those months, and in the end I took 18 cans of film home. In contrast, the new Polaroid was modern and fast, and I kept it with me all the time.

However, there were some things even more enjoyable things than a new Polaroid. One afternoon, I was just sitting down to read some German newspapers that I had bought at a street kiosk when the telephone rang. It was Anne Gardner.

Wow! I hadn't counted on that. Although I was always thinking of her, I had no idea that she would ring me up; I thought that I would have to take the initiative. Anne was also unsure; I could hear that. "Hi, Wolfgaaang," she drawled. "I've heard you're back in town. How you doin'? How's the tour goin'?" She was polite and didn't give anything away.

I asked when we could see each other again, and I also let her know that I had been thinking of her often. In the end, she invited me to have dinner with her. We could choose between the Eidelweiß, a German restaurant in Germantown, or an Italian pizza palace in Little Italy. I also suggested that we could go to Chinatown and eat real chop suey. After some discussion, Anne suggested that I visit her at home, and that I bring a bottle of white wine with me. That was a much better idea, because I was always eating in restaurants. Also, a visit to her apartment would be much more intimate. We'd seen each other so rarely because I was on the road so much, and so something would have to happen then. To spend such a lovely evening in a public restaurant would have been a waste of valuable time. We arranged to meet at nine o'clock in her apartment in a distant part of the city, which I could only reach by taxi.

I looked forward to the evening, as expectant as a child. I bathed and put on my most attractive clothes, including my new white spats on my big feet. I was ready much too early, and sat in front of the window, dressed to the nines, killing time. Anne was the most beautiful woman I had ever seen. She struck me as being a mixture of Johnny Weissmüller's Jane and Walt Disney's

Pocahontas. The air was filled with eroticism, the city was bathed in rain and melancholy, and my jacket lay ready for me to slip on.

Suddenly, the phone rang. I thought at once that Anne had changed her mind and wanted to cancel. I had such little self-confidence in those days that I was constantly questioning everything positive that was offered to me.

As it turned out, it was Karl. I asked him what he would do if his girlfriend's lover came back unexpectedly. He would probably get beaten. I made him promise to move to a safer hotel outside the city and behave more discreetly with his beloved. I was seriously worried about him, but he reassured me that he had everything under control. When I told him about my approaching rendezvous with Anne, he wished me a passionate evening.

I travelled to Anne's apartment in a yellow cab, stopping at a shop on the way to buy a bottle of Italian white wine. After a journey of about 20 minutes, the taxi stopped in front a small house roughly in the same area as the one in which I'd got lost after nearly being attacked. So this was where the right-hand woman of Famous Music lived! The houses in the district were no more than four or five storeys high. Anne's apartment was on the second floor, and I had to take the stairs because there was no lift. The staircase was narrow and dimly lit, just like they are in American gangster movies. Music and television noise echoed from the doorways on each landing.

I was trying to appear relaxed, although I was very excited. Anne didn't open the door as soon as I rang the bell, but then various locks and bolts were shifted and there was Anne, standing before me in a fluffy, sky-blue bathrobe. Her long black hair was wet and she was still holding a towel in her hands. She stood barefoot, and her beauty took my breath away. She said that she'd still been in the shower when I rang, and invited me in, smiling seductively. She walked across the thick carpet with light steps, her long bathrobe opening a little at every step, allowing me glimpses of her slender brown legs and delicate feet, which totally aroused me.

She took the brown bag with the white wine from me and immediately uncorked the bottle in her small kitchenette, obviously enjoying teasing me. She didn't lose any opportunity to grant me more glimpses of her graceful body, and it was a pleasure to look at her. She didn't make any move to put on more clothing, either. It appeared that she intended to make it easy for me! She poured wine into two long-stemmed glasses and we toasted each other. She crossed her slender legs and smiled at me seductively. We talked and talked, drinking continually, and I marvelled at her revealing bathrobe... Drops of water from her damp hair ran down her neck towards her breasts. I knew precisely that I only needed to reach out for what she was offering – the drops of water were showing me the way, and Anne wanted it. She let the collar of her bathrobe slip lower down her shoulders. I sat there on the sofa, unable to stop myself from admiring her firm breasts. Her eyes were enticing me.

Why didn't I do what we both wanted? What was making it so difficult for me to take the initiative? I felt inhibited and paralysed by her beauty. If she had been less delightful, it would have been much easier. Nevertheless, I was on my guard against falling in love with Anne Gardner, because at that time I would have been consumed with love for this woman. I lived in Düsseldorf and Anne lived in New York, thousands of miles away. It couldn't work out.

At any rate, it was an evening full of delightful conversation, intense looks and mutual compliments. There was a breathtaking eroticism that hung in the air. Late that night, when we were both tired from talking and from the wine, I asked Anne to call a taxi and went back to my hotel, tired and depressed, dissatisfied with myself. Had I disappointed her? Perhaps I had...

When Karl flew in from Memphis several days later, we excitedly told each other about our experiences. He was happy, having been given everything that he'd wanted, but he had to laugh at my adventure. In his eyes, I'd failed completely, although I didn't think of it like that. I thought that I'd achieved a victory over my desires.

85

# 12  Worn-Out Speakers And Stoned Roadies
## 'Autobahn' In The Wilds

LINCOLN, NEBRASKA, 2 MAY 1975

It wasn't all happiness during our tour of the USA. From the beginning we had trouble with the loudspeaker equipment that we'd hired. The company that Ira Blacker had used normally travelled around the country with guitar bands, and their loudspeakers weren't up to the frequencies that our synthesisers put out, with their merciless sinus tones, and we were plagued with burnt-out oscillation coils. The speakers had been built for rock bands using guitars and keyboards. In contrast, our instruments were new to the world of pop, and we suffered from unforeseeable problems because of this.

If our rich sound was to continue to thrill audiences, we had to carry replacement speakers with us all the time, but these were expensive, the huge bass speakers particularly so. At that time, there were very few hire companies around that were carrying the high-class JBL Professional series of speaker, which we wouldn't be able to buy for ourselves for some time. We reached the stage where the company we were using was no longer willing to bear the high costs of the constant repairs and spare parts.

Another company was commissioned, but we had to sack its roadies after several concerts because they were always loafing around behind the scenery, stoned or coked up, not keeping an eye on the show for possible equipment or instrument failure, as had been contractually agreed. It was weeks before we had assembled a practised and reliable team with a new crew, who were also experienced in handling the loudspeakers.

In the beginning, the construction assistants and stage technicians – who were only ever on the road with the goods vehicle to take the instruments and the stage structures to the next venue overnight – weren't particularly impressed by our music. They were accustomed to American guitar bands, so they had difficulty in getting used to our techno music, which evoked so little emotion. To them, Kraftwerk was just a good job.

Apparently, though, on one occasion they had to undertake an extremely long journey, from the east coast into the interior of the country, which lasted several days. During this time, they passed through an isolated Indian reservation, far removed from civilisation, while looking urgently for a petrol station to fill up their truck. They found something like a gasoline pump in front of a corrugated iron shack in a tiny, run-down hole. A toothless Indian filled the tank with diesel, and one of the roadies went into the hut to get some chocolate bars, coke and beers from the ramshackle vending machines. Then he heard 'Autobahn', recorded at 16 Mintropstraße, Düsseldorf, on the Indian's portable radio. He could hardly believe it. He'd already heard the song every day during the concerts. But here, in the middle of the wilderness, with native Indians?

It was hard to believe that the songs broadcast from the large cities reached across the entire country. Indeed, every place, however small it might be, has its own local radio station. Our roadie would have been more inclined to expect country singers like Johnny Cash or Emmylou Harris on the radio than us. It must have been an astonishing experience for him, because he later told the story again and again. After this, the roadies actually became quite proud to work for us. New sounds always need time to be accepted, because they change people's listening habits.

# 13 Electronic Music,
## Like Air Conditioning

In May, the baking Californian summer was at its shimmering height when we reached Los Angeles. We stayed at the Regency Apartment Hotel on Hollywood Boulevard, a building on a luxurious, low-rise residential estate enclosing a kidneyshaped swimming pool. As usual, Karl and I shared a room, on the ground floor, from which we could go directly from our door onto the terrace if we wanted to swim or to enjoy the sun. We had some days free, and were able to have some time to ourselves, but it was so hot that we only went into the city a few times to do the rounds of the record shops, always looking to see whether they had our LP and single in the shop, which they almost always did. We also visited Universal Studios, but for most of the time I preferred to lie at the poolside, recovering from the stresses of the tour.

Perhaps we were a little naïve, but we always kept the apartment door open so that a little air could circulate through the rooms. There was air conditioning in every room, but we switched it off because we couldn't bear its constant noise, and we weren't used to the stream of cold air. News of who we were quickly spread around the hotel. Pretty girls in tiny bikinis would often walk across the terrace, passing our windows conspicuously slowly. One afternoon, I had a shower to cool down after swimming, and I heard the bathroom door being closed behind me. I was thinking that it had to be Karl returning from the town when suddenly the glass door opened and a girl I'd never met before, stark naked and with long blonde curls, joined me under the stream of water. Apparently, you had to expect anything in Hollywood! The girl raised a finger to my lips so that I couldn't protest. I managed to lose the power of sight and hearing as the young woman ravished me, and the cold water had no chance of cutting short my growing passion – this anonymous encounter, about which every man fantasises about at some time, was too arousing. In my case, fantasy had just become reality.

I'd never come into contact with a woman in such a brazen way, and I didn't know what to think of it. At the same time, my thoughts were always with Anne Gardner, but she was far away on the other side of America. In Los Angeles, everything was a movie, a production, a surprise attack, and anything was possible. Today I sometimes think that what I experienced then was all a dream. Later, the girl told me that she'd had her eye on me from the beginning. She'd been spying on me when we arrived on the hotel grounds, and had made a bet with her friend. So that was it. I was the basis of a bet. Mind you, I was glad to help her win!

It didn't stop at that surprise encounter. Sometimes she would pick me up in her large red convertible and take me shopping. It improved her image to visit her favourite shops with me. She loved taking me into shops that sold luxurious lingerie, where she would show me terribly sinful fabrics. She would coerce me into the changing rooms with her, and she would get undressed in front of me in the narrow cubicles. The face that only a thin curtain separated us from the saleswomen and the customers excited her. She couldn't think of anything but sex, and was always groping me. This reached the point where it disturbed me so much that I forbade her to do it. Then she wanted me to fancy her girlfriend and indulge in a threesome, which was really too much for me, so I tried to shake her off, although this wasn't so easy because the foxy lady was always popping up somewhere unexpectedly, demanding that I "keep company, Wolfgaaang, darling, please, be patient". I was beginning to look forward to the night of the concert, because after that we could fly away and I could be rid of this persistent groupie.

The Village Bowl in Santa Monica accommodated 3,000 people, and on that night it was filled to capacity. The next day, the headline was "Kraftwerk – Electronic Music Like Air Conditioning Over Hot Los Angeles". Once again, we were described as being unemotional, cold and unmoving. Californians were used to a radically different music, which was warmer and more rhythmic, with more emphasis on guitars.

Even so, many people had turned up in spite of this. They were curious how we "four from the autobahn" – from a distant country with no speed limit – would look and perform. Actually, they didn't know any of our other songs, apart from 'Autobahn'. That May, 'I Want You' was released by the handsome and curly haired singer Peter Frampton, who made his guitar perform wah-wah pedals by way of a tube that he operated with his mouth, and this was a typical American hit and was played almost constantly on the radio in LA.

That was more the Californians' thing. Our success was actually an exception because it tapped into the Americans' love affair with the car. Apart from this, they thought that we were singing "Fun, fun, fun on the autobahn", a homage to 'Fun, Fun, Fun', the surfing anthem by The Beach Boys. Because of the way that Ralf sang "*fahrn, fahrn, fahrn*", the Americans must have thought that the song was a tribute! Nevertheless, the linguistic misunderstanding helped to send our song high up in the US charts, and also helped to get the Americans accustomed to our music.

90

# 14 As Free As A Pelican
## I Become Sick

I found the constant flying another problem. Towards the end of the tour, perhaps just after our 40th concert, we were on a flight to New Orleans in southern Louisiana when I felt sick to my stomach. I was really ill for the whole day, and didn't feel up to going onstage in the evening at all. I just felt like being sick, but the others didn't take my problems very seriously, because it was a simply beautiful day in the old jazz town, which seemed so French and romantic. The houses were particularly endearing, with their balconies and cast-iron railings. The streets were dominated by lively happiness, nothing at all like the usual hectic rush of most North American cities. In New Orleans, everything was friendly and delightful, just like it was in Mediterranean countries.

That afternoon, we went out to a restaurant. Because my stomach was still not right, I ordered only consommé. When Emil asked for pepper, two waiters came hurrying up, carrying a metre-long pepper-mill over their shoulders like a tree trunk, one in front and one behind. They held one thick end over his plate and indicated to him that he had to say how much pepper he wanted. Then one of the waiters turned the big wooden wheel at the back, and freshly ground pepper fell gently onto Emil's meal from the

91

front. We laughed at the performance; they obviously had a sense of humour in New Orleans.

The evening of our appearance drew closer. The venue was a low hall with many thin iron pillars supporting the broad roof, and a large audience awaited us. It was a warm evening, and on the street there was a real sense of well-being. If only my stomach hadn't messed up our plans! After the meal, I'd started to feel increasingly wretched, and I started the show feeling nauseous. Nervously, I played my simple beats on the drumpad board. Karl stood near me, as usual, also equipped with a percussion board and his vibraphone. As we played through the set, I was also increasingly aware that the stagefright I always felt wasn't exactly helping. Quite the opposite: I was feeling worse and worse, and quite quickly.

As we were playing 'Autobahn', a song in which I had a lot to play, my stomach suddenly lurched. I felt bile rising, and knew that I couldn't complete another song. I tried to catch the eye of one of my colleagues, but they were all busy with their instruments, and if I was ever able to catch a short glance from Ralf or Florian it was never long enough to attract their attention to my situation.

I thought that I was about to vomit over my percussion board at any minute. It was dreadful. How could I deal with this onstage, in the middle of a song and in front of the whole audience? I no longer had a choice. In the middle of the song, I dropped my sticks, went to Karl on my right and whispered into his ear that he had to take over because I had to go right then and be sick. He looked at me in shock and saw that my face was ashen and my forehead was glistening with a cold sweat. He nodded briefly, and I quickly ran straight to the back of the stage and down the steps towards our dressing room.

Emil followed me, having observed the whole scene from his position behind the curtain. He was always observant, and always in the right place if any of us needed help. I threw myself into the corner of our dressing room and vomited again and again.

It didn't stop; I was at the end of my tether. My nerves had been worn down by the stresses of the tour, the weeks of eating foreign food, the constant jetlag and distress about my pointless infatuation for Anne Gardner. Everything had come to a head and was now being thrown up in this miserable dressing room at the tail-end of the tour. I was almost in tears, and having something like a nervous breakdown. It was so bad that a return to the stage was unthinkable. I was shivering violently in spite of the heat, and I asked Emil to call a taxi. I just wanted to get back to my bed at the hotel, and to be left alone in quiet and darkness.

Thank God the journey was short. When I got back to the hotel, I had a cold shower at once, and I felt better for a short time, but I continued to be ill all that night and the next day. I was continually shivering violently, my joints hurt and I was sick goodness knows how many times. We flew back to hot Miami Beach, Florida, a few days later, and we had a few free days there, but my condition didn't improve at all, which made us worried about the forthcoming concerts in Tampa and Gainsville. And as well as this, we still had to conquer Canada.

We were staying in a hotel that backed directly onto the beach. With the temperature at 33°C, while my colleagues lay stretched out beside the swimming pool below and had cold drinks mixed for them, I lay freezing in my bed on the twelfth floor, waiting for the doctor that Henry Israel had called. Henry knew the addresses of all essential people in every city for every eventuality, and he knew the doctor from previous cases.

Through our apartment window, I could see a brilliant blue sky and flocks of pelicans flying majestically over the Atlantic. This picture impressed me and calmed me. I would have liked to have been as free and healthy as them once more. For the first time, I thought about the meaning of our tour, how quickly everything had become routine and how much this powerful connection with Kraftwerk was limiting all of my other activities. I also thought about the enormous effort involved in staging a tour like this, and about the artistic and social inequalities within our group, which was actually Ralf and Florian's band, as they both made us feel often enough.

The doctor came in and diagnosed a bacterial infection, which many tourists had recently brought with them from their flights to Florida. In his opinion, it was distributed through air circulating in the air-conditioning system in the aeroplanes. My defences had already been weakened by extreme exhaustion, and I needed peace urgently because we still had some important dates ahead of us. It was important to us all that I made a rapid recovery.

The doctor and Henry whispered suspiciously to each other in the adjoining room for several minutes, then came back in. The doctor took out a thin needle, and told me that the injection that he was about to give me would cost an extra $50, in addition to his fee. I told him, "I will agree only if it helps." I felt a short prick in my left arm, and I immediately began to experience a welcome sense of well-being. I felt a very warm glow around my heart, and the pain disappeared. It was amazing how quickly my nausea and my other ills disappeared, and within only an hour I was feeling so much better that I even wanted to join my friends down by the swimming pool. Nevertheless, Emil forbade me to do this, and kept me in my room for the rest of the afternoon. I was told to drink as much root beer as possible over the next few days to wash the toxins from my stomach. I didn't have a problem with this, because I'd developed a taste for it when we first visited the USA. At any rate, I had rarely felt like this. I was constantly grinning, and when I walked I felt as if I was floating on air. I had no idea what the mysterious doctor had injected me with, and Henry didn't want to tell me. Even today, I don't know, but I have an idea…

The following day, I was lying with Ralf on a sun-lounger by the pool and we were talking about my "marvellous" recovery and, as so often, about girls. We felt safe talking in German, and were certainly not over-scrupulous about our language, until suddenly an amply built, fashionable lady next to me protested angrily in a Bavarian accent, "You could talk a bit more quietly.

They are dirty little so-and-sos, the men from Germany. Don't think that you're alone here in Miami!" We were shocked, but we had to laugh out loud. We apologised to the conservative southern Germans. We'd gone too far, expressing our intimate desires too loudly. When you're travelling, though, there's no more pleasant theme than love and desire.

Between the concerts in Florida and our flight to Canada, we found the opportunity to take a day trip to Disneyland with some young people that we had met in Miami, and to have a good time. We were always able to make friends. Wherever we were, there were always people who wanted to show us the surrounding area and their city, or to invite us home to a barbecue or a party, or to hit the clubs with us.

While we were in the south, we'd also attended a concert by The Beach Boys and Chicago, who were appearing in the same city, and who were also staying on the same floor of the same hotel as us. The concert was held in a giant stadium. To start the event, and between performances, a German troupe by the name of Traber demonstrated breathtaking high-wire acrobatics. One of the acrobats flew from the taut steel tightrope high above the stadium, propelled by a rocket strapped to his back.

Staying so near to my earlier musical idols was an awe-inspiring feeling, but we didn't get to meet them. We were too unknown to each other, and my colleagues and I were too self-conscious of the cultural differences and the strangeness of our music. I'd attended a Beach Boys concert once before, in the Düsseldorf Stadthalle in the mid '60s, along with The Beathovens. The band had just had a hit with 'Good Vibrations', and they had played the tune of this with a remarkable little box – you only had to move your hands close to it and it would sound like a singing saw. This was a theremin, invented by the Russian Leo Termen in the '20s. It was a fore-runner of electronic instruments, although it never found a proper role in popular music.

We played three concerts in freezing Canada, which weren't much fun because we'd just been in the warm south and then had to go back to the cold north, and we were all looking forward to going home. It was the beginning of June, and we still wanted to see some of the spring in Germany. Two months of touring had been enough for us all, and we'd had enough of living out of suitcases, flying every day and checking into hotel after hotel in order to start our evening shift like musical civil servants. It was also destroying our private lives. We were no longer able to cultivate relationships, and we also wanted to record some new music. Ira Blacker asked us to return in the autumn in order to consolidate our breakthrough in America, but it was the wrong time to think about this.

On the plane back to Düsseldorf, I talked about our future with Ralf for a few hours. After everything that we had experienced in the States, we believed that there was a rosy future before us. America had discovered German bands and was calling their music krautrock – a dreadful concept, the half-witted unimaginativeness of which I still find stupid today. Bands such as Tangerine Dream, Atlantis, Randy Pie, Nektar, Triumvirat, Frumpy and even Hanover hard rockers The Scorpions also toured the States, more or less successfully and independently, and Peter Maffey was also touring there with his people at the same time as us. Not one of these bands had a song played constantly on the radio, however, or reached the top of the charts like us. We were proud of our own style. We weren't copying American rock music or English pop. We were playing electronic music with German precision, and we were Kraftwerk, a completely new musical dimension. Ralf, who like me had studied architecture, said to me, "Wolfgang, I tell you, neither of us will need to work as architects any more."

For the first time, I also heard him talking to Florian about the many radio stations in America, the distribution system for news and music long before there was local radio in Germany. It was through these radio stations that our music had first spread across the country and made us famous, and Ralf and Florian had given many interviews to innumerable local stations. Suddenly, there was a theme in the air, the activities of the radio stations, and the title of 'Radioactivity Is In The Air For You And Me' was born. All we needed was the music to go with it. However, this had nothing to do with Marie Curie's discovery of radium. The ambiguity of the theme didn't come until later.

# 15  Me? A Hunted Terrorist?
## Police In The House!

9 BERGER ALLEE, DÜSSELDORF, 26 AUGUST 1976

It was late morning, and I was lying in bed in my large room, resting from a studio session the previous night, when someone rang at our front door. I didn't stir because people often called – salesmen, postmen or other visitors – and I just turned over to go back to sleep. I wasn't expecting anyone, so it could only be for Karl or Emil. Then I heard the apartment door being opened and mumbling.

A short time later, Emil knocked at my door and crept quietly over to my bed. He whispered to me that two policemen were on the landing and that they wanted to speak to me urgently. They were very nervous, and said that it would be better if I got up and came out at once. When I asked what they wanted, Emil said that he didn't know. I found it quite tiresome, but I got up, grumbling, and pulled on my pink (!) bathrobe. In the hallway, the sharp eyes of a trim young officer and his older, more experienced colleague scrutinised me. Almost in unison, the pair asked me if they could talk to me. I assented hesitantly, but still made them show me their identity cards before inviting them into our large kitchen.

I offered to make tea, saying that I had only just got up, but they politely declined, as they didn't have much time and were there on a serious matter. The older man pulled a photograph from his pocket, while his younger colleague kept his hands in his coat pockets all the time. I was sure that he had a loaded pistol there aimed at me. At any rate, he seemed very nervous and I thought it best not to provoke him. "Do you recognise this person?" the older man asked me. Frighteningly, the photograph was of me, or at least of someone who looked very similar to me.

"Yes, that's me," I answered disbelievingly to the policeman, who was still looking at me closely.

"So you recognise yourself, then?" he suggested, looking to his colleague significantly. When I asked him where he'd got the photo, he answered that that wasn't important at the moment, and went on to ask me where I was on a specific Monday afternoon. I didn't have the slightest idea. The date that he'd given was so far back that it was hard to remember.

"Shall I give you a little help?" Without waiting for an answer, he continued in the same breath, "Just before 16.00 hours on the Monday in question, you were driving over the Südbrücke in the direction of Düsseldorf in an S-Class, dark-grey Mercedes coupé. Is this correct?"

Light gradually dawned. Yes, I began to remember. I'd been on my way home from Vlissingen, a town on the Dutch coast of the North Sea, where I'd been visiting Marita, my current girlfriend, and her family during the holidays. Unfortunately, the fantastic coupé hadn't belonged to me; it had been lent to me by Peter Diepke, a friend who lived nearby. I explained all of this to the policemen, who expressed their surprise that I was remembering so accurately all of a sudden. When I asked where they'd come by information about my journey, they explained that a doctor driving on the autobahn in the opposite direction had recognised me just by the Südbrücke and had called the police, claiming that he'd seen Christian Klar on the autobahn. The observant doctor had even been able to note my registration number.

I found it hard to believe what people are capable of if they believe that there's a reward on the end of it. At that time,

Christian Klar was one of the most hunted terrorists in Germany, a member of the Rote Armee Fraktion, and the explosive nature of the situation immediately became clear to me. I also realised why the young policeman was keeping his hands in his pockets. It was known that RAF terrorists didn't fool around if they felt that they were discovered, and there were constant warnings about their dangerousness on the television and on the radio. A short time previously, Christian Klar had taken part in a murder in a Chinese restaurant in the Oststraße, and the policemen probably assumed that he was still in the city, possibly hiding under my name. They weren't sure whether they had the fugitive before them or not. What could I do to convince them otherwise?

Then Emil, who had been listening in the hallway, came to my aid again. He walked into the kitchen and asked the men whether they knew the group Kraftwerk. Troubled, they answered, "Yes, of course. 'Autobahn, wir fahrn, fahrn, fahrn.' Great song."

Emil replied, "And that is Wolfgang Flür, the drummer of the band, and he's certainly not a terrorist. Come into his room and he'll be able to prove it to you."

Rather surprised and uncertain, they followed us along the narrow hallway to my room, where my turned-back bedclothes were still waiting for me. A gold record with my name hung on the wall by the window, and the policemen admired it. They'd never seen anything like it close up before.

Still not sure if I was Christian Klar, they nevertheless asked me to sign a record establishing the explanation for my car journey on the day in question. We gave them a Kraftwerk single and signed it for them. As he saw them out, Emil grinned at the younger policeman and audaciously advised him, "Take care of yourself. Life is very dangerous out there."

I was concerned that we had such "observant" fellow citizens in the area. At that time, everyone distrusted everyone else. Every young person who behaved unusually or drove an expensive car was suspected of being a terrorist. The mugshots of RAF members were posted on every street corner, and they looked just like many other normal people. Who wouldn't like to get so much reward money? Consequently, there were constant denunciations, surveillance and spying in the Federal Republic. Little by little, I began to feel less comfortable there. I wanted to get away again as soon as possible.

Emil told me that, on another occasion, the police had appeared in a similarly alarming fashion. It was the year before I came into contact with the group. At that time, Kraftwerk were still unknown and making short tours and appearances in Germany. After concerts and tours they would usually meet in Florian's apartment, in a three-storey house owned by his father near the Theodor-Heuss Bridge. One night they came back from a gig very late, turning up in their Ford Transit and unloading their instruments, loudspeakers and microphone stands into the apartment and an adjoining garage. They remained in the flat for some time, refreshing themselves and discussing the evening. It must have already been very late when Emil looked out of the window and saw a pair of hands on the balustrade of a second-floor balcony.

Suddenly, the door of the apartment was kicked in with a loud crash and police swarmed inside. Two more men sprang over the balcony in one bound and pushed through the door. They were members of a special task force, and they proceeded to herd the musicians up against the wall, gesturing with their weapons. The band members had to spread their legs while they were searched.

An over-meticulous search of the apartment ensued, followed by an endless interrogation. The police wanted to know who they were, what they did, where they had hidden the weapons that they'd previously unloaded and the terrorist organisation to which they belonged. Of course, it was possible to clear the matter up after some time, but because Kraftwerk were still unknown at that time they had no celebrity status to fall back on.

Apparently, a neighbour had noticed them unloading their vehicle at night, thought that he'd seen them carrying weapons into the house and called the police, who immediately thought of a terrorist group or a bunch of arms dealers and reacted with practised force. In this case, someone else had probably wanted to hit the jackpot.

> "You have to do something to avoid the guilt.
> For this, we need a strong spirit and a gentle heart.
> We have all our standards in ourselves;
> We just don't search enough."
> *– Sophie Scholl, victim of the Nazi regime, killed aged 22*

# 16 *Percussion Through Gestures*

AMERICAN AIRLINES FLIGHT TO PHILADELPHIA, 8 APRIL 1975
On our first American tour, we'd messed around a lot during
the flights to help pass the time. New and crazy ideas for our
stage show would constantly occur to us all at the same time.
We understood well that, in the vast land that had spawned the
song 'That's Entertainment', people had become very inquisitive
about us four strange types from the land of inventors, poets and
thinkers, the home of Wernher von Braun and Siemens.

Our shows always gave good value for money, and were at least
as exciting as a visit to the New York Museum of Science and
Technology. Of course, they were more an attraction for young
men, and we rarely saw girls at our concerts. The flat percussion
board was of particular interest at our appearances, which I (and
later Karl) played standing up. I was playing it so often, and with
increasing enjoyment. On the flight from Chicago to Philadelphia,
probably inspired by the pleasant feeling of swaying, the idea
emerged that it would be even crazier if a percussion kit functioned
simply through hand signals or movement, giving rhythmical
commands without impact.

The exciting feeling of having only to indicate to an imaginary
drum in order to elicit a sound immediately took hold of me. I

103

thought about that Beach Boys concert in Düsseldorf back in the '60s, when they had used a theremin – which gave a continuing tone, rather like a singing saw, determined by the proximity of a hand – in their song 'Good Vibrations'. This early invention was more interesting to me now, and the thought that something like that could also function in my drumming, allowing me to sound drums without impact, persuaded me to allow my imagination full rein as I swayed. Florian would later come up with the idea for Kraftwerk's "drum cage", completely unaware of my thoughts during this flight.

# 17 *The Mercedes 600*
## *Bollig*

Florian had rung us up in the Berger Allee, wanting to drive us out for a coffee, but he was late. Then Emil knocked on my door and called me over to the window in his room, which looked out onto the road. "Just look out and see who's just driven by," he said.

A huge, dark-blue car was parked outside. It was unbelievably big, and had a Mercedes star the size of a beer-mat on its bonnet. I thought that the federal president had just driven up, and was flabbergasted. At the same moment, the front doorbell rang. We opened the door and there stood Florian, grinning impishly. He invited us out for a spin, and when we got into his new limousine we couldn't believe how ostentatiously luxurious it was. Florian explained to us that he had purchased the car at a very reasonable price at a used-car dealership at Becker in Düsseldorf called the Second Hand. He loved big cars, and I think that he wanted to prove something to his father.

The fact that he was earning so much money at that time made me think. Of course, I enjoyed being driven around by him and parading our celebrity status with his luxury motor, but there was suddenly an invisible barrier between us. I must confess that I felt envious of him, and apart from that his showy demonstration seemed to be solely for the benefit of Karl and me. "I just have to park the motor in front of the garage door when my father is driving his 280 SL to the office in the morning," he said, "so that he finally understands that you can earn money with pop music."

Florian's father had been deeply disappointed that his son hadn't followed in his footsteps and joined his architectural company, as Florian's sister, Claudia, had done. For this reason, Florian obviously enjoyed flaunting his financial success to his father with the purchase of this presidential vehicle.

We were all suffering from a lack of recognition because of our strict fathers, linked by the experience of a futile expectation of praise. In fact, our whole generation had waited in vain for encouragement, love and tenderness from our weak fathers, who were incredibly strict and prey to exaggerated expectations of their sons, while our mothers – the protagonists in our families – projected an image of strength, love and attention. As a result, we all had a marked feminine side from having these women as our role models. However, from an early age I found men who don't show any feelings, and who see themselves in competition with their children and unable to ask them for their opinions, particularly stupid. They just don't have anything worthy of admiration.

As we travelled in style in the fashionable 600, Florian also introduced to us a young man who had patiently sat and waited on the front passenger seat while he had rung our doorbell. The man was Peter Bollig, from Heimerzheim, a stocky, powerful 25-year-old student of electronics who seemed very cheerful, and whose healthy, ruddy cheeks gave away his country origins – his father owned a farm in Lower Eifel. Peter appeared to be a person who could not be quickly rattled. "He still makes his transformers by hand," Florian praised him. Peter later became an ingenious problem-solver and a cheerful friend to all of us, although I still don't know where Florian had met him.

We drove to a café on the bank of the Rhine at Düsseldorf-Benrath, where we sat on very solid chairs and where they served

Rhine fruit and cream gateaux and tarts in the most delicious varieties. A uniformed waiter had observed our arrival in the 600, largely because Florian had driven up very close to the terrace. He served us suspiciously and extremely reluctantly.

"Peter has a fantastic workshop for his electronic experiments in the yard of his parents' farm," Florian told me. "You absolutely must see it. You'll love it." Florian knew how fastidious I was with my own workshop. "He can realise everything that we can devise," he continued. "He's an enthusiast, an ingenious craftsman, and he even has an idea of how he can build an impact-free percussion kit."

Of course, that made me curious, and I urged Peter to explain how he intended to achieve this. He eagerly suggested using photocells – a transmitting cell and a receptor cell arranged some distance apart and which, when mounted on a framework, should function as photo-electric beams. The light beam between them would serve to maintain contact. "If you break it with your hand, it'll break the contact. It's like the doorbell in some shops, where a light beam is interrupted by someone stepping through the door. The receptor cell will register the interruption and transmit a gong or a *ding dong* sound. You can connect whatever you want. In your case, it'll be the sound of a drum."

This made it clear to me, and we constructed an imaginary space around me, in which I would be able to stand and make movements with my arms and legs that would interrupt such invisible light beams rhythmically. It occurred to Florian that the space around me would have to be an open cube – a thin framework of iron tubing, for example, with enough surface area to install the contacts – which would look good onstage. Still at the table, we drew plans of cubes in which I would stand and "dance" my percussion ballet, sketching on a paper serviette among plates of strawberry gateau, cutlery and silver coffee pots.

This didn't sound bad at all, and Peter promised to take care of everything. I got deeper into conversation with him, and discovered that he was also crazy about cars. He told me that he had a proper

107

hydraulic lift in his father's barn that he used for renovating cars. He enjoyed doing things like that with his elder brother in his free time, and they liked doing up vintage cars most of all.

This was great for me, because I'd recently bought a 1962 black Mercedes 190B in a private sale for 1,600 DM. I was proud of this car because it was a rare model, and it was also in outstanding condition. There were several details that weren't quite right, though, and Peter seemed interested in having a closer look at it. We arranged to meet up in the following week, and I drove to meet him at his farm in Heimerzheim in my old car. I drove along the Cologne-Bonn-Koblenz autobahn in the direction of Euskirchen, and then finally, after several attempts, I reached Peter's parents' farm. Like all farms, it comprised several buildings: a house on the road through the village, a stall, a huge barn and, further back on the site, a large, open vehicle shed, which was packed with agricultural machinery. The howl of an old farm dog brought Peter's mother – a small, kindly woman who spoke with a Rhineland accent – out of the house. Frau Bollig took me to a door in the barn and called to Peter from outside. When he didn't come out, she said, "Peter must be doing delicate work again. He doesn't like to be disturbed. Just go in quietly."

The low room looked like an experimental electronics lab inside. Transformers, electronic components, cables, measuring instruments and cannibalised circuit boards (the components of which Peter could still use) lay everywhere. It was dark and damp, and smelled of oil, solder and electricity. I made out the master craftsman in a back corner, under an iron window frame, working on something long and narrow. He came over, obviously pleased to see me, and gave me the most powerful handshake I'd ever felt, almost bringing me to my knees. Cheerful and painful, that was Peter Bollig. "What do you think of this, then?" he asked, pointing to a long, narrow tube of transparent plexiglass, into which many colourful, narrow cables had been inserted. Soldered onto the outer surface at regular intervals there were a number of tiny metal plates, which looked like impact contacts. "That's Florian's new flute," he said.

I'd had no idea that Florian was working on an experimental flute with Peter on the quiet, and I felt hurt in some way. So Florian was now messing about with his ideas with Peter. I was very sensitive at that time. If I had even the slightest sense of being ignored, and even if I was only imagining it, I would feel wretched. I had no self-confidence at all. However, I didn't let Peter see this. In any case, I was looking forward to inspecting my car with him and being able to talk shop about the technology of our "drum cage".

Initially, however, he was so busy with the flute that I didn't dare disturb him. He proudly explained to me how it was supposed to work, which in fact was rather like the "disc percussion", which he also admired greatly. The only problem was that Florian was unable to play the flute with sticks. He had to trigger electric contacts – which were all arranged in the same positions as the holes on a classical flute – with his fingertips. Peter explained that this was actually the smallest problem. "We only need to copy and arrange the body and the air-holes of his proper flute, but the contacts that Florian will have to trigger with his fingers are more complicated. Unfortunately, I've had to construct them all myself because there aren't any available to buy, and these don't work very well yet." He explained to me that they were still much too insensitive, and were triggering uncontrolled contacts. This was caused by the tiny relay inside the two-and-a-half-centimetre-diameter tube. Even so, he didn't seem at all dissatisfied with the situation – he had faith in his own ingenuity. The transparent, tubular flute looked ultra modern, and I found myself looking forward to him completing the instrument, choosing to forget my personal resentment.

We left his laboratory and went over to my vehicle. Peter was lost in admiration for the beautiful car, and wanted to have a test drive immediately, so we got in and he drove like the clappers through the dusty farm tracks and small nearby villages in Lower

Eifel. His racing-driver style scared me out of my wits, but this was common among young men in the country – there were souped-up Capris and Mantas with lowered suspension parked in front of houses everywhere. I pleaded with him to drive more slowly, though, because I was afraid for myself and for my lovely car. He tried to reassure me, and explained the workings of the old-fashioned, four-cylinder, naturally aspirated engine to me. "Now and again you have to give it a real burst so that it's cleared by air flowing through it. I can feel that it's flooded by your short journeys in the city." He often enjoyed making fun of us "elegant city types".

Back at his parents' farm, he praised my car and the deal that I had got it with. He told me that he'd have to do something to the wheel bearings some time soon because there was too much play with them, but that it wasn't dangerous at the moment. In the following week, he was intending to come down to the studio in Düsseldorf with the photocells for my percussion chamber. When I explained to him that there was still no framework for it, Peter told me that Florian had ordered one ages ago from an instrument manufacturer, and that it was supposed to be delivered in the following week. The fact that Florian was no longer discussing such matters with me was also new.

I was very confused on the drive home. Unfortunately, Emil was also unable to give me any explanation for Florian's actions. An uncomfortable feeling was growing in me. Perhaps he just wanted to surprise me. Florian was unpredictable, and he was always good for a surprise.

Some days later, a gleaming framework of tubing stood in the studio, fully assembled. The packaging still lay next to it. "I've already bought it from an instrument manufacturer," said Florian. "It can be screwed together very easily." I stifled my objections because the cube simply looked sensationally futuristic. The fact that Florian had ordered the individual parts so quickly was vindication of my idea.

That same evening, Peter came chugging along in his father's red diesel with a bag full of electronics equipment. He'd brought with him the photocells for the percussion chamber, with screw sockets and long cables, and proceeded to screw the individual components – one transmitter and one receptor for each cell – onto two opposing rods, at hip height, after asking me to take my position in the middle of the cube. Then he attached the long cables to a relay box and linked this up to the amplifier. The light in the studio had to be very subdued, and I was supposed to make vertical movements with my arm in the free space between the two vertical rods. Each time I broke the invisible light beam, the relays in the station triggered the selected instrument. The snare drum was connected up on the left side, with the bass drum on my right and the loud crash of cymbals to the front. The device worked to a certain extent, but it was rather hesitant and, frustratingly, it sometimes didn't work at all. When it did work, however, it was always a spectacular addition to our stage shows.

# 18  A Novelty In Liverpool
## Giving Signs

NEWCASTLE, 5 SEPTEMBER 1975

That summer, we hadn't had much time to rehearse with our new attraction, the percussion chamber, as we had to dredge up our earlier songs and also learn the ones on our current album, *Radioactivity*, which we had recorded quickly after our tour of the USA. Our next tour was about to start on 5 September in Newcastle, and I was looking forward to finally being able to travel to England, the land of my earlier idols, through whom I had found my way to pop music in the first place. "England" had always been a magical word to me. I thought of all the radio and television programmes about The Beatles, The Hollies, The Pretty Things, The Who and so many other famous bands that I'd seen ten years ago. Now that I was travelling there myself with my own band, one of my greatest dreams was about to be fulfilled. Also, the fact that I would be able to use my new percussion chamber had me almost crazy with anticipation.

We all travelled to England together – including Peter Bollig – in a second-hand black Mercedes 250S. After warming up in some small towns in Scotland, one of the first of our larger concerts was scheduled to take place in Liverpool, home town of The Beatles. On that evening, of all evenings, Paul McCartney was playing in

112

the city with his Wings Over Britain tour. It was unbelievable. I would have given so much to have seen McCartney's Wings play live. I'd read in the paper that he was touring with his band in his own private jet, and that he was playing in England for the first time in years. He also had a new song called 'Jet' in his repertoire. I wanted to ask him how he was feeling, touring his home country.

I was feeling great, at any rate! Everywhere we looked, our posters were stuck right next to those of Wings. The theatre in Liverpool in which we were to give our concert that evening was one of those plush old halls from the turn of the century, built in an ornate baroque style with red, upholstered seats and two or three rows of balconies – the usual layout. The auditorium smelled of floor-polish and linoleum, and the wardrobes and backstage area smelled strongly of detergent and stale alcohol. It was so neglected, cold and musty back there that I understood why musicians were unable to stand months-long tours in such impersonal surroundings without lots of alcohol!

We still had some time to relax in our hotel rooms before rehearsal. The organisers had actually booked good hotels in every town in which we were to appear, and we always had three double rooms: one for Ralf and Florian, one for Karl and I and another for Emil and Peter. We were governed by a fixed hierarchy. Emil was present on almost all our tours, fulfilling his tasks as tour manager. He and his assistant always made sure that there was enough money in the appropriate local currency with which to pay people or to organise replacement materials onsite in the relevant location. He greatly enjoyed doing this, because it was like being a kind of manager. He wasn't actually able to stand on the stage at night and be applauded by thousands of fans, but in this way he still had an important task to perform during our journeys and was able to smoothe over arguments and settle disputes. This was his great skill – he always seemed so well balanced, but he was also looking for recognition.

I would often spend the few hours before rehearsals cleaning my shoes or grooming myself in the hotel. It didn't take long to run a bath, and I was sometimes able to retreat and enjoy myself for half an hour or so in this way. There were few enough other pleasures on the road. Far from their homes, musicians had a tremendous need for love and tenderness. I know this from my colleagues – and, of course, from my own experience.

Florian suffered most from the stress of touring. He didn't like travelling at all, and after a few days on the road he would yearn for a familiar environment. For this reason, we would always spoil ourselves with a leisurely shopping expedition or two and dinner at a good restaurant. Emil told us that he often found Florian sitting alone in nearby Indian restaurants just before our concerts. Florian rarely told us that he would do this, and we were often unsure whether he would come.

Initially, everything ran according to plan during our rehearsals in Liverpool. As with the gigs in the small towns in Scotland, the English crew performed some outstanding construction work. In any case, the British were better technicians than the American roadies, whom we had to let go because of their drug consumption. We began the soundcheck by playing a selection of songs, including the new pieces 'Radioactivity', 'Antenna' and 'Airwaves'. After this, the evening soon arrived, and we drove with Emil and Peter to a nearby restaurant to eat.

We always got ready in our dressing room just before the performance. We had a flight case set up for our stage clothes in each of our sizes, and that night we were sitting there nervously. Every now and again, Emil went out onto the stage and looked through a small hole in the curtain that we'd brought with us (because not every stage had one) to see how many people had come. On this occasion, there weren't many in the audience. Emil told us that only about half of the hall was occupied, although he always exaggerated the numbers a little so that our mood didn't plummet through the floor. The worst thing was if only a few rows were occupied, although this was unusual in England, because from the beginning this was the country in which we had the most and the most enthusiastic fans. The situation that night was obviously a result of the fact that Wings were playing in the same city. In spite of this, Kraftwerk were bringing a new kind of pop music to Liverpool. We were the most modern act in the city, although many people weren't aware of this.

Just before eight o'clock, Emil fetched us from the dressing room and led the way to the stage with his torch, through the narrow passages and stairways of the old brick building. When we arrived on the stage, we took our positions behind our own instruments and devices and very quietly tested the tuning of the synths and the preset sounds of the keyboards and the drum machines one last time through headphones. I put on a pair of silver gloves and took my position in the chrome framework of light sensors. The cage stood in a prominent position in the centre of the stage, and was intended to be the main attraction for 'Radioactivity', our latest hit in the UK and the first song to be played. In those silent few seconds, the tension was nerve-wracking. As the house lights were dimmed, the noise audience became quiet immediately. At Ralf's curt nod, two roadies opened the heavy curtain. It moved metre by metre, because they had to get hold of the lines again and again.

We looked out into a large, black nothingness. Then a spotlight from the balcony shone onto the cage with me inside it. I lifted my right arm, moving it up and down through the front light beams in the rhythm I had practised for the beginning of the song. The plan was that my silver gloves would be illuminated by the front light cell and would flash every time I broke the beam.

Nothing happened. Absolutely nothing at all. How awful! How embarrassing! What was going on? I tried the snare drum on the left. Nothing there, either! Absolute silence. I stood petrified and alone on the stage, more lonely than ever before, in full view of everyone, pinned in the spotlight in the middle of the chamber, and they were all expecting something from me! The others were in darkness. I had no idea what they were feeling, and no time to think much about it, because I was occupied with my own predicament.

Something in the system had failed badly. For me, of all people! Why did we have to go on tour with such sensitive electronics? How reliable a Ludwig drum set would have been then. What a disgrace! The only consolation was that the audience couldn't have had any idea what they were missing because nobody had understood what I had just "performed". So, with an elegant gesture, I lifted my still-raised hand to smoothe my hair and stepped adroitly from the cage over to my drumpad, which had been set up nearby. The man operating the tracking spotlight didn't understand that I wasn't coming back to the cage, and he stubbornly kept the spotlight trained on the empty frame, so I was back in the darkness myself, but I switched on the board's lights and began to beat my rhythm there. Thank goodness the rest of the band understood what was going on! At that point, our neon lighting came on and we moved quickly into our new song, a stream of sweat running from my armpits down to my bottom. Apart from that, the evening went really well, but I was incredibly disappointed that my wonderful machine had failed. In Liverpool, of all places.

In our dressing room after the show, while we were taking off our shirts, which were completely drenched in sweat, the promoter introduced a few young men who wanted to meet us. They introduced themselves as Orchestral Manoeuvres In The Dark, a still-unknown student group from Manchester. They were impressed with our performance, and were very happy to be able to meet us in person. They excitedly told us that they had understood their musical future at once, through our synthesiser music, and said how happy they were. From then on, Andy McCluskey, their leader, cultivated a close friendship with us, particularly with Karl, who worked with him during the '90s.

The next day, we bought the morning papers at a kiosk before our departure, hoping to find a review of the concert. We found one. "With their new hit, 'Radioactivity'," it read, "the four electronic musicians from Germany have shown once again who is setting the synthetic tone in contemporary pop music. However,

116

the remarkable hand movements of their drummer, which resembled those of a traffic policeman, were incomprehensible. The quietness at the beginning of their concert was rather oppressive. Did Flür want to give us a sign? What message was he intending to transmit?"

We had to laugh about the article, and from that point on my friends constantly teased me about my traffic policeman's signals. Unfortunately, the technical breakdown occurred at some later concerts, too, and so later we didn't bother erecting the frame, resorting to the more reliable drumpad instead, totally frustrated.

Eventually, Peter found the cause of the fault. He noticed that the light sensors were too sensitive, and that even a spot of light onstage or on me was enough to disrupt their functioning. Although it was possible for their sensitivity to be calibrated more precisely, it was also possible that they would over-react unpredictably if we made them too precise. There was no time to repair them or change them on the road, and Peter said to me, "Don't be upset, Wolfgang. When we get back, I'll reconstruct it completely and install ultra-violet sensors. Then you'll be able to play it wherever you like, because those transmitters aren't affected by normal light." So the instrument wasn't finished yet, and I could look forward to an improvement.

After the concerts in England, we made some appearances in France, where we experienced a logistical mishap. Driving to Lyon in our black Mercedes, we drove straight into the rush-hour traffic jam. Time passed, and it got later and later. I can't remember where we'd played on the previous day, but I know that it was a long way from Lyon, and that we had a very long journey, during which we changed drivers constantly. At any rate, one of the trucks had got stuck somewhere, and when we arrived at the large, unfriendly hall, in which cattle auctions took place on weekdays, we were very late.

Fortunately, the audience had waited for us and no one had left, even though we turned up a whole hour late, and didn't have any stage clothes because these were in the clothes case in the

117

lost vehicle. We also didn't have time to have a soundcheck of any description. Everything was completely improvised, out on the open stage because we hadn't hung a curtain. We built up our instruments, amplifiers and the heavy loudspeakers ourselves with the stagehands and some roadies, and performed the concert without more ado in our normal clothing, which we'd been wearing all day. During the show, a synthesiser gave up the ghost in an acrid-smelling cloud of thick black smoke. In spite of this, however, the audience enjoyed the show, and honoured our come-as-you-are appearance with raucous applause.

This was the only concert we ever gave in jeans and leather jackets after the release of *Autobahn*. We looked like an electronic punk band. Strangely enough, on that occasion my percussion chamber functioned perfectly, goodness knows why.

# 19 Machine Men – Sex Machines?
## Four Large Ls

We didn't miss any opportunity to go out and have a good time, and we certainly weren't against having fun at all. Although as artists we were presented as having a stoic, unmoving and unemotional image, we were still young and full of energy and we had to let off steam somehow. Many people came to regard us as technocratic, unfeeling, cool, calculating and, worst of all, hostile to women, even though we loved women very much, and indeed pursued them. At weekends, and also usually on Wednesdays, we would stalk new prey in the clubs of Düsseldorf and Cologne, meeting regularly at about eleven o'clock in the Rocking Eagles in the Talstraße and then driving to Malesh (later Checkers) in the elegant Kö region.

At weekends, if that wasn't successful, our search would carry on into the night. There was a lot more going on in Cologne, which was only 30 minutes from Düsseldorf, and it was easier to satisfy our urge to exhibit ourselves ("we are mannequins...") and to pick up girls. The girls there seemed to be more interested, and they had a lot more zest for life than the stuck-up model types of Düsseldorf.

To start an evening, we usually drove to the Morocco, on the

119

Cologne Ring, where we were friendly with the DJ there, Carol, who would sometimes play our demo tapes for us, testing their suitability for dancing. Afterwards, we usually went to the Neuschwanstein, or to the Alte Wartesaal in Cologne's main station, a saloon bar which was very *in*. It was enormous, offering two dance floors and several bars to lean against. We would quickly establish a position at the bar furthest towards the back, which was raised a little higher, and so offered a good view of the dance floor, where we could look at girls. It wasn't that we were constantly picking up women, but sometimes one of us would make a dazzling conquest.

Later in the morning, anybody who hadn't had enough would visit the 42, or the Overstolz in the Südstadt. I often picked up girls myself, or rather I wangled it so that they picked me up. I can't remember how many women I danced and necked the night away with in Cologne. Thank God no one was talking about AIDS then, or it would have been a very frustrating time. At that time, my life was characterised by affairs with women, going out, making music and having fun with old cars. I was living hard and enthusiastically (although rather superficially) for the day, and was happy with myself and enjoying going out.

Because I was earning hardly any money from Kraftwerk, I sometimes had to find ways of earning extra cash. I didn't even shrink from having myself photographed naked for a men's magazine, which went by the title of *Don*. When the magazine published my photos, a gay friend of Florian's saw them and slipped them to him when the opportunity presented itself. Florian held the page under my nose, assuming that I would be embarrassed. "So?" I said. "Are the photos bad? At least I like myself!" Because I'd always had a healthy relationship with my body, I also saw it as my capital. I never regretted anything I did. We lived and loved hard, especially me. As young men (and ultimately we were nothing else, in spite of our fame), we were trying to find out what life could provide in the way of fun.

Things really got going when we held parties in the Berger Allee

120

MACHINE MEN – SEX MACHINES?

or in Florian's parents' house. Friends from all around would turn up to these, and each of them would bring food and drink. The rooms in the Berger Allee would be cleared of furniture and decorated by myself and Karl, and the large apartment always became packed with people very quickly. Two of the rooms were linked by a double door, which could be opened wide, and the two rooms provided a huge parquet surface that was good for dancing. The fashion was for disco and funk, and the hit of the day was James Brown's 'Get Up, I Feel Like Being A Sex Machine', which was symptomatic of our youthful needs. We also played popular dance hits from The Isley Brothers and Earth, Wind And Fire, envying these groups very much for their groove. My stereo system would quickly become overheated, and it often failed.

In the wee hours, the rooms would sometimes become dark because Emil would throw the fuse every now and again when he came back late and if things became too heavy for him. He would disappear into his room and lock the door from inside while things got going in the other rooms, mine in particular. People would make out and get it on for all their worth. Ralf and Florian unfortunately had always left the place before this time came – what they missed! A super-eight projector would be playing sex films onto the wall next to the bathtub. Everything would be covered in bubble bath and red wine, and candlelight would dimly illuminate the sweaty scene. These parties were like Sodom and Gomorrah. I was in the middle of it, always looking for girls and sex. I don't know what drove me on then, but I was (*was?*) certainly addicted to sex.

Karl was also one for the girls, and lost no opportunity to seek out pretty women. For fun, we took pictures of ourselves in the summer garden, featuring me posing with flowers in my hair, using mine and Florian's new SX-70 cameras. No, we certainly weren't cold robots then, but rather inquisitive young men, eager for adventure and the pleasures of life, and the photos are evidence of the quality of our friendship.

There was also a swimming pool in the garden of Florian's

parents' house. When we held parties there on warm summer evenings, couples and naked people would romp around in it, offering their bodies to one another. All of our friends enjoyed these parties, and we often asked Florian impatiently when his parents were going away again. To our satisfaction, they were often in St Tropez, or visiting their country houses in the south of France. We also liked cooking at the parties, while we slurped up Florian's father's champagne. We were all good cooks, but Florian was the best, having mastered the Mediterranean cuisine of his parents. Whatever he cooked was always a treat and something for gourmets. He's still a gourmet today.

We also listened to a lot of music at the house, where his father – an architect in the city – had embedded hidden loudspeakers into the walls. We would loaf around in his comfortable armchairs (which he had designed himself), listening to music by James Brown, The Beach Boys, Earth, Wind And Fire, The Ramones and, above all, The Isley Brothers, really analysing the music. It was there that I encountered the music of avant-garde artists Terry Riley, Steve Reich and Moondog. These were completely new sounds for me, far removed from my favourite pop music. Florian's mother, Eva Maria, liked us all a lot, and was often there when we were listening to music or philosophising. She would give her own reasoned opinion and then spoil us with her superior gateaux and chocolates bought from Café Bittner, a luxury café in Düsseldorf.

Looking back, I'm glad that I was able to experience such a carefree and enjoyable youth, which was above all free from fear. It was the time of the four great Ls: love, life, lust and laughter. At the same time, I was occupied in the search for a stable relationship with a girl, but it was a long time before I attracted a woman like that.

When that did happen, it was in the year in which the first dreadful reports of the new scourge, AIDS, dominated the papers. Our great Computer World tour of 1981 was behind us, and suddenly our chaotic lifestyle disappeared. Everyone was

122

panicking and starting to be very careful about encounters with the opposite sex. I remember reading the first headlines about AIDS in the publication *Stern* as I was lying contentedly with my new girlfriend on the grass in the Düsseldorf Rheinstadion. I was glad that I'd met Constanze, and although our meeting hadn't been an easy or a quick matter I also knew that she was the one I wanted. She entered my life at precisely the right time, at five minutes to midnight, to love me and to make my departure from Kraftwerk (which she never liked) easier for me.

# 20  The Sequencer Creates Unemployment

### The Electro Blues Starts In Paris

PARIS, MAY 1977

In the middle of the year, we had begun work on a new LP. In my opinion, *Trans Europe Express* is the best and most melodic album that we ever recorded. The idea of the title had occurred to Ralf, Florian and the French journalist Paul Alessandrini as they were eating a meal in the restaurant Le Train Bleu at the Gare De Lyons in Paris. Because of its theme, and because of the illustration of us on the front cover and the poster insert, this album contributed significantly to our unique German image. The cover was a gentle colour reproduction of the four of us created from a skilful photocollage made by the celebrated Paris photographer J Stara during a complicated photo session. We had discovered the photographer's studio next to the Arc De Triomphe back in 1974, during an earlier concert in Le Bataclan, a bar wreathed in marijuana smoke on the Boulevard Voltaire. We were enthusiastic about his montage technique and soft hand-colouring. In his shop window, Stara had advertised largeformat photographs of monarchs, heads of states, kings, first ladies and famous show and film stars for the whole world to see.

He took group shots in a process that he had developed himself, photographing each member individually in a separate corner of his studio in front of a black molleton cloth. Intimacy and the mental concentration of the artist on himself or herself were extremely important to him. For this reason, the separate lighting was absolutely necessary. If we'd all been photographed together, we would have ended up looking at each other, which would have been a stupid group dynamic, and certainly wouldn't have been the strong projection of our personalities that can be seen on the album cover. Stara took shots from all perspectives, in both colour and black and white, later developing the best negatives and mounting them into a dynamic grouping, taking care that there was no one at the back who didn't have a smaller face than anyone at the front. Everyone had to have the same significance in the picture. If you look closely at the picture, it looks like we're all a little distant from each other, as if we didn't know each other, and each of us has his own aura.

Stara realised that we weren't a band in the classical sense but were instead a group of four individual personalities. After he had finished taking the photograph, he coloured it in with a special spotting technique that he had also developed, which he executed with a brush less than a millimetre thick. It made the finished work look very soft and artistic. An enormous amount of work had been involved with our commission, but that was his particular speciality, and we admired him for it. The fee for his laborious work was horrifying, but the outstanding result was worth it.

A large poster folded up and included in the album shows a comfortable group sitting at a table with a red-and-white checked cloth in a coffee house under an oak tree on the Rhine, a romantic setting. This work was also a montage, from a photograph and an oil painting created by Emil. The poster later became a cult item, because it was only included in a limited number of records. It was pure irony, and a counterpoint to the tousled image of the punk scene that was then emerging.

Meanwhile, a serious technical innovation had taken place in the studio. Commissioned by Ralf and Florian, the Bonn synthesiser studio Matten & Wiechers had developed a device called a sequencer, a large, heavy, 16-track device. (It was always the same old story: we had to have the equipment that we needed custombuilt. There was hardly anything on the market. Unfortunately, this always cost a fortune, but thankfully we'd sold many more records since 'Autobahn'.) The sequencer could be linked up to the Minimoog synthesiser and control it by means of synchronisation equipment (which had also been commissioned). Ralf was then able to key in the individual notes of melodies into the sequencer. This device made it possible to regulate the tempo and the levels of notes, which could be changed independently during the sequence by means of a small, notched wheel.

The machine was revolutionary, and appeared long before MIDI technology, digital sequencers or computerised music programs came onto the market. It made it possible for bands to replace at least one musician. When programmed, it could play a looped melody for as long as required. The age of technologically controlled sounds had dawned.

We were now able to record our melodies and rhythms much more precisely. We had previously had to record everything manually onto the tracks of our MCI tape machine, which required a good sense of timing and a good feeling for the dynamic of the music as a whole. Now everything could be left to the machine, which was also linked to the tape and always started at the right time, at the beginning of a song. As a drummer, I became less and less important during the actual recording, because the patterns and fills were all programmable. The only things that were still important were composing the patterns and setting the style and tempo. I sometimes found this alarming, although rhythm programming is now a normal everyday studio technology – a drummer is no longer actually needed.

The idea of 'Metal On Metal' came from me. In my workshop, I was always manufacturing objects from large metal sheets, and it sometimes grew really loud in there. The others loved the idea of using these sounds. I would cover our devices in thin steel sheets fitting them with a hammerblow to the surface, and this led to my suggestions to use this harsh sound for the snare drum. We even considered using enormous metal sheets and an over-sized sledgehammer to beat out the number on stage. For that reason, we experimented with the most diverse types of metal sheeting in front of microphones in the studio. 'Metal On Metal' therefore became our first industrial song, as they were later called. However, we gave up the idea of performing it in public because it appeared to be too much fun. It would have meant that we would have had to present ourselves in action on the stage. This kind of thing was much more suitable for heavy metal bands than for our prosaic image.

Nevertheless, we did make a 16mm film for this song, which would be projected onstage. This was some time before MTV and video clips, but we had fun with short musical films. To make these, we hired the Düsseldorf film-maker Günther Fröhling, an extremely cheerful and experienced man who had learned his craft at the DEFA in Berlin. We took the familiar stationary shots on the platform of Düsseldorf's main station, and Fröhling filmed us in a light-hearted atmosphere in the compartment of an express train on the way to Dortmund. During this, the poor man lay huddled up in a luggage rack under the roof of the compartment, where we had stashed him, cradling his heavy Arriflex video camera.

In these recordings, you can even see me smoking a cigarette. This would never have occurred later, because I gave up smoking. Apart from this one vice, we all lived in a very healthy way, not wanting to set a bad example for our fans. Smoking and boozing were better suited to rock groups than to philosophising technocrats with a well-developed sense of responsibility.

Fröhling and his assistants, who worked for Märklin Model Railways, built a futuristic landscape in his studio with miniature skyscrapers and other buildings, reminiscent of Fritz Lang's film *Metropolis*. Florian was even able to buy a functioning model of one of the streamlined, propeller-driven trains that had been developed by the Nazis from a nearby toy shop, a rarity on the toy market. In our film, simple aluminium tubes like those used in air conditioning served as tunnels, and the Deutsche Bundesbahn served to make the realistic scenes of moving locomotives on tracks.

Our friend Maxime Schmidt, the manager of our French label, had organised a grand event for the release of *Trans Europe Express*, inviting journalists to travel with us in restored carriages on the *Orient Express*, from La Gare Du Nord, Paris, to Reims. Our new album was played continually through loudspeakers on the train during the journey. We sat in one of the most luxurious compartments, furnished with valuable intarsia work and mother of pearl, answering questions gladly. Of course, there was plenty of alcohol for the journalists, so most of them were drunk upon our arrival in Reims. There we were quickly transferred to waiting buses, and the local police provided us with a motorcycle escort. We drove through the inner city and out into the country, heading for the vineyard of Moët Et Chandon – the famous champagne manufacturer – at high speed, where an atmospheric, torch-lit supper awaited us. The waiters of the champagne company hovered everywhere, bearing heavy magnum bottles, skilfully pouring the fine foaming drink into our glasses one-handedly.

The constant refilling of our glasses encouraged us to relax to the point at which we became very foolish, and soon the journalists and record-company employees – 60 of them, at least – were all thoroughly tipsy. That night, accompanied by raucous singing, we took the buses back to Reims Station and then made the short train journey back to Paris. When we got there, we all took a taxi to the exclusive Parisian club Le Palace, where we met the singer Grace Jones. I made a date with her (although unfortunately nothing came of it, dammit!) and we danced into the early hours of the morning.

If I have to make a journey these days, even if only to visit my management company in Cologne, I like to take a similarly

128

Winfried and Wolfgang. Frankfurt, 1947.

Family happiness. Koblenz, 1953.

Hildegard Flür.

L–R: Great-grandmother, Gregor, Winfried and Wolfgang at the age of seven. Filsen, 1954.

First love, Brigitte. Düsseldorf, 1965.

Winfried (L) and Wolfgang (R) in an
early thespian encounter.

The Beathovens in Dahme,
Eastern Sea, 1965.

The Beathovens, smoking like chimneys,
just before supporting The Who in concert.
Düsseldorf, 1966.

The Beathovens on tour.
Eastern Sea, 1965.

The Spirits Of Sound at the Teenage Fair. Düsseldorf, 1969.

Drumming with The Spirits Of Sound in 1969.

The Beacon Theater, Broadway, New York, in 1975.

'Kraftwerk: The Man Machine.' US poster, 1975.

Karl (L) and Wolfgang (R) on stage at the Beacon Theater in 1975.

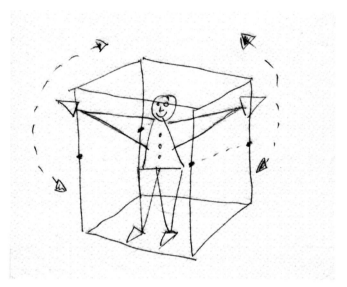

The first ever drum cage, designed on a napkin in July 1975.

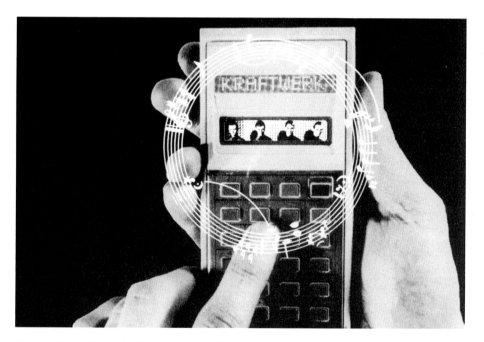

One of the pocket calculators from the 'Computer World' tour, which played the melody of the song.

Tiny instruments – what a release!

Playing *boing, boom, tschak!*

Ralf and his stylophone.

'Pocket Calculator', somewhere in Europe, 1981.

At the Lido, Venice, in 1978. The band's neon name-signs are clearly visible.

The gleaming chrome and sharp angles characteristic of a Kraftwerk concert.

The electric quartet.

Karl, triggering sounds on his customised keyboard with a metal pen.

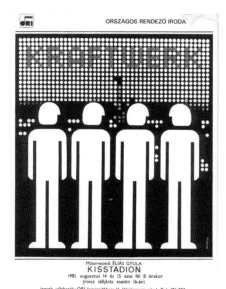

Painting the video screens with Emil at Popkomm, 1993.

Poster for the concert in Budapest in 1981.

Constanze peeling fruit in St Tropez in 1983.

MTV's Steve Blame, announcing the release of 'Little Child', the first Yamo song, in response to the Bosnian war in 1993.

Jeannine Flür (niece) in the 1997 video
to 'Stereomatic'.

The doorway of the apartment at
9 Berger Allee, 1998.

The dog from the 'Stereomatic' video.

George Clinton testing the 'Stereomatic' headphones in 1997.

large, solid train, such as a Euro-city or an intercity, but never the super-fast, nerve-shattering Intercity Express. I like to recall our time on the Trans-Europe Express, which travelled through the Rhine Valley. That was always my favourite route, along the mythical river, alongside the castles, fortifications and the ancient villas, which dated from the Wilheminian period, some of which had been built by my great-grandfather, Josef Rindsfüßer, for rich industrialists and politicians at the turn of the century. For this reason alone, *Trans Europe Express* will always be my favourite album, because it has so much to do with me and my love of German romanticism and melancholy.

Paris was the epitome of a chic metropolis, even for the sons of cultured and prosperous families. I always thought that Ralf and Florian felt most comfortable there and were in their element. They were like spiritual and cultural tourists, only too glad to press their noses against the windows of the elegant shoe shops, where you couldn't simply walk out with a pair of shoes; you had to be measured and then wait weeks for your shoes to be made by hand. The prices were accordingly high – in such places, 700–1,000 DM (£250–£350) for a pair of shoes was quite normal.

The restaurants and cages in Paris were also very classy, and such elegance drew Ralf and Florian as bears to honey. They took every opportunity to throw on stylish suits and give clever answers to young journalists in some of the most blasé interviews, which I have read as translations (I could speak hardly any French), and I believe that people understood our music and its philosophical content best over there. At the same time, the pair usually kept a polite but discreet distance from the person they were talking to in a very stilted, rather shy, almost ethereal way. They were more like culture diplomats or the representatives of a humanitarian organisation than musicians. If we went out together – not always the case, by a long way, because I usually couldn't afford to – we were always welcome guests, and people would look at us as if we were demi-gods. I liked that a lot then, too; Ralf and Florian had infected me with their style. And the idolising gave my ego an enormous boost.

We always got into discos like Le Palais or the more outrageous Bain Et Douches without delay, and the brasseries and restaurants drew us like magnets if we lingered in the metropolis, where the lights never went out, apart from the street lights that appeared at night. The enormous 2,000-capacity La Coupole, the country-style Au Pied De Cochon in Les Halles and Le Train Bleu in the Gare De Lyon, decorated with kitschy ceiling paintings, were just some of the restaurants that we – some of us still meat eaters – visited.

At La Couploe the maître d'hôtel was a German, of all things. He was an extremely organised but entertaining man who had worked there since the basserie opened, in 1925. The décor of the place – with its ceiling high, *schliere* mirrors and wall paintings full of social motifs – expressed a *joie de vivre* from a time when people still danced the Charleston.

The headwaiter was usually standing conspicuously in the centre of his gourmet temple. With discreet calls and hand signals incomprehensible to the diners he directed his hierarchy of senior waiters and their subordinates, down to the humble garçons, who were only allowed to change the paper tablecloths and place fresh bread and water on the table when new guests sat down. His eyes were sharp and woe betide you if he caught sight of someone impatiently hailing a waiter; he would send a minion over to the table with authoritarian tongue-clicks and a snap of his fingers.

There were at least 100 waiters working there. They would move through the passageways with breathtaking speed, laden with enormous metal trays carrying full dishes or crockery that had been cleared away. It looked bizarre to see them plough through the doors to the enormous kitchen, carrying plates and dishes with never a mishap. It sometimes looked like a dance when, fully loaded, they followed the movements of the swinging doors so that the crockery wasn't swept out of their arms. They

130

would move back and forth in their black waiter's trousers as if they were dancing the two-step on their thin legs, and then speed through quickly, just when the doors were swinging the right way. It looked simply priceless: forwards, backwards, through quickly. The torsos of these men – most of whom were considerably large – seemed to stand still in the air as they moved, stiff as boards, and only their legs moved. To and fro, ahead and back, wait for the passage and… *through!* They obviously knew a lot about the physics of the pendulum, and I admired that.

La Coupole was entertainment to fill the evening any time, practised and executed in the long-standing tradition of the house, perfectly organised. We felt a strong connection with this degree of organisation, as we were known for being arbiters of perfection, too, with our technically clean Germanic sound. And the maître d' was often in the habit of giving his customers neck massages while they were eating at the endlessly long tables – and of course, out of our group, he selected me. His hands were very sensitive and effective, and I basked in his flattering remarks – for which he was famous – while he recommended that I try their delicious *steak au poivre verde sur asperge gratinée au sauce Béarnaise.*

The maître d' liked us especially because we were German, too, and because we were cheerful and quiet celebrities who knew how to behave and didn't let our hair down like some other people from the world of showbiz or the city's intelligentsia, who enjoyed carousing there loudly and simply tolerated the food, which wasn't always that great.

On one occasion, our restaurant visit became a matter of survival. From a distant table, we heard a sudden, very loud noise. Boorish thespians from a local theatre – who were probably drinking after a première that had turned out badly – were sitting a few rows away. Suddenly, a scrawny actor leapt onto the table and wrenched open a can, showering the foaming contents in all directions while shouting hysterically in French. The swine had sprayed tear gas, and we didn't notice until it was too late, when the corrosive acid cloud floated over to our table. Everyone immediately got the most horrible attacks of tears, coughing and retching.

All the neighbouring tables were affected, too, and widespread panic erupted. Everyone in the restaurant – and there must have been 100 people there that night – tried to squeeze through thr revolving doors into the street at once, out into the fresh air. Such recklessness was simultaneously grotesque and alarming. People were stampeding towards the plate-glass doors as if it was a matter of life or death, and indeed I had the feeling that I wouldn't get out alive. Everyone around was coughing, and I watched, nauseated, as some people vomited on their tables.

Later, I saw waiters and their strict boss wildly gesticulating and coughing loudly on the pavement of the Boulevard du Montparnasse. All the delicious food had been left and now it was getting cold and spoilt between torn-off tablecloths and vomit. No one really wanted to go back inside and, besides, it was only possible to go back to your seat after about half an hour, when the restaurant had been ventilated and the tables cleaned hastily. You'd have to order *completement nouveau*, and it certainly wouldn't have arrived *tout de suite* as usual.

We hailed a taxi and rode back to the hotel. We'd lost our appetites, but that was just Paris – you could never be absolutely sure something like that wouldn't happen. I don't know what became of the actor.

Things became just as exciting on a quiet Sunday morning while we were brunching on the Champs-Elysées. We would often stroll alongside the great fashion houses between Place de la Concorde, with the pointed obelisk in the idle, and the Place de L'Etoile, with the Arc de Triomphe to the north, looking at the shop windows and having dinner. On this particular sunny morning, we were sitting on the terrace of the Café de Paris opposite the drugstore, not far from the elegant Citroën, Simca and Renault showrooms. We haad already been served with our baguettes and cafés au lait and assumed that we were in no particular danger when a violent bang suddenly thundered through the city. Shockingly, it came from our immediate vicinity, and it was followed by several echoes from all around. Thunder – rumbling – and thunder again, a huge clap. I've never felt such a huge vibration in my life. The shockwave of a massive explosion rolled up the Champs-Elysées, and I can still remember that I could actually see it coming with a time delay. The compressed air glinted with menace, looking somehow both milky and sparkling brightly. With it came a cloud of dust that looked as it if was composed of the finest sugar crystals, but it wasn't sugar at all – it was pure glass dust! A billion tiny fragments from countless shattered windowpanes of the US TWA offices came flying towards us.

I later learned that a bomb planted by the OAS had exploded. At that time, the French were having huge problems with the left-wing terrorist organisation, just as the Rote Armee Fraktion was making people fearful and scared at home in Germany.

There was a deathly stillness after the explosion and we were enormously lucky that we'd been sitting behind a wall made of thick Plexiglas. Otherwise, we would have been grinding curshed glass between our teeth or suffering ever worse injuries. Looking into the stillness, I could make out buildings of the US airline still standing a few hundred metres down towards the Place de la Concorde. It was eerie but also beautiful to behold – on one side of the building, the curtains were hanging at the same angle as the street from eery window. It looked like there was a sudden draught in the building. I'd never seen anything like it before, and neither had I ever seen a street shining in the middle of spring as if under a fine layer of ice. I shall remember that terrible bang and the fear I felt for the rest of my life.

However, we were safe in our hotel. We usually stayed at the Royal Monceau in the Avenue Foche, a fine establishment near the Place de L'Etoile. Fortunately, the hotel belonged to a chain in which our French recording company had a share and was thus able to subsidise our stay a little. That was quite all right with us, because the hotel was stylish and expensive – first class. However, a small, comfortable bar at the reception remained wallpapered in a green, red and yellow tartan and intimately lit by table lamps with small cone-shape shades decorated with paper cigar bands, just link in the whisky bars of the '60s and '70s. I saw a lot of hotel bars with such décor in Europe on our travels. Lots of conversations, ranging from the important to the extremely banal, took place there at that bar, and you would always be served peanuts and olives with your drink, even if you'd ordered only a fizzy drink or a tonic. High-class prostitutes also often waited for their guests there.

The rooms were furnished most elegantly, and it was all genuine, not throwaway rubbish like we found in some American hotel boxes, which always looked the same. At the Royal Monceau, European culture was dominant. The bathroom was the showpiece, with walls clad in marble and fittings including two heavy washbasins, a shower, a bidet (for the lady) and a bath big enough for three, as I once told everyone, happily and quite naïvely. An American publicist staying in the hotel at the same time, and with whom we were friendly, exploited this after a turbulent night at the disco. In fact, she sneaked next door into my suite, where I was necking very intimately with my girlfriend, who had come into the bath with me. The intruder was so outrageous that she immediately undressed in the bathroom and stepped into the bath behind me to busy herself with me as well! This was not at all unwelcome to me or my girlfriend, who had a weakness for pretty women anyhow, and the American was simply stunning, with black hair as striking as her own. The pair were soon enjoying each other *tout de suite*! And so I was actually initiated into a real *ménage à trois* quite unplanned – in Paris of all places. Oh, la la – you probably *do* travel there because of love, don't you?

# 21  Ja Twoj Sluga – Ja Twoj Rabotnik
## The Robots

MONTPARNASSE TOWER, PARIS, 1978

In the many reviews and articles that appeared in the international music press, and in their analyses of our synthesiser music and appearance, we were often described as puppet-like, cold and robotic. This gave us the idea to build on our theme of being window dummies. This theme had already been going around in Ralf's mind since our first American tour, and suited our formal, puppet-like image. As I said, since *Trans Europe Express* we'd decided to refrain from staging action-packed performances, using huge metal sheets and suchlike for percussion. In 1978, Fritz Lang's film *Metropolis* presented a world of mechanised people and servants, and the continuing mechanisation and automation of our own musical production in the Kling Klang Studio lent itself to the robot theme. Ralf and Florian still had the "Kraftwerk – The Man Machine" poster from the US tour in their minds, a phrase so strong and rich with associations that it simply had to be developed into the title for a new album.

As it turned out, work on this album was carried out more and more by our enormous analogue sequencer. Melodies and rhythms sometimes ran automatically in the studio for days on end in minimised forms so that we could test their effects. From time to time, Ralf would play variations on his synthesisers and would then transfer them to the sequencer, which would mean that his hands were free to play another keyboard, to add accompaniments or anything else that he wanted in the composition. It was an unending cycle of trying out and resetting our electronic slaves. The music of Kraftwerk didn't actually emerge spontaneously through emotional group sessions, like that of normal bands; instead it tended to be created via a procedure one might find in a research laboratory or on a musical research programme, as if an academic professor was making up a new musical format for the needy in the world.

We often carried out tests to determine the effects of the new formulae that we were developing, playing the music on the stereo system in Florian's car during journeys on the autobahn to Cologne, or getting Carol to play it at the Morocco. My personal influence on the work was becoming increasingly limited to the providing of advice and short drumming sessions against which to test styles. Subsequently, the programmed sequencer could reproduce rhythms that had been played only once on the pad boards, and for as long as required. Consequently, Karl and I didn't have to stand at the percussion kits and drum for half the night.

This was a very practical arrangement, because it gave me more time to concentrate on the design of our instruments. I immediately rebuilt all of our new keyboards and the other electronic devices that we used in our work, providing them with more modern housings and covering them in sheets of stainless steel. We didn't want to show collections of prehistoric brown or black plastic boxes onstage, emblazoned with enormous manufacturers' logos and names. Everything had to look like an integrated whole, hidden behind metal trim and gleaming keys.

We also devised the first electronic keyboards, at a time when there were still none on the market. I built the prototypes, which hung around the player's neck, in a workroom next to the studio and in my workshop in the basement of the house in the

Berger Allee. In the same way, I designed and built an electronic vibraphone, which was linked to the master synthesiser and could be carried on a belt, like an ice cream seller's tray. The idea was to develop instruments that we could all hang around our necks and play while moving freely around the stage. We surrounded the edges of the keyboards, drumboards and the vibraphone with blue neon tubing. All of the upper surfaces were covered with reflective metal sheets, and the contact pads were mounted on discs of white plexiglass, which were in turn illuminated by thin, blue neon tubes. The whole effect was very futuristic, believe me. Nevertheless, we never used this complete instrumental genre because we later found other solutions that we preferred, and which were smaller and more portable.

We decided that we would have *Doppelgängers* made of us, and after this the idea of developing robots developed rapidly. We asked the leading fashion houses in the city if they could tell us who were the best manufacturers of window dummies, the name of the Obermayer company in Munich was mentioned again and again. It was said that the models in their shop window had the most realistic faces. After several telephone calls, Florian arranged for us to meet the manufacturers. We drove to Munich in the Mercedes 600 on a number of weekends, where we stayed in the elegant Bayrischer Hof. In the daytime, we each had a session in the boss's studio, which would last for several hours.

The old man was a true artist, but his studio was very creepy. There were piles of clay, plastic heads and body parts everywhere on the metre-long shelves and in the open cupboards, most of which were covered with a thick layer of dust, in various stages of completion, broken and unpainted. There were those with eyes and those without, and from every period of world fashion. The castings and pre-fabricated parts made them look as if they came out of a chamber of horrors. Most of them were casts of the heads of past and present female models that were supposed to represent the ideal of beauty of their time. The artist had modelled them all from raw clay himself (it could have been thousands in previous decades), absolutely true to the living heads that he had chosen reproduce.

When it was my turn to pose, he sat me on a raised chair very close to his potter's wheel, where he shaped, kneaded and pushed a lump of clay around until he had a shape similar to my head. While he was doing this, he occasionally measured the dimensions and distances of my skull with a large pair of compasses, constantly checking that the eyes, ears, nose, mouth, forehead and chin of the sculpture had the correct proportions and distances from each other. Subsequently, a negative casting of my clay head would be made in the plastics department of his company, and a polyester shell would be made from that. This would be sprayed with a skin-coloured material, and the master craftsman would paint it with reference to a colour photograph of my face and give it the right eyes and lashes. The man had a cupboard in his workshop with many small drawers full of glass eyes of every size and colour. Eyelashes in all shapes, colours and lengths also lay set out in drawers, ready for selection. If you weren't used it, the feeling of all of those thousands of artificial eyes staring at you from the drawers would be enough to give you goosepimples. Soon, each of us had his own duplicate head, and we had a lot of fun with the dummies. I found myself with a second twin.

## 22 *I Am Your Servant – I Am Your Robot*

After the exhausting and lengthy sessions, I enjoyed spending my evenings with Karl in the Trader's Vic, the cellar restaurant in the Bayrischer Hof, where they sold the most delicious – and large – cocktails. A large quantity of white rum, coconut milk, vodka and exotic fruits were mixed together and small, piquant canapés were added. The restaurant was furnished with cane chairs and we loved it, largely because of the very attractive Hawaiian waitresses, who served us attentively, and because the drinks had a wonderful effect. Also, if we were drunk afterwards, we only had to go up a few floors in the lift and fall straight into bed.

We found some standard clothes for our robots, which had wooden ball-andsocket joints at their shoulders, elbows and knees to allow them to be bent into position. Wooden bungs rose from the top of the models' torsos, and our finished heads were set on these. Now all we had to do was buy red shirts, black trousers and shoes for them. Peter Bollig welded small plates covered with rows of red LEDs behind the mannequins' black ties, which stuck out from tiny holes that he cut in the material, and these winked in a rapid rhythmical succession from top to bottom, powered by very small-scale electronics and a hidden nine-volt battery.

Our robots looked great, and we presented them for the first time – along with the song, 'The Robots' – in our spot in the ZDF show *19.30*, hosted by Thomas Gottschalk, on 29 May 1978. The show was filmed by Günther Fröhling, and he also shot the performance in 16mm. We were already building in little tricks by now, such as installing an electronic counter on the foreheads of the robots and movable mouths which spoke portions of the text: "*Ja twoj sluga. Ja twoj rabotnik.*" ("I am your servant. I am your robot.") It was obvious that we had to build this sentence into our song, particularly after Ralf (who had once studied Russian at school) found out that "robot" translates into Russian as *rabotnik*, meaning "worker". Fröhling had filmed these words from Ralf's lips and played them onto the face of his puppet by using a simple crossfading technique. Unfortunately, other electronic tricks, such as morphing, wouldn't be available for a long time.

Meanwhile, we were able to decorate our new robots, and they could be made to look just like us with masks on. In the film, we all appear together and play a game, exchanging identities with our puppets. For the album cover, Fröhling photographed us in the stairway of his studio. By a stroke of luck, the startling red banister of the staircase also appears in the picture. Our stepped presentation and our austere eastward gaze, combined with the static design of the cover, betrays our constructivist stance and our love of the movement. We commissioned the Düsseldorf graphic studio Klefisch to create this sensational design, imitating the '20s poster art of the Russian artist El Lissitskij. Many people later misunderstood the cover shot, finding it too fascist. They were unable to understand that it was pure irony to us.

In 1978, Maxime Schmidt, from the French recording company Pathé Marconi, had another great idea of how to promote our album *The Man Machine*. Journalists had been given glossy red invitations to a launch party high up in a new skyscraper, the Montparnasse Tower. Huge red posters were stuck up all over Paris showing the cover of our new album, as big as the posters for washing powder, and anyone who didn't know us might actually have found them quite fascist. At the party, we only appeared before

140

the journalists very briefly, and they had to put their questions to the robots. They already had the answers ready printed on paper. Everything in the room in which our presentation took place was decorated red, matching the Russian-style album cover, and of course there were also large quantities of vodka and caviar, and our new album was blasted constantly out of the amplifiers. The journalists grew rather unhappy, but whether this was because of their drunkenness or because of their disappointment in not being able to interview us personally (we had allowed the robots to represent us completely during the whole party) is unknown to this day. In any case, many souvenirs were removed that chaotic, vodka-soaked night. The next day, we had to pack our now almost-naked personal representatives back into their cases. Robots are patient; they don't object to anything or protest.

Something interesting happened on the way to the launch in Paris. In order to transport the robots and the small amount of equipment we needed in case we had to stage a short appearance there, we had to acquire a carnet to cross the border. This was a declaration of harmlessness, an official certificate of passage for our trucks and freight. After having the papers drawn up at the customs office in Düsseldorf, Karl and I drove to Paris in a rented VW van along with the luggage. Before we'd left Germany, however, the rented van broke down, and we had to wait in a car park for replacement transportation to turn up, which took several hours. After quickly loading our luggage into the replacement van, we drove on more quickly because we didn't want to drive through the night, and I was also afraid that I wouldn't be able to find my way around Paris at night.

Even so, it was already beginning to get dark and rainy when we reached the French-Belgian border at Valenciennes. A long queue of vehicles had formed at customs clearance, and this was moving forward very slowly. When it was finally our turn, we held out our passports from the van window, hoping to be waved through quickly. However, the French customs official seemed to be disturbed by something about us.

Perhaps the miserable weather was making him bad tempered and he just wanted to demonstrate his power to us kids. "What have you got in there?" he asked. "Where are you going? Do you have anything to declare?" After I explained that we were from Kraftwerk on our way to an important appearance in Paris, the official grinned and directed us out of the line of vehicles. "Drive over to the right and show me your vehicle papers," he requested sharply. Without further comment, I parked the van and gave the man the hire company's permit. Then he shone his torch inside the van, and on seeing the many black boxes and crates he became very curious, and wanted to know what was inside them. Our instruments and the stage set, I told him. He then told us that he wanted to see our customs papers. I gave him the German carnets and he disappeared into his hut.

When he came back, after a quarter of an hour or so, he said that we had to open up the back of the van and take out the boxes so that he could inspect their contents. After I attempted to protest – after all, we had an official carnet guaranteeing uninterrupted passage – Karl mollified me, saying that it would be best to show the man everything he wanted to see, or the chances were we would still be standing there the following morning.

I understood, although I was pretty angry. Karl and I dragged the heavy boxes out of the van for the second time that day and opened them one after the other, and when the customs official saw our instruments he couldn't make head nor tail of them. Growing impatient, he started working on one of the long boxes that was the size and shape of a coffin. After folding down the two twistlocks, he tore the reluctant lid back, and then got such a shock that he sprang two or three paces back. Eyes wide and staring, he looked into the interior of the van and, in the pale streetlight, saw my colleague Karl lying in black foam padding, decked out in full stage gear. The robot's fixed gaze gave the man the fright of his life! Even when we opened the other boxes, showing him the reproductions of the rest of the band, he wasn't particularly reassured. Our polyester puppets were just too real. Laboriously, we explained why we needed the figures, but the poor man didn't understand, and it must have been extremely embarrassing for him to have been so shocked by the robots in our presence.

To ease his embarrassment, and to smoothe the atmosphere, Karl shrewdly fetched some of our singles from the cabin and showed them to him. The man gradually seemed to understand that we were genuine musicians. He assured us that he already knew of Kraftwerk and some of our songs, and his face began to clear. We signed two singles for the distressed man, and he have us a hand loading up our van so that we could drive on. This was particularly satisfying, after he had initially annoyed us so much.

We arrived in Paris late that night, absolutely exhausted, and got a taxi from the northern part of the city to the Royal Monceau Hotel in the Avenue Foche, where the others were waiting with Maxime Schmidt, already deeply worried.

To my regret, we didn't go on tour to promote *The Man Machine*, although our robots would certainly have caused a sensation. I was always in favour of concert tours because I enjoyed travelling and playing live, but as my colleagues grew older they lost the desire to travel. I heard Ralf and Florian questioning more and more often the sense of such exhausting undertakings, and this worried me because the planning of everything to do with Kraftwerk was in their hands; they didn't even pass this business over to a manager.

Consequently, the idea of sending the robots on tour was born. The idea was that they could advertise our music themselves, seeing as we already had them anyway. This sounded fine in theory, and Ralf explained this idea repeatedly in interviews. However, I thought that it would be almost impossible to equip the puppets with the complicated technology needed to enable them to perform our show fully automated.

It turned out that the idea was also unpopular. We'd seen evidence of this in Paris, when we'd put the robots before the reporters as a replacement for the living musicians. The press had been thoroughly unimpressed, and had pulled our dummies apart over the course of the evening. I doubt whether our faithful audience would have been content with paying money to see motor-driven robots. Perhaps this would have attracted attention in some exceptional cases, at television performances or at special press events, but our human fans had an understandable need to witness the flesh-and-blood electronic quartet behind the music machines. Apart from this, fitting the robots with the necessary mechanics, which would comprise many motors and a substantial amount of electronics, would have been way too expensive for us at that time. Looking back, I thank God that this was the case, or we might have actually gone through with it.

Although for some time our assistant, Günter Spachtholz, played about with electrical motors designed by the automobile industry to raise car-door windows, hoping to bring the puppets to life, nothing came of this, and I wasn't at all inclined to help because I didn't like the idea. This was one of those situations where I had a chance to influence a decision in matters determined – nay, ordered – by Ralf and Florian. If I didn't like anything, I would just refuse and say "I can't do that" or "That's too complicated." Then other specialists would have to be called in, and these people didn't always achieve satisfactory results – not by a long chalk.

The infrequency of travel, of taking our primary resources on the road, made me increasingly uneasy. I was asking myself more and more often why we'd had the expensive puppets made in the first place. They were originally intended to make a spectacular appearance in our shows, actually starring in their own song. Instead, more often than not they stood in a corner of the annexe to our studio, where we watched television, along with many other things, waiting endlessly.

Late one evening, I found myself with a lot of time to work on some devices in my workroom. Fed up with my "homework", I decided to have a laugh with my Polaroid camera at the expense of the robots. Interestingly enough, in an interview about my current project, Yamo, in the September 1998 edition of the German magazine *Keyboards*, a fan (whom I assumed was female) asked me, "Were the robot puppets ever caught having sex? And, if so,

144

where are the baby robots produced by them?" As you can see, our fans have a definite sense of humour!

Remembering my earlier session with the Polaroid, I answered, "Our earlier robots were really lively. They felt that their bodies were complete, and certainly didn't want to just stand around in the corner if they weren't needed. They already had too much pleasure in their physicality and charm. It was inevitable that I would catch them in their corner of the studio one evening, when they thought that they were alone. I took a discreet photograph, so that I would be believed later, but then I withdrew and left them to themselves, knowing that only love counts in life. Unfortunately, no progeny can be expected, because our robots were all male. Today, their fun has been spoiled, when you see them without a lower abdomen, on such spindly prostheses and with such grumpy faces."

With this last sentence, I was referring to the robot generation of 1991, which Ralf and Florian had developed after Karl and I left the group because our faces didn't fit any more, at which point, without any further ado, two other musicians were hired. For the album *The Mix*, Ralf and Florian had new puppets made without any body from the waist down. They had metal rods for arms and legs that looked like prosthetic walking and gripping aids, and their faces looked particularly severe.

How did I find out about the new puppets? Well, in 1992, my friend Emil and I committed ourselves to the cause of helping the children who had been wounded in the appalling war in Bosnia, and I wrote 'Little Child', my first post-Kraftwerk song. It was the first song I'd written on my own, both lyrics and melody. Although the song takes the war as its subject, I was proud of my band's debut release, which was then still called Jamo.

One day, as I looked out of the kitchen window of my apartment in the centre of Düsseldorf, very near the Hofgarten, opposite the flat there was a pillar that was plastered with advertisements for all kinds of products. That morning, for once there weren't any advertisements for washing powder or sexy lingerie stuck up there;

145

instead, there was a huge, yellow poster of Ralf Hütter, made up to look like a robot. I didn't want to believe my eyes. The image shook me. I was doing what I could to help the most severely injured children in Bosnia, and to win public support for urgently needed medical assistance and prostheses for the poorest people in Europe, and the solemn face of Ralf's robot puppet was gazing at me all day from the other side of the road. On the poster, Ralf had twisted arms, spindly legs and no lower body, so no sexual organs. I still don't know what had got into my former colleague. In a time when war was raging nearby and women and children were having their legs and hands blown off while shopping at the market, Kraftwerk were advertising their product with prosthetic robots. Much later, just as I was recording my first Yamo album, *Time Pie*, and the last time that I arranged to meet up with Ralf over a coffee, I protested about this act, and let him know how angry I felt. Ralf listened to me attentively, and I believe that he fully understood.

# 23 Dancing At The Lido
## Ian Dury At My Feet – Too Much Bellini

Shortly after our German fans had caught their first glimpse of
our new robots, on a programme broadcast by ZDF, we received
an invitation to attend a big television gala at the Venice Lido.
This was to be a Eurovision broadcast by the Italian television
company RAI, and many internationally famous artists and bands
had been invited. The broadcast was special in that it was also
going to be transmitted live to Eastern Europe, and to the Soviet
Union in particular.

I hate flying, although the journey to the Adriatic was mercifully
brief. After landing in Maestre in the early afternoon, we travelled
directly from the Duke's Palace to Lagoon Island by water taxi,
a fast, sturdy Riva boat. The arranger of the event had booked
us into the splendid Hotel Des Bains, which I remembered from
Visconti's film *Death In Venice*, based on Thomas Mann's novel.
I was full of respect and wonder for the splendid buildings of *la
belle époque*. I wouldn't have thought that I'd ever find myself
staying in that magnificent building. Wandering through the fine
halls and the long passageways, which were soundproofed with
thick carpets, I expected to see Mann's beautiful Tadzio coming
around the corner at any moment, turning his sensitive face

147

toward me. I felt myself transported into the history of Gustave von Aschenbach's Venice, with its late-summer Scirocco and the reddish evening light falling across the smooth Adriatic and its well-tended beaches. In the melancholic mood of early autumn, I was able to empathise with the despair of the character in the novel. Here, time had simply stood still.

In the afternoon, we wandered around the small island a little, gazing at the peeling stucco walls of the villas and the romantic gardens. We breathed in the mild breeze, which smelled of chestnuts, leaves and the sea, and it warmed our hearts. After the flight, cramped in the cabin's narrow seats and breathing its dry air, it was very refreshing to be out in the open.

In the evening, we visited to the Casino Municipale, which was built in the style of the fascist architecture that was erected during the time of Mussolini. I like buildings like that. The enormous rooms and high stucco ceilings, and the equally high windows and ornamental polished mirrors, had the showiness of old government palaces. We had already slipped into our suits to meet the casino's strict dress code, and we also had to present our passports. We kept to the rules, and were admitted without any problems.

It was the first time I'd ever been so near to pure avarice. At one of the playing tables, we discovered a corpulent man in a dark-brown suit and black, horn-rimmed spectacles playing roulette, with piles of chips of all denominations stacked in front of him. Next to him, in an elegant designer evening dress, stood his attractive middle-aged companion, who constantly whispered to the man. He then put his chips on the green felt and won time after time. It was fascinating how confidently he manoeuvred his chips again and again onto the right field, which his muse had pointed out to him in a whisper. Florian was the first to recognise the man, a German industrialist called Max Grundig. He was smoking a fat cigar, and he must have been playing for a long time because he had a huge pile of chips. Suddenly, he picked them all up and he and his companion made for the cashier. Apparently, he'd had enough of gambling, and he'd certainly won enough. At least he knew precisely when to stop. The other players and watchers at his table – even the croupier – looked after him wonderingly and enviously.

Encouraged, Ralf and Florian changed a small sum of money into plastic chips and risked a short game. Their stake was swiftly lost, though, and we took this as a sign to return to our hotel. We had an exhausting day behind us, and we wanted to rest in our lovely rooms so that we were ready for our appearance the following day.

The next day was a stark contrast to the previous one. Our hotel was very near the ugly Palazzo Del Cinema, where the Venice Bienniale is also held. When we arrived at the Temple of the Muses, an assistant took us directly to our dressing room, which was one of many along a long passageway under the stage, which was already a hive of activity. Many familiar and unfamiliar artists were running back and forth, nervous and self-important. Make-up artists, cosmeticians, dress technicians and assistants were running around each other and gesticulating madly, accompanied by the sound of slamming doors, hectic clatter and shrill cries. We took possession of our room and were quite satisfied with it. It was furnished rather attractively and cleaner than most other dressing rooms we'd been in. A large bunch of flowers, a bowl of tropical fruit, various drinks and a bottle of champagne stood on the glass table. It looked like the management really knew how to spoil their artists!

Suddenly, just as we were putting on our red shirts and black trousers, the door of the dressing room burst open and a procession of people poured in. We were horrified and outraged. Who would dare disturb us like this, bursting into our sanctum with such poor manners? An excited, handsome-looking Spaniard with sharp features and very light hair waved his arms around and shouting the same thing again and again in his native language, which of course we didn't understand. This made him even more agitated, particularly since he also noticed our amusement. One of his companions had bags of clothes hanging over both arms, and their weight seemed to be almost bringing him to his knees. Like his idol, he also chattered away in Spanish.

It wasn't long before the stage manager arrived, but he only spoke poor English. (Just listen to Italians when they speak English – it's very strange!) Anyway, he apologised obsequiously, gesturing helplessly, and communicated to us that it was all a misunderstanding. Apparently, we'd accidentally been allocated Julio Iglesias's dressing room, and the stage manager actually asked us outright to leave the room. He must have been crazy. We were standing there half naked, and had already made ourselves at home, having hung up our clothes in the cupboards and eaten the fruit, and we had no desire to pack everything up again. Apart from that, there were four of us whereas Iglesias was on his own. It was only logical that we should stay there because we were in the majority and, apart from that, we were there first. The fiery Spanish crooner would have to look elsewhere. However, the stage manager didn't know which other room he should give to Iglesias. By this time, the backstage area was packed, and there were no more dressing rooms free. For better or worse, the angry Spaniard had to change and prepare for his act in the corridor outside. I have to confess that we did laugh at his misfortune, because we didn't particularly like the presumptuous peacock.

All of the artists and groups playing that night had a current hit in the charts, and I caught glimpses of Ian Dury and The Average White Band in the corridor outside. Dury's current number was 'Hit Me With Your Rhythm Stick' and The Average White Band had released 'Pick Up The Pieces', while we were there to promote 'The Robots'. Many other artists were also scheduled to appear in the show, a circus starring the international giants of showbusiness. Rehearsals were taking place all day, while camera positions were established and marked on the floor of the huge stage.

We had only brought a small selection of our instruments and equipment with us, as the performances weren't planned to be live, although we did bring the robots, our main attraction. However, at a screen test in the afternoon we found that there would be no opportunity to bring them onto the stage between sets during the performance that evening. We argued about just how we could pull this off.

Eventually, just before the audience was admitted that evening, we struck upon the idea of sitting our robots directly in front of us in the first row. In this way, they would sit opposite us and watch us during our set. It was as soon said as done. We placed the four fully-dressed puppets neatly next to each other on four seats in the middle of the first row and arranged their faces so that they were looking at our stage positions. It looked fantastic.

Later, we were told that seats were expensive and had been reserved for honoured guests, and even though it had been a good joke, the event organiser charged us for them afterwards. We also hadn't informed the cameramen about what we'd done, and during our appearance they were confused, shifting their cameras constantly between us and the robots. Nevertheless, it was a triumph of fashion and innovation, which was extremely well received by the public. We had no idea what would develop next from this variation of our "man machine".

After the show, most of the artists and groups congregated at a disco that had been set up in the basement of the grand old hotel. Everyone was on a high – the show was over, and now, of course, everyone had to celebrate. The party lasted until the following morning, and the barman really had his hands full. Bellini – a fruity, frothy drink made from champagne and puréed peaches which Florian had discovered in a Venetian café on St Mark's Square and which Johann Wolfgang von Goethe enjoyed drinking when he travelled to Venice – flowed in streams, and in no time at all most of us were cheerful and tipsy. The musicians became louder and louder and grew increasingly spirited.

We danced to disco music and international hits. Ian Dury didn't come down from his dressing room until late that evening, with a tall, heavily made-up black model on each arm. He was a short man with a congenital handicap, and he looked rather strange between the pair of "professional lovers". At the bar, Ian sat there throwing Scotch down his throat, and when he recognised me he hobbled over, leaning on his elegant walking stick, and in a thick English accent formally invited me to dance. I was already quite dozy from the Bellini, and I was ready for any nonsense. I accepted his invitation in high spirits, and joined him on the dance floor with all the other dancers. Suddenly, Ian positioned himself on my big feet with his hard shoes, put his arms around me and let me lead him in the dance. It must have looked really strange, and loud laughter broke out around us as our fellow revellers howled at the tipsy Kraftwerk robot dancing with Ian Dury perched quite happily on his feet like a spider monkey. At one point, very late, I saw The Average White Band on the dance floor with toilet seats around their necks. They were the craziest of all.

A huge hangover the following morning was an unavoidable side-effect of such a happy and relaxed evening. In spite of my buzzing head, I couldn't allow myself to miss the chance of having a solid brunch in the classical dining room of the Hotel Des Bains, just like Gustave von Aschenbach. Two liveried waiters attended to me most courteously. It was the most civilised meal of my life. Unfortunately, no Tadzio appeared, and I was unable to gaze into the brown eyes of his mother, the vivacious Polish countess, who in Visconti's film had been portrayed by the enchanting actress Silvana Mangano. Nevertheless, I was bewitched by the atmosphere of the island, and I vowed to take a private holiday there one day.

# 24 *Pocket Calculator Gets Us Moving*

DÜSSELDORF, 1978–81

Because there wasn't going to be a tour to promote *The Man Machine*, we decided that we really needed to do something about our equipment. During the last few appearances, we'd become increasingly aware of how difficult and inconvenient it was to set up our instruments and studio equipment each time we played. The faults and equipment failures that plagued us on tour had to be caused by faulty programming, because they cropped up every day. Compounding this was the fact that the structure of our band differed from that of rock bands to the extent that the roadies and technicians were finding it difficult to cope with our complicated cabling system. We had to supervise them the whole time, monitoring everything and issuing instructions. This had to change if we were to appear more professional in future and able to rely on our equipment without having to compromise.

At that stage, we were also working on ideas for a completely new stage show, while my colleagues were working on the tunes and sounds for the new album, *Computer World*. It occurred to us that we had to loop up all of our instruments, sequencers, drum machines and effects with a special cabling system. This meant that each musician had to have an individual unit, with heavy plugs protruding from it, which could be linked to the unit of his neighbour and was thus connected to all systems in series. These plugs were also interchangeable and had labelling symbols stuck on them clearly, so that errors arising from wrong connections could be minimised.

In 1979, although we were working hard on the most unusual devices, it was still unclear what the whole thing would look like. One day, we had the idea of packing all of the electronics into a kind of container behind us so that we didn't have to hide behind mountains of amplifiers piled up on the stage. Each of us would be given a keyboard or percussion board that was as narrow as possible, erected on a metal stand, and each of these would be linked to the essential electronic equipment via a cable protruding from the back. These devices could then create the relevant sounds. In order to stop people stepping on the sensitive cable, we built a platform out of a flat cable box and set all of the pedals that we needed for regulating and mixing our sounds into the front edge of this. This made it possible for us to walk about on a kind of catwalk through which the lengths of cable leading to the nearest band member to the left and right were running. The whole structure was arranged in a V shape, so that we could see and communicate with each other.

We started to develop the initial prototypes. I made a model of our new stage at a scale of 1:10, with small plastic men (which we'd bought from a toyshop called Comic) representing the musicians. Because two sets of fittings would have been too expensive, and because we had nowhere to store them, we used the new containers as studio furniture. What we really needed was order and reliability, both in the studio and on the stage. Finally, we chose the shape of the subsequent oblique console, which we built to the industry-standard 19-inch format.

Over the next few years, I carried out an extensive building project in the Berger Allee, including the construction of all of the necessary racks, instrument boards and pedal rostra. An electrician rebuilt and recabled a system of neon lights that I had originally constructed because it had often been scorched. I glued the control console boxes together from panels of laminated wood and then painted them grey, and I also built swivelling lighting units out of aluminium, which I screwed onto the upper side, directing them to cast light onto the fascias of the devices below. Meanwhile, the rest of the band often came to me with more new ideas, delaying production by peppering me with other suggestions. When they were completed, I took the consoles across to the Kling Klang Studio, where our electrical technician, Achim Dehmann, began to install the mixers, effects, vocoders and drum machines, along with the complicated internal cabling. We also installed a cassette deck into my console so that I would be able to fade in the sound of the departing Volkswagen on 'Autobahn' and the approaching train at the end of 'Trans Europe Express' when playing live.

One day, my colleagues came up with the idea of using a pocket calculator. Florian had discovered a small Texas Instruments translating device that could also be used for calculating. You could enter letters and numbers or whole words with a miniature keyboard, and the machine would then translate these into English, and would speak at the touch of a button. Although the sound was rather artificial, it suited the concept outstandingly. This was the start of the idea for "*Ich bin der musikant mit taschenrechner in der hand*" ("I am the musician with a calculator in my hand"). Of course, after that, we all had to have one. We had great fun with things like that.

We also found a stylophone in a music shop in Düsseldorf called Kunz. It was a miniature keyboard with a small metal surface on which piano keys were printed. You could trigger individual sounds by pressing the keys with a metal pen, although it only had one sound. We used it in the song, and later Karl played it onstage. Meanwhile, Ralf had found himself a miniature organ with tiny black and white keys.

However, there was no similar miniature percussion device available for me, so I had to build myself a mini-drumpad that was no larger than the other little boxes. I found a flat, aluminium

155

lunchbox that would serve as a housing and screwed three rectangular metal plates onto it, which were electrically insulated from the metal case with plastic foil. These three contact surfaces were connected by a long cable, which I linked to the console so that they could trigger the drum sounds. The three tones were triggered by a small metal rod, just like my big drumpad, although I could only play it one-handed, with one stick, because I had to hold the box with my other hand.

Also, the plan was to stop using the large screen on which Emil played his slide projections, which he always had to erect laboriously onto its wobbly frame each time we used it. The light of the projector wasn't bright enough to make the pictures very clear. We had also just begun to make films, and we wanted to find a way of projecting these effectively onstage.

In the meantime, video projectors had come onto the market. Sony offered us four large projectors, which were very heavy and extremely expensive. It was always the same: we wanted to use the latest technology and had to pay the highest prices, but what was the good of it? Florian ordered the four projectors, which had integrated reflex screens and were the size and weight of washing machines. We placed one of them in our TV room, and from that point on we had our own cinema. The projection surface was actually almost two metres diagonally, the largest that was available at the time.

Our new stage set became more and more like a shining control room in a spaceship – our "electronic living room", as Ralf liked to describe it. The album was also growing constantly as we developed new themes, and we were recording new material all the time. At the end of 1980, we had everything ready, and in the following year EMI released the album with a cover depicting a classic IBM computer screen with our facial profiles picked out in computer graphics. On the back, the robots are pictured working at the new instrumental consoles, connected up with plugs the size of irons. The robots were entirely appropriate to *Computer World* – thematically, at any rate – because, after all, home computers are nothing more than electronic servants, carrying out our orders and commands at the touch of a button, and this is happening in every office, in every household and in every child's bedroom, day and night. On the inner sleeve of our record – what an antiquated word! – we photographed our helpers in active poses with the new miniature instruments. The plan was for our live appearances with the new mini instruments to look just like that.

# 25 Resting

## Into The Scene

Between studio sessions and extensive construction work, we were also going out on all kinds of excursions and journeys. In 1976, we drove in Florian's Mercedes 600 to a concert by David Bowie, who was on his Station To Station tour in Frankfurt. I still look back on that concert with enjoyment; it was a real highlight for me, and I was deeply impressed by the androgynous artist's stage performance. By this time, he'd dispensed entirely with coloured spotlights and had only white lights installed. He used every gradation of luminosity; the lighting technician had tastefully arranged warm light bulbs, cold neon and blazing halogen rays to accompany Bowie's songs. Bowie himself appeared in an elegant black-and-white outfit straight out of the '20s, and his band also wore black evening dress, which I felt was much better than the garishly colourful Bowie from his absurd Ziggy Stardust period. I still enjoy listening to his deep, clear voice on songs like 'Golden Years', 'TVC 15' and 'Heroes'.

In the meantime, Florian had acquired a racy, anthracite-grey Mercedes coupé, which he enjoyed driving around to various events around the area at weekends with Sandya Whaley, his American-Indian girlfriend. One Sunday, the rest of us drove to

Spa, in Belgium, to watch a Formula One race and to find out just what was so inspiring to so many people. Was it the deafening noise of the cars, or the chances that there could be a spectacular accident on the track? Florian had already set out for Spa in his new coupé earlier that morning, because he liked to go his own way. The rest of us landed up in a long traffic jam near the Belgian border just before midday, stuck in a queue with lots of other Germans who also wanted to see the race. Suddenly, a black mushroom cloud rose up above the autobahn some distance away, and we assumed that an accident had been the cause of the traffic jam. We were inching forward, stopping and starting fitfully, but as we approached the scene of the accident we came to realise that there hadn't been a collision. Nothing quite so serious – a luxury car was standing on the hard shoulder of the empty opposite carriageway with its bonnet cranked up and clouds of thick, black smoke pouring from the engine. I was the first to recognise the car – it was Florian's coupé, and he was standing helplessly next to it, looking down at the blown-out engine. We hooted as we drove by, and Florian waved dejectedly to us but stayed with his smoking wreck.

I could imagine what had happened, for I'd often experienced Florian's driving. He would sit at the wheel, start the car and shoot off at breakneck speed, without even letting the engine warm up. We often told him to keep an eye on the temperature gauge and apply the revs carefully if the motor was still cold. The way he drove, he either had no understanding of technology or he simply had too much money to be bothered about damaging his engine. I have to admit that I felt a twinge of malicious pleasure when I saw him standing there helplessly by the roadside. At least now he couldn't keep trying to impress us with his fantastic car.

As it turned out, motor racing didn't appeal to me – it was simply too loud and fast. I've always been afraid of high speeds, however they're achieved and for whatever purpose they serve.

At this time, we enjoyed eating at one of the many Italian restaurants in Düsseldorf, and we would always visit the cinema when there was a new film out by Rainer-Werner Faßbinder. We all liked his films, mainly because of the actor Kurt Raab and his absurd humour ("*Fliegen ficken, Fliegen ficken*"). Faßbinder had devised a highly individual style, and told his tales of Germany with passion and imagination. We also enjoyed going to see Rosa von Praunheim's over-kitschy and garishly colourful domestic romantic dramas and John Carpenter's horror films, and after these spine-chilling movies we would often eat at a fashionable ice cream parlour on Graf-Adolf Platz called Palatini's, where they sold the most fantastic ice cream sundaes and sorbets. On the Konigsallee, the Café Bittner invited passersby to sample the creamiest and fruitiest gateaux imaginable on its terraced square. Florian particularly liked this place, because he could drive up there in his sumptuous Mercedes 600 or his fashionable coupé, pulling up to admiring crowds and playing the great game of chic Düsseldorf society. He enjoyed breakfasting there in the late morning, when he would eat fresh strawberries with chocolate ice cream (for which he had an unusual craving), washed down with a glass of bitter lemon.

There was a bar in the old town that had a delicious menu for those with culinary cravings in the late evening. For a while, the Heinrich-Heine taverns were our permanent rendezvous for supper. We would regularly turn up late at night on the first floor of the restaurant in the Bolker Straße, which was in the middle of the old town and was open until two o'clock in the morning, and when we turned up we were still able to order hot food. The menu was international, so there was always something to our tastes, and the waiters were also international in origin. A short, energetic Italian who worked there was particularly spry, although he didn't have much of a sense of humour and always seemed surly and in a hurry. He didn't at all like having late guests turning up.

One night in spring 1980, we stumbled hungrily up the narrow steps to the woodpanelled restaurant after more nerve-wracking sessions in the studio. As we tentatively ordered our meals, we saw that there were few other diners there. It was the asparagus season, and we wanted to study the varieties of vegetable dishes on the menu in some detail. While my friends had particular difficulty in choosing, I gave the waiter my order promptly and even told him what I wanted for dessert, because we'd already had the kitchen close on us in the past when we arrived late. The waiter accepted my order, muttering as he did so, then scribbled something onto his pad and quickly disappeared into the kitchen. My order was served incredibly quickly, and the waiter took the other orders. However, he also brought out my pudding, an ice cream dish called a Banana Boat, which he slammed down in front of me, along with the asparagus, and then promptly disappeared.

So I began to eat my Rhineland asparagus, which tasted excellent, but as I ate I saw my dessert melting in front of me. At last, I managed to catch the man's eye and called him over to me. As quick as a flash, he was at our table, enquiring about my needs, his eyes ablaze. I informed him that the ice cream was really a light, insubstantial thing, and wanted to know why he'd brought it to the table so early.

"Well, you certainly ordered it as if you were starved," he answered pompously, and then disappeared again.

We couldn't believe our ears, but we laughed because we were already familiar with his hot-tempered ways, although that evening he seemed particularly fussy. As I watched my dessert melt into slush before my eyes, I decided that I wasn't prepared to put up with his impudent attitude. I angrily called him back and asked him to at least put the dish in the fridge long enough for me to finish my main course.

He raised his right hand dramatically and snatched the crystal bowl full of ice cream and cream in front of me. I thought that he was about to take it back to the kitchen and put it in the fridge, but instead, cursing loudly in Italian, he threw the whole dish toward the ashtray next to the sideboard, on which stood the cash register. Unfortunately, he missed his target, and the bowl crashed against the wall next to the sideboard with a loud bang and its delicious contents exploded in a spray of milky drops. A breathless silence reigned in the restaurant. The other guests that were there that night had observed my complaint and the incident, and were both shocked and amused. We couldn't stop laughing – the situation was just too grotesque. The ice cream, cream and pieces of banana slowly oozed down the wall on a sticky tide of alcohol and dripped onto the carpet. So the waiter didn't like us. He was probably unwilling to serve us because he saw us as successful layabouts. Perhaps this was his way of demonstrating his contempt to us. If so, he'd failed completely.

On another occasion, it was my turn to lose my cool and throw an ice cream sundae at a mirror, although the circumstances were understandable. In June 1981, during our promotional tour for *Computer World*, we were in Lyon, in the south of France. A beautiful warm afternoon had tempted us out of our hotel and, after our daily soundcheck had been completed, we wanted to see something of the lovely old town. We drank a few espressos in an ice cream parlour and I ordered a sundae. It was a comfortable old '50s-style place, and I sat down on a precarious stool to enjoy the cold dish. We were in a good mood because the concerts were going well, and we felt very much at ease in the south of France, as we did in all Mediterranean countries.

Suddenly, a stinging pain lanced through my tongue. It was unbearable! I started to panic, because I didn't know what was causing it. Sticking my tongue out, I ran over to the mirror on the wall, where I saw a long splinter of glass sticking out of the middle of my tongue. It had penetrated it completely and now stuck out of it both above and below as my mouth filled with warm blood. I quickly gripped the thicker end of the splinter with my fingertips and yanked it out as fast as possible, causing blood to pour out of my mouth and onto my chin and shirt.

In a fit of rage and shock, I called to the sales assistant behind the counter, "*Monsieur! C'est glas! C'est glas, monsieur, c'est glas!*" My French isn't very good, though, and in my anger I'd forgotten that *glas* is phonetically identical to *glace*, meaning ice cream in French. Of course, the man didn't understand at all, and smiled at me kindly and said, "*Oui, oui, monsieur, c'est glace. Naturellement, c'est glace!*" I was beside myself, and couldn't help feeling that someone was making fun of me, because at that point the others – who hadn't seen the incident – joined in with cries of "*Oui, oui, Wolfgang, c'est glace. C'est glace, à votre plaisir.*" They thought I was proud of finding the French word for ice cream, and were calling it out at the tops of their voices to praise me.

Their laughter made me even more angry, and I snatched up the silver bowl and threw it at the mirror behind the counter. Terrified, the sales assistant ducked, obviously thinking that I was about to attack him. Here, too, the sauce dripped down the mirror, and it didn't look at all appetising. When I opened my mouth to show my friends my bleeding tongue, and showed them the glass splinter between my fingers, they weren't particularly worried about me, though, and just giggled. "*Oui, oui, Wolfgang, c'est glace. Naturellement, c'est glace...*"

My appetite for ice cream completely disappeared after that, and I was angry at them for their lack of sensitivity. Over the next few days, I really didn't want either to speak to them or eat anything – my tongue was throbbing too painfully. If I'd been the singer in our group, we would have had to cancel the following concerts, and that would have been an expensive pay-out for the ice cream parlour's insurance company. On the other hand, I felt sorry for the sales assistant, because he obviously hadn't been able to do anything about the accident, and was very sympathetic. For this reason, I didn't take any legal action and just accepted my painful mouth.

Between our studio sessions and construction work, during the evenings we took refuge in the discotheques of Düsseldorf. Although I drank hardly any alcohol, I'd begun to enjoy sweet cocktails and a drink called sekt, a delicious sparkling wine, which I'd discovered helped me lose the inhibitions against which I was still struggling – it was much easier to flirt with champagne.

Our favourite discotheque, the Mora, lay in the Schneider-

Wibbel Gasse in the middle of Düsseldorf's old town, and there was a waiter who worked there who always greeted new guests with the words "*Hallöchen! Sekt? Korrrrrrekt!*" You didn't have the chance to contradict him, because he always answered himself. He loved selling champagne to the guests, largely because it was the drink on which he earned the highest commission, and he forced it on everyone.

We'd heard him so often, and he was such a fine example of Düsseldorf chic, that we invited him into our studio when we were recording 'The Model' so that he could speak his smug slogan directly into the microphone. That's why his pithy "*Sekt? Korrrrrrekt!*" appears in our most famous song.

There was a new disco called the Bagel on the edge of the old town, almost on the Rhine. It was a fashionable meeting place for models, advertisers, photographers, playboys and wannabes, but above all it was the place to go for voyeurs and showoffs. The biggest social game of all is to see and be seen, and every city has its own appropriate areas. Düsseldorf's old town is very much like the fashionable district of Schwabing in Munich. With its innumerable bars, restaurants, steak bars, chip and pizza stalls, discotheques, shopping arcades and fancy bistros, it's a powerful magnet for the surrounding towns in the Ruhr district and the whole of the Rhine area. At that time, the Bagel had an Ibiza theme, because tanned models who were temporarily between photo shoots in the Balearics or the Canaries were always hanging around there. In the '70s and '80s, advertising photographers and hordes of young models favoured the islands of Ibiza, Majorca, Lanzarote and even the Seychelles. Düsseldorf, the city of trade fairs and fashion, swarmed with advertising agencies that gave a huge number of photographic commissions for fashionable youth products.

With an artistically worked stucco ceiling, which was under a preservation order, the Bagel was very comfortable but much too small to accommodate the hordes of people who wanted to be seen there. In summer throngs of people would loaf around on the pavement in front of the windows, reaching as far as the other side of the road. Among them were muscular bikers with Harley Davidsons, who liked to show off their tanned biceps, and the owners of Porsches, who were always under pressure and would ostentatiously wave their keys around to entice any girl eager to go for a spin. A new group of stylish bikers also attracted attention, equipped with extremely expensive racing bikes and euphoric, triumphant, fanatical stares. They were more interested in 24-gear derailleurs mounted between two gleaming titanium forks.

Among them romped the perpetually tanned Ibiza girls and smart-looking but effeminate young men with raffia bags hung from their narrow shoulders, colourful scarves tied around their hips and skin-tight linen trousers that ended in a short slit near the ankle. They looked like hippies. The lovely model Christa Becker was in great demand at that time, as was her older sister. And there was also Bea Fiedler, who had an enormous mouth, the loudest laugh and the firmest breasts, and brought many men's fantasies to the boil in those days. My favourite, the boyish, slender Britt, was also often there, as supple and flexible as an exotic creeper. The girls' foppish photographers would also hang around in this licentious environment, trawling for fresh meat – that was, of course, if they weren't driving in front of the Café Bittner's terrace on the Kö in the pink Chevrolets, black Corvettes or Land Rovers befitting men of their social standing, ready to steal the show from "ordinary" men.

These bars exerted a magical attraction for us Kraftwerkers, and we were only too eager to mix with the fashionable who frequented them. Quite simply, we were part of the Düsseldorf scene. Ralf and Emil were totally obsessed with Christa Becker. She must have had a sphinx-like effect on the pair of them, because I was continually hearing them talking about her and going into raptures about her. I couldn't really understand it myself because, although I found her very attractive, I quickly sensed whether someone had a rather uncomplicated nature. I only found people who also had emotional intelligence sexually attractive, and this didn't appear to be Christa's thing at all. I sensed no such aura around her; she was just beautiful, nothing else. Ralf and Emil, however, went to the Bagel to gaze at Christa again and again, although she never granted them so much as a glance, Nervertheless, they wrote a new song about her: "*Sie ist ein Model, und sie sieht gut aus. Ich nähm' sie heut' gerne zu mir nach Haus.*" ("She's a model and she's looking good. I'd like to take her home, that's understood.")

We found ourselves up against many social barriers, and our formal, unapproachable image pushed us further and further into isolation. Who would ever want anything to do with a cold window display dummy? Certainly not Christa, Bea or Britt. For this reason, a private liaison never occurred. Nevertheless, unrequited longing and hope have always been an inspiration in music, and 'The Model' became one of our best songs – along with 'Autobahn' – largely because of this. It was quite an unusual one for Kraftwerk, though, wasn't it?

I only relate such incidental stories to show the pattern of events. We wove our musical stories and embellishments from everything that we heard and saw, our ideas, and sometimes what we only suspected or felt. However, I'd also like to convey the concept that Kraftwerk tried to communicate to the outer world. It wasn't that we all thought we were wonderful, not by a long chalk, but even so there were plenty of people who saw us as arrogant or thought that we dressed too formally, and we were often on the receiving end of resentment, envy and malicious gossip, unfortunately even from friends.

Düsseldorf is a small city. Although elegant, and apparently prosperous, it's also a narrow-minded and intolerant place. If you want to work undisturbed, you have to keep away from all the social circles that operate there. We'd been able to get on with each other for years because we hadn't allowed ourselves any kind of adventures, and behaved quite normally in public. In spite of our fame, we were able to live in the city, go shopping and walk down the street like anyone else without being harassed.

I even went to the public baths and to the nudist beach at the Unterbacher See in summer with my girlfriend. I felt particularly at ease in that natural environment, among all the other naked people there. There was no prestige nor ornamentation there; only the individual and nature were important.

It's true that all of us (with the exception of Karl) had a great weakness for luxury cars, although this was the only external evidence of Kraftwerk's financial success – Florian's Mercedes 600 and his elegant 280 coupé turned many heads, even on the elegant Kö. For a while, Ralf also let himself be seduced by luxury, and in 1976, while we were in England on tour, he bought a beautiful, old, dark-green Bentley, and when he got it back to Germany Peter Bollig did it up in his yard. However, the car caused no end of trouble, and was always suffering from technical faults. It wasn't much fun cruising around the country in it because we were always afraid it would break down. It also used a great deal of petrol, and Ralf sold it on and treated himself to a nearly new Mercedes. That, at least, was reliable.

I'd since sold my 190B long ago and bought a light-blue 1966 220S for 6,000 DM. The car was in fantastic condition, with an ivory-coloured steering wheel and a stick-shift topped with an ivory knob. Nevertheless, the "Tail-fin" had 110hp and ran at a smooth 170kph. Although the car was old, it was 100 per cent reliable, and I travelled across half of Europe in it without it ever breaking down. However, for the same reason as Ralf, I later sold it to a doctor in Hamburg who needed it to complete his collection of a fleet of Daimlers from the '60s. Now, although they could afford any luxury car in the world, because of common sense and environmental reasons Ralf and Florian drive small-town cars that use very little petrol.

# 26 Computer World *On Tour*
## *Not All Fun And Games*

DÜSSELDORF, MAY 1981

We embarked on an extensive phase of musical development. Because every concert was just like the last, and because they always ran in the same faultless way, here I want to write about a few stops on this tour that were unusual, exciting, gave us great happiness or even took us to our limits.

For days we'd been rehearsing our set in a rented hall, with amplification and lighting provided by Sound & Light, a company from Hanover. We had to spend some time rehearsing with them, as after every gig they had to pack all of our gear into flight cases and load them onto trucks. To do this, they followed a plan that we'd given them, and they spent time learning where everything was needed onstage. The heavy crates were all numbered, with their contents marked clearly, and the crew had to know where each one had to be unpacked on the stage with their eyes closed in order to avoid traffic jams when the trucks were loaded and unloaded.

This wasn't so easy, because this was the first time that the company had gone on tour with an electronic band. The instruments and our shining, modern-looking stainless steel containers weren't the usual pieces of equipment used by conventional groups. The

V-shaped construction of our elegant containers, with the thick connecting cables and iron-sized plugs, was also new to them, and the roadies and stagehands had to learn some extra details. This always took time, and in the first few days we were highly dissatisfied, but we were willing to wait for a routine to slowly develop.

Finally, when everything worked, we practised our songs. We adopted the same running order for all of our concerts:

1. NUMBERS
2. COMPUTER WORLD
3. METROPOLIS
4. THE MODEL
5. RADIOACTIVITY
6. COMPUTER LOVE
7. AUTOBAHN
8. NEON LIGHTS
9. HALL OF MIRRORS
10. SHOWROOM DUMMIES
11. TRANS EUROPE EXPRESS/METAL ON METAL
12. POCKET CALCULATOR
13. THE ROBOTS
14. HOMECOMPUTER
15. IT'S MORE FUN TO COMPUTE

All of the foreign trips were organised and managed from London by the British company Wasted Talent, whose Ian Flooks did a brilliant job with the logistics. There were hardly any incidents or delays over the next few months – the tour rolled and flew around the whole world like an oiled machine. At that time we were travelling around Europe with a company called Univers, a professional travel company from the Rhineland, and their most experienced rep, Erwin, became a trusted and helpful friend along the way. His bus was the most comfortable form of travel that we'd ever experienced. It was air conditioned, and was equipped with some very comfortable seats in the front section, while in the rear section there were groups of seats, tables, heavy chairs and a sofa, all protected from prying eyes by thick curtains. In the centre of the coach were four stacked beds, which we could separate with the curtains provided, giving us all our own private areas for when we needed peace and quiet. There was also a small onboard kitchen, so we were able to make coffee and heat up small meals *en route* or fetch cold drinks from a fridge. As well as this, the coach was also equipped with a nearly odourless chemical toilet and tinted windows which reflected the sun.

Since our departure from Düsseldorf, we'd enjoyed gliding through Europe in such comfort. I'd bought some particularly comfortable clothing for the long journey, including woollen tracksuit trousers with an elasticated waistband, comfortable sweatshirts and soft trainers, and dressed in these I could lounge around on the fluffy seats and loaf around in complete comfort, or read or nap in bed if I sometimes used the nights that we spent in hotels for activities other than sleeping!

There were five men who were essential to the success of the tour – Emil Schult, Joachim Dehmann, Peter Bollig, Ha-Jo Wiechers and Günter Spachtholz – and they were nearly always with us on the stretches between dates. Emil was the MC of the whole enterprise, responsible for money, organisational and personal matters and all our gear. He was just as important as the musicians, keeping the highly sensitive egos from fraying in tense situations and acting as a mediator between us.

Achim Dehmann was responsible for connecting up our new consoles and solving any problems that arose. In previous years he'd inserted and soldered kilometre-long wires and finger-wide cables into my home-made boxes. He was the best at diagnosing connection problems, and to this end he'd devised a special system of colour coding by which it was easy to follow each link and pinpoint faults by referring back to lists.

Peter Bollig also travelled with us for a long time. He was also responsible for technical concerns, but his concerns were more

170

for the amplifiers, synthesisers and particularly for the e-flute that he'd built for Florian. Hans-Joachim Wiechers, from the Bonn synthesiser studio Matten & Wiechers, also accompanied us to Japan, and it was his responsibility to monitor the performance of the micro-electronics – the sequencers, synthesisers, synchronisation, drum trigger and other electronic specialities that he'd developed for us.

Günter Spachtholz had been hired as a Man Friday, and he was also responsible for erecting the stage set. He monitored the transport crates and, together with Emil, he was a sort of construction manager. He also supervised the stage hands onsite and the roadies onstage, and during our concerts organised the merchandising in the foyer of each hall, where we sold small pocket calculators made specially for the Computer World tour which played the tune of 'Pocket Calculator' and could also be used to perform calculations. We also sold black T-shirts with calculators printed on them, posters, sweatshirts and records.

During the tour, Günter took on another responsibility. Because he was very goodlooking, and because he was also onstage immediately after our concerts, supervising the dismantling of the equipment, he often attracted crowds of female fans in his wake. He was our contact with our fans. He would often smuggle girls back into our dressing room, if they told him which one of us they wanted to meet. Because he knew our individual tastes in women, he also separated the wheat from the chaff, and would only smuggle back those girls who seemed interesting or attractive enough. It sounds unbelievable, but even an electronic band like us was often pursued by female fans.

# 27 Italian Shoes

ROME, 26 MAY 1981
What a crazy encounter we had with Helmut Berger! On 26 May, we found ourselves in Rome, an elegant, beautiful city. Although I was the most southern-looking member of the band, and although I had a great fondness for Italian women, I'd never been there before. I felt like I could fall in love on every street corner. Almost everyone was beautiful and tastefully dressed. I must say that the Italians are the connoisseurs of Europe. Just look at their shops, and see how elegantly and finely fitted out they are. Today, their style is copied everywhere in Germany, and over the last few years Italian restaurants – especially the small trattorias and osterias – have become enormously fashionable.

There were comfortable espresso bars on every corner in Rome, which was simply fantastic. The fashion boutiques also had their individual chic, and even the smallest ones were charming and elegant. These journeys and experiences were always the most enjoyable part about being a member of Kraftwerk.

That late May, Rome was very hot. We'd been invited to a fashionable club near the Via Veneto after the concert that evening, and so in the early evening we sauntered along the street together, lost in admiration for the stylish men and women strolling along

172

it. The street was reminiscent of Federico Fellini's famous film *La Dolce Vita*, about the pleasures of life in this metropolis.

Things really got going later, when we hit the sweltering club. I remember being in a place of gloomy corridors and dimly-lit side rooms and bars. Glass lamps shaped like erect penises protruded from the walls, throwing a dim light on the good-looking male couples leaning against the walls, who embraced each other tightly, showering each other with caresses and groping each other lecherously. We were amused by this, and quickly realised that we'd been taken to a gay club. It seemed that the Italians, too, had thought that we were a gay band, and obviously thought they'd done us a favour by taking us here. We were also curious, though, so we didn't leave immediately. Instead, we even went onto the dance floor to dance to one of our own songs, 'The Robots'.

Apparently, another artist had observed this display with some amusement. Later that night, we were introduced to the Austrian actor Helmut Berger, who had made his career with the great films of his friend Visconti, and was now living alone in Rome after the director's death. It didn't seem to suit him well. That night, he'd drunk a little too much, but he was very pleased to meet us, grinning at us complacently, and we couldn't get rid of him. In the early hours, he invited us back to his flat in an elegant part of Rome, driving us there himself in his Mini Cooper, still drunk, while the faithful Erwin followed behind us in the tour bus and waited for us.

When we arrived at Helmut's place, he began to touch me up on the stairs. I quickly understood what he wanted – he did have a certain reputation. Naturally, the others also saw what was going on and pushed me toward him, giggling. They wanted to see how I'd get myself out of the situation. The atmosphere remained cool in Helmut's flat. It was furnished with period furniture and heavy curtains, decorated with an unbelievable collection of expensive-looking, decadent interior fittings. There was art everywhere. The man had taste, I must grant him that, and he also had the money to realise that taste. I felt great respect, walking through his flat, almost like a "man machine" myself. A heavy picture frame hung on the wall containing an oil portrait of the narcissistic actor standing naked before a mirror, looking down lovingly at himself, and there were also photos of him with Romy Schneider.

We sat down in his comfortable living room, and he unsteadily offered us drinks. After several embarrassing attempts to begin a conversation, he became sentimental and told us how much he envied our independence and artistic autonomy. He'd only been able to express himself artistically with Luchino Visconti, who had been his great love, and now that he was dead Helmut didn't know what to do. I felt incredibly sorry for him, especially when he began to cry. I think that he was overcome with an urge to belong, and was perhaps longing to return to Germany and his home but didn't know who he would meet and who he'd work with when he got there, because he didn't have any friends there. Nevertheless, he'd already experienced how working and co-operating as part of a team could make him successful, and he evidently saw this in us. He was right; in the years that followed, we were never as strong and close to each other as we were then. Our most effective period in the rapidly developing world of computer technology and dependence on technology was the era of *The Man Machine*. The idea with the robots was ingenious for that time, and the Italians loved our image, which parodied fascism with pseudo-fascist colours.

Later, Berger lured me into another room, gesturing furtively and telling me that he wanted to show me something. I was nervous about leaving my friends, but I was also curious. I also noticed the others raising their eyebrows and grinning at me meaningfully. Of course, the other room was his bedroom. Oh God, I thought, now what? I was quite a good-looking young man then, and I'd already had many advances from men, but I'd never accepted any because I was simply more interested in girls. Either that, or I was too afraid to have a go with a man. I don't like very excitable people, either. Surprise attacks don't do it for me. In my case, everything has to occur voluntarily and develop slowly, with tenderness on

174

both sides, if there is to be any sexual activity between men and women.

Helmut, however, was greedy and passionate. As he later wrote in his own biography, after Visconti's death he was without restraint, having sex with anyone who pleased him, and I soon experienced this myself. He grabbed hold of me, hurled me onto the bed (straight from Visconti's villa), threw himself upon me and began to cover me with kisses. Apart from the fact that he smelled terribly of alcohol and was unshaven and prickly, I was shocked by his directness and his unsophisticated approach. I only succeeded in getting out from under him and escaping to the corner of the room by forcing him off me. Angrily, I told him that I wasn't into that kind of thing, and didn't have those kinds of feelings for other men, however attractive. However, I wasn't quite honest with him, for if he hadn't been drunk and clumsy my desire for tenderness with a sensitive man could have been realised with Helmut, whom I admired. If he hadn't reeked of alcohol – which struck my sensitive nose like it would a child's – and if my friends hadn't been waiting with gleeful anticipation for me in the next room... Perhaps there were just too many inappropriate circumstances, preventing what could otherwise have been an exciting experience.

Helmut was completely shattered and close to tears. I felt sorry for him, but what could I do? I sat down again next to him on the edge of the bed, stroked his hair and told him that he should come back to Germany to make new contacts with other filmmakers. I also told him how much I hated drunkenness and its consequences. I'd heard a great deal about what he'd got up to under the influence of drugs and alcohol and the scandals that had resulted. I went on that I didn't have anything against homosexuality in principle, although I was one for the girls myself, but told him that I hated to see the way he was destroying his reputation. Surprisingly, he listened to me quietly. When I'd finished, he said that no one else would be allowed to talk to him like that, and that anyone else who'd tried to lecture him like that would have got his face smashed in.

175

Suddenly, he sprang up and staggered towards an expensive-looking wardrobe. I thought that he was about to attack me again, but when he turned around he held out a pair of shiny Italian shoes. "There, take them!" he said. "You've earned them, my dear." He then cut his gaze away, like a shy child. I was baffled. What on Earth did he mean? Until that time, I'd never heard a man say "my dear" to me while offering me a pair of shoes. What was I supposed to do with them? Wear them? I wasn't so keen on the idea, but he was very eager that I should take them. He said that he really wanted to give me something, and that I shouldn't be so prissy and coy. I was moved, and saw it as a gesture of apology, so I didn't want to disappoint him again. "I could try them on," I answered. "They probably won't fit me, anyway." However, they did, and extremely well – like a glove, in fact. I couldn't believe it. They were very elegant, and Helmut noticed my big feet. "It seems you're like me, both psychologically and physically," he said. "Someone with such big feet should also have a big... You turn me on."

I was just standing there, eager to be free of this evil-smelling man and his bizarre lechery, when Ralf came to my assistance. He'd been puzzled because we'd been in the bedroom for so long, and had come to look in discreetly. I whispered angrily to him behind my hand that we had to get away quickly because things were so embarrassing with Helmut now.

Even so, for some time after that we sat with him in the living room, where he swung frighteningly from attacks of rage and tears to gazing adoringly at me, panting for affection. Ralf told him that, with young directors such as Rainer-Werner Faßbinder, Volker Schlöndorff and Wim Wenders, the new German cinema was very successful at the moment. We advised him to make contact with Faßbinder, whom we admired and whose films we enjoyed, attempting to encourage Helmut to make a comeback in the German film industry, but he waved the idea aside apathetically and said, "No one will want me." I think he just didn't want to try any more. He didn't have the courage to go to the young intellectual film-makers, whose ideas were so differently from those of Visconti, his discoverer and friend. Helmut preferred boozing, and seemed to have given up long ago. By the time we left, at first light, it was terrible to look at him.

It was still warm in Rome, and the birds were already twittering in the scented gardens of the respectable quarter when we left. I instinctively knew that Helmut had chosen to spend the rest of his life there. Tragically, he had been behaving destructively for so many years. I'd always enjoyed seeing him in films such as *The Damned*, *Ludwig II*, *The Garden Of The Fitzi Continis* and *Dorian Gray*, and admired his beautiful face, his fine gestures and facial expressions, and in particular the way he acted fits of rage, but I now realised that he'd lost his place as a world-class actor. He was too weak, his lifestyle too chaotic, and he'd spoiled too many things. Although I took the shoes with me, I never wore them because, however elegant they were, I didn't want to wear the shoes of the man whom I'd once admired so much.

Interestingly, I later read in Berger's biography that he'd had a very similar background to my own. All his life he'd longed for the recognition and love of his father, who hadn't wanted to recognise his talents and had forced him to train as a salesman. In my case, an apprenticeship had been forced upon me, too. I'd also dearly wanted to be an actor, and during my schooldays I'd secretly been trained by the Düsseldorf theatre actor Adolf Dell before I fought to be allowed to pursue a career in music, which after all isn't that far from acting. Neither Helmut nor I had been given any support at home, and Helmut had crept out of his parents' house during the night with a packed suitcase to follow his own destiny, leaving his beloved mother behind.

Helmut had accepted the support of Visconti, and in the same way I accepted the support of Kraftwerk, at least in the early years. However, the difference between us today is that I've become independent and now produce my own music. If he hadn't been so erratic, I'm sure that a director's post wouldn't have been too ambitious for Helmut, considering his relationship with Visconti and his experiences in the international film industry. On the other hand, a person is defined by the mixture of his or her characteristics. I marvel at Helmut Berger on German talk shows (particularly at how much sekt he can down), and I'm still hoping for a great new film from him. I envy the German group Blumfeld, admiring them both for their great lyrics and for the fact that they were able to persuade him to perform with them in their video. Helmut and I are also similar in this – he would never commit to doing anything that didn't fit his passion and his taste. If he enjoys something, he'll do it for little money or for nothing at all, like me.

# 28  Almost Flying

When we arrived in Bologna it was a warm spring day, and it was pleasant to sit outside sipping espressos. Our fourth concert in Italy was scheduled to take place in an uncovered football stadium where a stage had been constructed from scaffolding with a high canopy of tarpaulins stretched over it in case it rained, although it didn't look like it was going to. In the early evening, we retreated to the stage and tuned our synthesisers, hidden away from the public, then went back to our dressing room and waited for the audience to turn up.

The stadium filled quickly, and hordes of excited and expectant people swarmed in. The Italians crowds were lively and impatient. When we climbed onto the stage and played our first song, twilight had already descended, bringing a change in the weather, and a wind sprang up. To begin with, it was only a pleasant, gentle breeze that suited the mild evening, with purple light glowing on the horizon. However, the breeze grew and grew, and quickly developed into a storm that ruffled our hair and made the enormous tarpaulins above us billow upwards. The immense strength of the wind turned the fabric into huge sails that pulled the stage upwards. Soon, the whole contraption was creaking and banging so loudly above us

179

KRAFTWERK: I WAS A ROBOT

KRAFTWERK: I WAS A ROBOT

that we were spending more time looking fearfully skyward than we were at our instruments. A side tarpaulin had come loose and was flapping continually against a row of spotlights above us, and I became so anxious that I gestured frantically to the others. Eventually, we had to break off the concert because the stage area had become too dangerous.

It was bedlam in the audience. The crowd was forced to struggle with gusts of dust and whirling sand, and things grew quite restless down below. When we finally aborted our performance, all hell broke loose. The whole stage structure was shifting in the storm and began to twist to the right, and we fled from the platform to an adjacent patch of grass a safe distance away, afraid that everything would collapse.

What could we do? The organiser of the event was completely distraught, frantically telephoning the police and the fire brigade from his car. After a quarter of an hour, a number of red emergency vehicles with flashing blue lights and sirens came racing towards us from the direction of the town. Confusion reigned on all sides of the stage. A ghostly light flashed over the scene and men shouted to the Italian soldiers across the wind. Then I saw two daring souls climb up the scaffolding bearing heavy ropes. When they reached the canopy, they attached one end of the ropes to the crosspieces and climbed down quickly before the whole thing collapsed, then tied the other ends of the ropes to the fire engines and drove very cautiously against the wind and away from the stage, which was by now leaning perilously. They managed to pull the enormous framework almost back to its original shape, working together extremely carefully. Then the fire trucks stopped and their axles were blocked with large wheel chocks, stabilising the stage.

After extensive discussions under the pleading gaze of the event organiser, we decided to return to the stage and continue our concert. In the meantime, we had to don warm jackets against the freezing, penetrating wind. When the audience saw us climbing back onto the stage, they went berserk. We eventually had to abort the concert for safety reasons, so that the fans didn't riot, which was the organiser's greatest fear. We were still in danger, though – we looked up and saw the spotlights swaying back and forth above us. The storm later abated a little, and in the end we were able to turn our fourth concert into a fantastic success, although it was certainly the most dangerous one we ever gave.

# 29  In Budapest

## A Love Nest

BUDAPEST, 13 AUGUST 1981

We arrived at Budapest on the day before our concerts were scheduled to start, and so we had some time to relax a little and go exploring. I quickly fell under the spell of the old city on the Danube, which left a romantic impression on me like almost no other town. Budapest is unlike Vienna or Prague. It's much more mysterious and inscrutable, and has a debilitated elegance, and my heart burst with love for it.

The organisers of the tour had pulled out all the stops to ensure that we felt comfortable, and had booked us into the historical Hotel Gellert on the left bank of the Danube, under the castle. Despite the afternoon heat, I went strolling through the narrow lanes and ancient squares of the old town, and became increasingly captivated. The reddish light of the August day matched my own idealistic picture of Hungary. We were scheduled to give two concerts over the next two nights at the Kiss Stadium, a sports ground situated in the middle of the forest, but there was still enough time to relax in the hotel, which had a classical 19th-century hot-tub. You could really relax there – we'd been on our world tour for three months, and it was pure, blissful relief to take a sauna, indulge in a massage and swim in natural spa waters. The huge stone, domed halls with ceilings supported by high, polished marble pillars provided a cool and elegant ambience for people who came from all over Europe seeking refreshment. We'd already experienced a lot, but I felt so comfortable that I could have gladly stayed there for a fortnight.

On the first evening, I was coming out of the baths with one of the hotel's terrycloth towels under my arm when I saw Erwin, our driver, sitting in the tour bus, parked directly in front of the hotel with the doors open because of the heat. When he saw me, he waved at me excitedly. I climbed up onto the driver's seat through the front door and asked what was going on, and he told me that there was someone waiting for me. I walked down to the back of the bus and saw a slender girl sitting on one of the back seats. She looked very young, and had big blue eyes and golden hair that was combed back and knotted together, with a single blonde strand hanging down her forehead. Erwin told me that she'd been waiting for me in the bus for the whole afternoon and couldn't speak a word of German or English, but she had repeated my name again and again. I went to her and saw that she was trembling. She gazed at me with clear, innocent eyes, and it was almost unbearable. What a delicate creature! My God, I thought, what beauty there can be in the world. And she was waiting for me! I introduced myself, and she nodded eagerly, relieved. She offered me the smallest wrist that I've ever seen and gave me the most gentle handshake, but it was also very self-confident. "Lena," she said, and pointed to herself.

It turned out that Lena knew about 13 words of English, and it didn't take long for me to find out something about her with this limited vocabulary. Apparently, she'd seen me at our concert in the forest. She must have been extremely impressed to seek me out so boldly. I took her hand and led her from the sweltering bus, feeling sorry for her because there were little beads of sweat standing out on her forehead. I was just about to ask her to come with me back to the hotel so that she could freshen up when Erwin called after and told me that this was impossible – she wasn't allowed in the hotel with me under any circumstances. They were very strict there, and anyone without a passport or an official social security card wasn't allowed to go into my room under any circumstances.

I couldn't believe it. I asked myself what century we were living in. I told Erwin that it should be up to me who came back to my room. No, no, no, he replied, it wasn't allowed under any circumstances. Ultimately, the girl was still a minor, and her motives weren't clear. Budapest was teeming with prostitutes, who weren't allowed into the good hotels. That was enough for me. There was no way that Lena could be a prostitute. Couldn't he see for himself that she looked very respectable, more like a daughter from an aristocratic family? She was tastefully dressed in a thin, white, short-sleeved cotton blouse and tight, beige poplin trousers, with flat, white tennis shoes and a dark-grey woollen pullover tied around her hips. She touched something deep in my soul. As a child, I'd seen the film *Ich Denke Oft An Piroschka* on television, starring the young Liselotte Pulver, who had played a young rural Hungarian woman and who had enchanted me with her fair plaits and her light laughter. I'd fallen head over heels with light-hearted Lotte, and she'd left me with an undying image of Hungarian womanhood. Now this image was standing before me in the flesh, beaming at me sincerely.

What could I say? What could I do? How could we communicate? A thousand words were spoken as we gazed into each other's eyes. I was melting, and we knew that we both wanted to love each other. I indicated to Lena that she should wait, that I'd be right back, I just wanted to fetch my swimming trunks. Back in my room, I quickly put on fresh clothes and ran back down to the forecourt, and then spent the whole afternoon with Lena. We walked along the Danube and she showed me the most beautiful views of her city.

In the early evening, I met the others back at the hotel lobby and we decided to eat our evening meal with Erwin and our friends. Lena told us that she knew of a good restaurant nearby, and we followed her there. Yes, she did have good taste. The inn that she took us to was in a quiet cul-de-sac away from the tourist area. It was furnished rustically, and the menu offered a selection of regional delicacies. We didn't see any tourists there; most of the people eating there were local. The meal was outstanding, but we had to rush off immediately afterwards because they were expecting us back at the stadium for our second concert.

Of course, we took Lena with us on the bus and even allowed her into our dressing room. She was very proud and didn't leave my side, and I felt the same way. Our performance went just as it had on the previous day. The stadium was crowded again, and there were rows of policemen in front of the stage, which was unavoidable, as they'd refused to comply with our request for a less obvious police presence. What were the authorities afraid of? Perhaps they were confusing us with heavy metal bands? If so, they would have been accustomed to dealing with restless audiences. They probably assumed that all western bands were the same, and their guardians of the law and spies were here as a matter of course. Nonetheless, it was a wonderful evening, and the mood of the people and the tone of our synthesisers couldn't have been better.

Later, after the concert, I walked with Lena along the bank of the Danube, near the Hotel Gellert. We held hands continually, as if we never wanted to let each other go. Nevertheless, we both knew that our encounter would be brief, as our departure was already fixed for the next morning. Near the hotel, we saw Erwin strolling through the warm evening, smoking a cigarette. When he saw us, he came over to us and deftly slipped the keys to the bus into my pocket, and then explained to me in whispers which button on the dashboard would lock the doors from the inside. That was the idea! I hadn't thought of that! We already had a travelling hotel with us, without a reception desk and, on top of that, it was sovereign German territory, where we were the masters of the house. There could be no checks. Immediately, Lena and I went looking for the bus, which Erwin had parked in the shade of a large willow tree, out of the heat.

It was still stiflingly hot inside. The evening hadn't brought much of a drop in temperature, but I opened the skylights and closed all the curtains and it gradually became bearable. We put our arms around each other and went to the comfortable bed in the central part of the bus. As soon as the curtains were drawn, we couldn't take our clothes off quickly enough. Our bodies were still hot from the heat of the day – or from desire. At any rate, we melted into a burning German-Hungarian passion for the next few hours. Only the moment counted; we weren't thinking at all of the morning, nor of the day after, only of the feeling of the sweetest minutes and the most tender hours that I'd ever experienced. I felt so young, so carefree and so loved. Even though I was 33 years old, I was still able to experience love like the first time again and again.

We didn't sleep at all that night, and we had no need for words. Our fingertips and our eyes communicated for us. Our bodies knew all of the physical languages in the world. They paralysed our reason, enabling a tempestuous communication of seeking and finding, of a tender give and take.

At around nine o'clock the following morning, there was a gentle knock at the driver's door. I quickly slipped into my clothes and opened the door for Erwin, who had kindly brought over a tray with two delicious breakfasts from the hotel. What a sensitive ally we had in him! I gave him a grateful look but he waved it aside magnanimously.

An hour later, the others came back to the bus with their cases and we prepared for our departure, and I went back to the hotel to fetch my things from my room, freshen up and pay for my extras at the reception. When I returned to the bus, I felt bad that I couldn't offer Lena a refreshing shower in my room, but she gestured to me that it was no problem, that she would be able to bathe at home. We were both in tears as we parted. Oh, how glad I would have been to stay. We'd already exchanged addresses, and we promised to write to each other when I got home, but unfortunately nothing ever came of this, as I lost her address *en route*. Besides, I was an employee of an electronic band and had to fit into the mechanism of this music machine. I couldn't abandon myself to sentimentality or the structure would collapse. I was a musician, an actor and a traveller, and of course I was manipulated like a marionette. I had to obey and I had to work, like an employee from Fritz Lang's mechanistic Metropolis. On that day, I hated this situation. When we left for Poland, I knew instinctively that there wouldn't be much there.

# 30  In Poland

I have to report that the concerts in the land that borders Germany to the east were rather frustrating for us. In the late summer, the exhausted country was in a state of political upheaval, from Lech Walesa's hopeless Solidarity movement to General Jaruselski's military government. A system had failed, both politically and economically. There was nothing but strikes in the country, and no one wanted to carry on working. There wasn't any help from abroad, either. On the contrary, other countries demanded that Poland repay her debts, but the Poles only had agricultural products with which to pay them. The general who had been faithful to the regime was already in power, and the agricultural co-operatives weren't supplying anything else.

There was nothing to buy anywhere. People were standing outside bakeries and grocer's shops in long queues. I had seen terrible pictures of this on TV at home, and we were now able to experience it in person, in every village and town through which we drove on the bus. In Germany, people would perhaps queue at cinemas or at the ticket booths in football stadia, but not like this. It must have been like this during the war, with rationing. I thought about the crowded markets in German towns, where heaps of

188

Polish agricultural products and fatted geese were sold, while here the people had nothing to eat. I didn't feel right, and I was deeply ashamed. It struck me as unfortunate that we were playing here at this particular time, bringing our themes of a modern computer world to these poor towns, with such ringing and venerable names as Katowice, Zielona-Gora, Gdansk, Bydgoszcz Warschau and Opole. I let these names dissolve on my tongue, even though there wasn't a great deal else that you could have bought there that would.

The Orbis Hotel that had been booked for us, part of a state-owned chain, also served miserable food. Cubed sugar and tinned milk were painstakingly rationed and served with thinly brewed coffee. Again and again we dined on tinned vegetables and hot cakes made from some kind of some unknown cereal. On top of this, the weather was always poor, and it was dirty and draughty in the halls and auditoriums in which we performed, just as it was in the streets. Weeds grew through the paving stones everywhere; handrails had been broken off; broken-down trams lay derelict and rusting away at the sides of the roads; and paper and rubbish was strewn everywhere. No one cared for the towns, and no one seemed to be responsible for anything.

We were continually accosted by shady types asking us to "Change money?". The Poles were so eager for western currency that they offered ten times the fixed exchange rate. We were offered 1,500 zloty for one American dollar. Of course, this was officially forbidden, and if you were caught you were sent straight to prison. We never succumbed to such risky transactions, however, because what would we have been able to buy with so much Polish currency? There wasn't anything attractive there, apart from in designated tourist shops, where you were only allowed to pay in western currency anyway. Even so, the Poles were eager for it. Luxury items such as Walkmans, American cigarettes, French perfume and champagne were all very popular.

We didn't need any of this, though, and only exchanged a small amount of money for the purchasing of odds and ends at the hotel receptions *en route*. Even so, being continually and openly harassed by the locals – particularly just outside the hotel – really got on our nerves. Prostitutes also followed around us in droves and approached us blatantly, asking if they could come up to our rooms. To cap it all, it was always drizzling. The long coach journeys over narrow, bumpy country roads grew more and more irritating, and our mood worsened daily.

On one afternoon, our bad mood escalated hideously. We were standing on a twolane paved road in a traffic jam in the middle of the rainy countryside. Next to us, in the fields that stretched over the horizon, they were still ploughing with oxen. A short distance ahead, an HGV had had an accident right before our eyes. Its right rear tyre had burst and the vehicle had skidded at full tilt into the field and then back on to the road, where it now lay on its roof. Other motorists had pulled the severely injured lorry driver from his cabin, and they were now waiting for the ambulance. We couldn't move, and we had a performance that evening. As usual, Florian had slipped away to the back of the bus, where he crept under his coat. The rest of us were fooling around together, one thing led to another and I made a stupid remark to Karl, who was sat at the front with the driver.

Suddenly, he threw a full can of coke at my head. I was terrified! I'd never expected something like that. It was enough to make you weep. Had things come to this? Thoroughly depressed, I slipped into one of the beds, closed the curtains and clutched my painful head. What had I done that had caused Karl, my friend, to react so violently? I had already been irritable and dissatisfied since our departure from Budapest and my separation from dear Lena, with whom I would have been able to have such a wonderful time if I hadn't had to cross an exhausted Poland in the drizzle. I'd probably been pestering Karl again about my relationships, and the subject of love in general. Now I'd been given a clear sign that we were all on edge, and I decided to hold my tongue in future.

It was relatively bearable in the smaller towns, where matters were more personal. The local organisers had sensed our mood and had taken the initiative, pooling their resources with friends and acquaintances to provide simple buffets and teas which they served in large aluminium cans in our dressing rooms. They were touchingly concerned about us, and you could see how embarrassing it was for them that they had nothing else to offer us. It was equally embarrassing for us to eat the pitiful amount that they had painstakingly gathered. For this reason, we regularly invited them to eat with us, and in this way things became a little friendlier.

During a journey from Warsaw to Opole, we passed through a large forested area where men and women carrying baskets full of fresh chanterelle mushrooms would stand at bends in the road and on the edges of fields, so we stopped and bought some and had them cooked for us later at the Orbis Hotel there. We sometimes helped ourselves in this way, in a country that shouldn't have suffered hunger at all in the first place.

At the end of our dubious adventures in Poland, the tour management company in London had the great idea of depositing all of our accumulated fees in an account of the Polish airline company, which actually operated alongside Swiss Air. By placing a deposit in foreign currency with the Swiss airline company along with the Polish currency, and later purchasing tickets for the Japanese and Australian legs of our tour, the zloty that we'd earned didn't lose as much value as they would have done with a regular exchange into western currency.

# 31  The Land Of Laughter

Our time in Japan was the most thoroughly organised stay that
we'd ever experienced. We flew with Swiss Air from Zurich to
India, where we had to change to a jumbo owned by the Japanese
airline JAL. However, the Japanese flight crew seemed to have
problems piloting the enormous aeroplane. The only time I'd
been on a more turbulent flight was on a BA plane travelling from
Berlin to Düsseldorf. The JAL plane was filled to capacity, and
the pilot landed it so roughly in Tokyo that it bounced on the
runway several times, and had a distinct inclination to the right. I
was frightened to death, and we consoled ourselves with gallows
humour, saying that maybe the Japanese pilot's legs were too short
to reach the pedals.

All three concerts in Tokyo, Osaka and Nagoya were sold out,
and the audience was very enthusiastic, which was something that
we'd never expected of the Japanese. At home, we'd heard that
audiences in Asia were quiet and reserved and never gave free rein
to their feelings, but the fans here showed their wild side. Again,
though, as in Hungary, we were annoyed to find that the stages
were protected by ranks of policemen. Although all of the concert
halls at which we played were seated throughout, the audience

192

didn't stay in their chairs for long, and would run up to the front of the stage to see us at close quarters or and dance. When they did this, though, the police would lunge at them with their rubber truncheons, driving them back to their seats. After the first concert, we considered making it a condition at future concerts that the presence of the police wouldn't be tolerated, and that dancing wouldn't be forbidden, but it was impossible to get the conservative Japanese organisers to agree to this. Nevertheless, we were later able to meet some of the fans at close quarters, in our hotel beds.

In fact, hordes of boys and girls would regularly congregate in the hotel lobby after our appearances, hoping to catch us and beg for autographs or to come up with us to our rooms. The hotel managers and the security chiefs weren't very well prepared for this, and fans were constantly slipping into the lobby, crying, "Party! Party!"

I was very interested in Japanese girls, who were delicate and often very beautiful. You only had to point to the woman of your choice and she would come to your room to spend the most wonderful and imaginative night of love. So as far as love was concerned our needs were well catered for in Japan, although the others weren't as active as me. But as far as the vivacity and the imagination of Japanese women is concerned, my politeness as a drummer will keep me silent.

The organisers thought that they were doing us a favour by inviting us to dine out at traditional Japanese restaurants, but sometimes I felt sick at what there was to eat, dip and drink at these places. I'd never eaten Japanese food before, and I didn't really acquire a taste for this delicate cuisine until I was back in Düsseldorf. It's actually something quite different if you eat locally in Japan. In most cases I couldn't eat what I was served, and I could only manage the green tea and would eat the rice out of politeness, after sprinkling it with sweet soy sauce.

In the evenings, we would hurry into the craziest clubs that we'd ever seen. There were skyscrapers in the entertainment quarter of

Tokyo that had a disco on every floor. Temples of entertainment had been set up to cater for every taste, musical style and age group, and all of them were packed to the rafters with dancers. Whenever we visited one of these, everyone would stare at us as if we were creatures from another planet. Of course, we also danced the most energetically. On one occasion, we met members of The Yellow Magic Orchestra on the dance floor. They were extremely smart and hospitable, and stayed with us for the whole night, and even sent us some lovely nylon rucksacks afterwards. I'm still using mine as a washing bag! Apparently, nylon sacks are still a common promotional gift in Japan, because I was given another when I was there again recently to promote my *Time Pie* album. On that occasion, it was from Pizzicato Five. It's attractive and extremely hard wearing, and I use it for my daily supermarket shopping.

Something unusual occurred to me just after our arrival in Japan. On the long journey from the airport to the city we were stuck in a traffic jam. It was very warm outside, and when I wound down the window I was expecting exhaust fumes, but instead it smelled unusually fresh in the crowded city. The organiser was sitting in the car with us and spoke very good English, and he explained to us that a law had been passed decreeing that all public transport – particularly taxis – had to run on natural gas, which produces hardly any noxious exhaust fumes. Apparently, not long ago it had been impossible to breathe in the cities because of the smog, and the police had been forced to wear masks and oxygen tanks when directing traffic.

Apart from this, the streets were obviously clean and tidy. There was no litter or trodden-in chewing gum on the pavements – it's against the law to throw rubbish onto the street in Japan. There were even ashtrays under the streetlights. I'd never seen anything like it, and I approved wholesale. The underground stations and trains were also extremely clean. No one had slashed the seats or graffitied the carriages or the walls, as they do in Germany or in America. Apparently, the environmental consciousness of the

Japanese is cultivated during their upbringing in the family and during their time at school. I also didn't see any alcoholics, tramps or anyone begging, because that was also forbidden. It was good for us to be able to walk through welltended streets safely and without being accosted. I still enjoy going to Japan. Europeans could learn a lot from the laws that they have there, and the way in which people live together in Japanese cities.

However, in the colourful suburbs, what amazed and dismayed me the most was the fact that all of the electricity and telephone cables were hanging unconcealed above the streets, attached to the walls of the houses in fat bundles. The view upwards – and it was worth looking upward to gaze at the lovely old houses – was obscured by tangles of black wire. Apparently, the Japanese no longer noticed the tangled wires.

Our performances went smoothly. Every tiny detail had been taken care of. Sony had heard about our problems with their video projectors and had sent a technician to every city in which we were performing to take care of the huge, washing-machinesized boxes. They obviously weren't built with such a hard tour in mind, and were illsuited to being continually packed and unpacked. The flight cases were also manhandled at the airports, and were probably pushed around quite a bit, and so the picture tubes – the most expensive components of the projectors – were constantly failing. Each of the projectors had three tubes for the primary colours, and if one of these failed then that projector would produce a different colour. In Japan, the defective tubes were replaced at every concert. Perfect service!

Fans invited me into their homes on two occasions, and so I entered a Japanese residence for the first time. When I walked inside, I had to take my shoes off and put on slippers that were placed ready, which immediately created a private atmosphere. I also had to sit on the floor while the food and drinks were being served. I slept on hard rice straw mattresses and was given delicate, meditative, erotic massages.

We found the most crazy comic strips about us in the

newspapers. For example, there was one hand-painted storyboard that depicted a day in the life of the band. Apparently, we all got up together in the mornings and went to work in the Kling Klang Studio all day. In the evening, we were depicted lying in an extra wide bed, again as a cosy quartet, waiting for the night. However, in the illustrations we had discreet, slit eyes, probably because they couldn't draw European faces. The media saw us as conventional workers who did everything together and only lived for the company, as disciplined as the Japanese themselves. And they assumed that we went to bed together. We found this hilarious. Another magazine cover showed a full-sized colour drawing of the four of us biting into a over-sized slice of melon and spitting out the seeds. It seemed that the press had heard that we were vegetarians and were making fun of it.

The nine days in the land of laughter passed much too quickly and we all vowed to return soon.

# 32 *Florian Presents A Puzzle*

Our reception at Sydney Airport in Australia wasn't at all pleasant. The passengers and the crew had to wait for what seemed like an age after the plane landed, not knowing what was going on. While we were sitting in the narrow seats, filling out the disembarkation forms and getting annoyed about the many personal questions they demanded of us, several officials from the local health authority appeared in the passenger compartment armed with large aerosols and started to shroud everything in spray, including the luggage in the open compartments. It was outrageous! After a long, tiring flight we all wanted to get out of the plane, and now, to top it all, we were being covered in powder! The human disinfectant they were using made us gasp and wheeze, while those with the sprays wore white masks and gloves so that they didn't have to breathe in the poison themselves. We felt like lepers. The image of the disinfecting process in German concentration camps sprang to mind. They would probably have liked to have put us into quarantine for a few days as well. I don't know what the Australians were afraid of.

What a great reception. All we wanted to do was bring our music to the continent. Florian suffered most from such humiliation. He

197

was extremely sensitive to everything that was imposed upon him, particularly anything that happened against his will. For him, everything seemed to go against him in Australia. He even seemed to stand in his own way. He cut himself off even more than before. Much as we liked him – and we continually made him aware of this – he simply couldn't stand the strain of being on tour for so long.

The rest of us thoroughly enjoyed getting to know the world. The evening appearances and short soundchecks in the afternoon had long become routine, and we found more time to become interested in our perpetually changing environment. It was an almost ideal situation: we could enjoy the travelling, explore foreign cities, visit exhibitions or just spend enjoyable hours on the beach; we could stroll around shopping and eating in fine restaurants; and in the evenings, we were acclaimed and applauded. Can there be a more wonderful life, when the whole world loves you?

If Florian hadn't been there, you might be inclined to think that this was a rhetorical question. He didn't seem to appreciate any of the positive aspects, and couldn't enjoy the things that the rest of us did. He was continually going his own way, becoming increasingly isolated. Ralf was coming into our room more often, because he obviously had more fun with us, and we ended up communicating with Florian through poor Emil.

Florian was becoming very puzzling to us. He simply wasn't suited to touring in general, and I felt so sorry for him when he was obviously suffering so much from homesickness and lovesickness. On these occasions, he would eat alone in other restaurants, or he would sit in the furthest corner of the tour bus during long road journeys. Even on planes he would look for unoccupied seats in another row. He was so introverted that he didn't even say hello if you met him in the hotel lift. Was it really only homesickness? Longing for a familiar environment, his girlfriend and peace and quiet?

We had performed in Sydney on 16 September, and the concert had been, as expected, very successful. The next evening performance was to be in Melbourne. It was a beautiful day. I can still remember things exactly. On the free day before the gig, I sailed on a ferry from Sydney to an offshore island, where I spent the whole day swimming, sunbathing and reading. It was like being on holiday. There was a deep blue sky and a layer of heat lay over the city. Our concert in Melbourne was scheduled to take place in the Princess Theatre the next day. We had no idea of the surprise that waited for us there.

Everything had been set up in the large hall, which could seat at least 4,000 people. We had rehearsed for a short time in the afternoon, and of course everything had gone fine. The roadies were thoroughly practised, and each of them knew his position and the contents of every flight case perfectly. They had memorised what belonged where, and where everything had to be plugged in, so we left the hall that afternoon in a good mood, intending to relax for a while in the hotel. That evening, we ate at a restaurant near the concert hall. We'd got used to eating a small amount before our concerts, because it was usually too late to eat afterwards. If we ate then, we didn't sleep very well, and would be exhausted for the following day. By this time, we'd become accustomed to the fact that Florian would eat on his own. He usually went out to find an Indian restaurant, so the fact that he wasn't with us that night didn't worry us at all.

Back at the hall, we took our time preparing for our appearance, taking our shirts and black trousers from a clothes rail fitted in our costume case and putting them on, and removing our ties from their compartment in the lid of the case. The shoes, which we'd bought in a shop on Broadway in New York, were kept in one of the lower drawers. My brass drumsticks and the small pen torches for the dark stage, our crib sheets with the set-list and Ralf's synthesiser settings and prompt sheets were always stored in an orderly way. All we needed to do was glance quickly in the mirror to make sure our hair was combed and then we were off through the passages to the darkened stage. The crew always positioned our robots behind a curtain so that they could quickly move them to our sides when we went into 'The Robots'. We checked our doubles to make sure that they were correctly dressed, and that their adjustable joints were all positioned properly. On the stage, we tuned and warmed up the synths and the e-drums a little, listening to them through pairs of headphones. Each of us was busy with his equipment.

Each of us except Florian. He still hadn't arrived. We were gradually becoming uneasy, and so we sent Emil out to scout the nearby restaurants in the hope that he might find Florian there. After what felt like an endless 30 minutes, Emil came back, quite breathless and quite alone. What were we going to do? It was only a quarter of an hour to the beginning of the concert. Emil looked through a small hole that we'd cut in the curtain. "It's completely sold out," he said. "People are getting rather restless."

We'd already realised this ourselves, after hearing catcalls and whistling while Emil had been out looking for Florian. Things were looking bad. We discussed how we could get through the songs without Florian, but his roles were too extensive for any of us to take them on in addition to our own. Apart from that, it would be obvious if the fourth member of the band wasn't there. We thought about cancelling, sorely confused. It had got to the point where we were no longer prepared to accept this kind of behaviour from him. It just wasn't funny any more – it was incredibly frustrating.

Disappointed, Karl, Ralf, Emil and I stood on the stage in semi-darkness, not knowing what else to do. Then, amazingly, Emil peeped through the hole in the curtain and excitedly whispered across to us, "There he is! There, in the back row! Thank God! I can see him quite clearly. He's sitting there in his stage outfit. Has he gone completely mad?"

We were horrified and relieved at the same time. At least he was there, although we didn't know what on Earth he was doing. We sent Emil into the hall to fetch him, and I peered through the curtain and watched Emil run up the aisle to the distant row of seats where Florian was sitting in the middle of the audience, waiting for the show to begin. Emil stepped carefully over the legs of the fans, struggled through to Florian and stopped by him, then bent and whispered something in his ear. Florian then whispered back. They began whispering back and forth. I couldn't hear what they were talking about, of course, because they were too far away, but after a few minutes Emil came back to the stage and said to us, "Florian wants to see the show from the audience for once. We might as well start without him. He says that he isn't needed, and that we won't miss him at all."

That hit home! So that was what he wanted to say to us. He thought that we didn't pay him enough attention, or give him enough affection, and was obviously feeling deprived. What were we going to do? We had another quick conference, and decided that we wouldn't start without him under any circumstances, even if it took another hour to get him onto the stage.

Emil volunteered to go to Florian to persuade him that we couldn't start without him, demonstrating once again what an important, faithful and helpful friend he was when it came to solving problems on tour. Unflagging, he set off again to struggle through the crowds. I was so frustrated that I couldn't look through the curtain again. I looked into Ralf's and Karl's faces and saw only grey. Our fun was spoiled. We were cross with our friend, but we could also sympathise with him. He had to have been suffering considerably to have done this. After an endless wait, Emil returned to the stage through the side entrance with Florian at his side, who murmured something like, "What am I doing here? You don't need me. I'm not interested in any of it any more, anyway." Angry whispers flew back and forth on all sides, and then we started our announcement tape. "Ladies and gentlemen, tonight, from Germany, the Man Machine – Kraftwerk!"

I've never played in a fouler mood at a less enthusiastic concert on a more beautiful day. We didn't become the slightest bit more cheerful as the show progressed, and none of us even looked at each other. Thank God that we didn't need to, and that we were rehearsed enough just to play together. We never found out whether our fans had grasped anything about our problems. They probably hadn't even realised who'd been sitting in their midst.

In any case, we couldn't go on like this. In spite of our sympathy for Florian, Karl and I were almost ready to abandon the tour and fly home at that point. Thank God we didn't, though, because the most exciting stage of the tour came next.

# 33  Escape From Bombay

Bombay, 28 September 1981
We were halfway home from the Australian leg of our tour, and
we were provisionally scheduled to give the two final concerts of
the Computer World tour during a stopover in Bombay. We knew
from our timetable that we had four days free when we got there
(the two concerts had been planned one after the other at the end
of that week), and so we were looking forward to visiting the
Indian city of a million inhabitants, which was the most exotic
location in which we'd ever played. We also wanted to see the Taj
Mahal and immerse ourselves in every aspect of the culture, as we
had always enjoyed doing in other countries.

However, on landing in Bombay, we immediately had problems
with the sultry heat, and during the long taxi ride into town we
were simultaneously amazed and horrified when, at every corner,
where the cars had to stop because of traffic jams or junctions,
hordes of children would gather around our vehicle, thrusting their
mutilated limbs through the windows, which we'd wound down
because of the heat. It was deeply shocking. So much suffering, so
immediately and so widespread was too much for us. The sight of
the misery was a huge culture shock; we weren't prepared for it at
all. Children and adults with amputated legs and hands, horribly

bent fingers or ragged stumps for arms were begging for their very existence. Although these injuries were all healed, they were also horribly exposed.

It was just pathetic to behold. Some hobbled with wooden crutches while thrusting their grinning, open-mouthed faces into our car, displaying their mutilated tongues so that we could see their wretchedness. The sight was unbearable. Even so, the eyes of these children were beautiful and proud, and I shall remember their gazes for the rest of my life.

I later learned that these were bands that were maintained, mutilated and trained by gangsters. The children were taken away from their families or sold cheaply when they were still quite small, then mutilated by some dreadful means – often while they were fully conscious – and trained to beg and seek out foreigners, and also to keep a look-out for taxis carrying tourists or business people. At junctions where vehicles had to stop, they surrounded the cars, holding out their hands (if they had any) and showing their dreadful wounds to arouse the pity of the tourists. It was the general view that this was better for such children than living with their own families, but surely this couldn't be true? At the end of the day they had to give their money to the gangsters, and anyone who hadn't begged enough was beaten. The worst thing is that this hasn't changed to this day.

I felt sick when we arrived at the Holiday Inn on the west coast of Bombay. American conditions prevailed there, complete western luxury, everything that you could expect of a five-star hotel, although of course it was run by Indian staff. Our rooms were furnished in just the same way as they would have been in America or Europe – typical, standard Holiday Inn furniture, everything according to the blueprint. After relaxing for a while, we met in the lobby in the evening to find somewhere to eat. Our tour guide warned us against drinking the tap water, and advised us that we shouldn't even clean our teeth with it. Instead, crates of mineral water were delivered to our rooms by the hotel management. That was a great start – unlike everyone else, I hadn't found the time to get vaccinated against cholera and typhoid back in Germany. I was at risk.

We ate at the hotel restaurant for the sake of simplicity, and coincidentally I met a former German girlfriend, of all people, who was eating there with an Indian businesswoman. I couldn't believe it. I hadn't seen her in Düsseldorf for years, and then I met her on our very first night in Bombay. We were both amazed and pleased. She told me that she'd found a career as a textile designer in a German company, and was always travelling through India, visiting textile mills, where she selected materials for her collections and carried out inspections. It was her dream profession, she explained, although it turned out that she'd already had malaria and a number of other diseases. I invited her to our concert, but unfortunately she had to be miles away by then. Also, she explained that it would then be the rainy season – not a particularly good time to be visiting India. She urged me to come back in the summer and travel around with her, when I would surely understand her passion for India and would perhaps be musically inspired. That wasn't a bad idea. I recalled that The Beatles had discovered the sitar and the eastern influence for their songs during their trip to India.

After the meal, we took a taxi into the city centre to have a look around. However, we never got there, at least not that day. After we'd been driving for only a few minutes, the heavens opened. The downpour was torrential. I couldn't believe how much water fell that night. It just didn't stop – you could hardly see your hand in front of your face. A thick, green wall of rain poured over the city. The taxi didn't stand a chance against the deluge and it just stopped there, its engine drowned in water.

We were stuck. Four musicians in the middle of Bombay in a worn-out, fourwheeled tin can, which seemed to be slowly sinking into an enormous lake. The water in the streets rose rapidly because there was hardly any drainage. In the end, we were sitting and our feet up on the seats with water seeping into the car. The taxi driver had rolled up his trousers and had his head under the bonnet, looking for the fault in the middle of the driving rain. Did he really believe he could get his flooded car going again? I assumed that it was more likely to be a cursory action, because he was embarrassed at being stuck. To him, we were educated, well-dressed foreigners, and he didn't want to let us down for the *baksheesh* alone. Actually, he didn't need to be embarrassed about his taxi.

After 20 minutes of frenzied attempts at breathing life into his engine, the unbelievable happened – it suddenly coughed into life. We just looked at each other, baffled. There was an important lesson there: it pays never to give up! Keep on trying. If you believe in something, and behave positively, success is inevitable at some point. We drove back to the hotel, our feet up on the seats.

We forgot about the city for the time being, and thought about what to do next. At least we had a wonderful view of the Indian Ocean from mine and Karl's room, which was on a higher floor. Of course, you couldn't see much during the downpour, but every now and again the rain would stop and the sun would come out, and then it would be possible to see the ocean and the tall coconut palms. The wet coastal landscape before the hotel and the surface of the ocean shone in the sunlight. It would have been a fantastic view, if only…

…Yes, if only it hadn't been possible to see what was happening down there next to the hotel wall. It was dreadful. Directly adjacent to the hotel, with its beautiful gardens and romantic promenades, there was an enormous, filthy slum. Shacks and shelters were built directly against the high, implacable wall of the hotel. I saw entire families, emaciated and almost naked, attempting to rub their wet brown bodies dry with sopping rags and tarpaulins. Children and toddlers lay around in puddles where packs of stray dogs had left their excrement. Between these plastic shelters I saw dogs lounging around with tapeworms hanging out of their behinds. No one was looking after the dirty children. The collision of cultures there was truly dreadful.

I found it impossible to come to terms with this. I lost my

appetite for the entire week, and ate only rice and peas out of a sense of shame and revulsion, as well as from fear of infection. I drank the hot peppermint tea that was always available, freshly made, in the restaurant or available for room delivery. On one occasion, I even ate an Indian chicken, but it was so spicy that I've never tried it again. Even today, I have no appetite for Indian food, but that actually has more to do with the conditions that I witnessed there than the nature of the food. Florian, however, has always loved it.

It was still raining hard the following morning. The wind had been roaring all night, and I was also feeling quite cold and damp. Every now and again, the clouds would part and the rain would stop for a short time. We tried to get into the inner city a few more times, but it was always the same: begging children and torrential rain. Whenever it stopped, a merciless tumult and bustling activity immediately dominated the streets. Bodies lay everywhere on the ground – sleepers, the sick, alcoholics and probably the dead, too. They were simply overlooked, and people just stepped over them resignedly. I noticed that the houses were almost all the same greenish-black colour, but this wasn't paint; it was shimmering mould. With the constant, oppressive rain, the cheap paints that were available there, with their high casein content, were a feast for mould spores. Even so, this made a very colourful and exotic impression on us.

The gaudy film posters that we saw everywhere – some of which were as high as the houses themselves – also added colour to the city. People stood in long queues in front of the cinemas, and Bombay has a lot of those! People queued up there at all times of the day, even in the rain, among them many slender women with colourful saris wound closely around their bodies, black plaits, brown, glistening skin and sparkling eyes set below spiritedly curved eyebrows – a feast for the eyes. I've rarely seen such proud women anywhere else in the world. Even Italian women seemed pale in contrast. I couldn't help but stare at them, and irritated my colleagues with my constant rapturous appreciation of them.

I would have dearly loved to have got to know an Indian woman and tried out the Kama Sutra with her! At that time, I hadn't had a girlfriend for a long time, and I was hungry for love, tenderness and sex. Unfortunately, because we were so strange to the Indians, there was no possibility of this kind of contact.

We often saw the Indian swastika on balustrades and railings in front of the houses, which was very similar to the swastika of the Nazis, and Emil explained to me that the Nazis had copied it from the Indians and perverted it, adopting it to represent their own symbolism.

The week continued in much the same fashion. We grew impatient, and in frustration bought things in the nearby bazaars and the hotel lobby, where there was a tailor who had huge quantities of very fine materials and who would make up trousers, jackets or complete suits at short notice. We found another shop that sold cassettes, and we even found some by Kraftwerk there. We couldn't believe it. This was totally illegal, because our record company had no representation in India. There were no official imports at that time, either, so these were either bootlegged recordings or contraband, and apart from that the sound quality was miserable and the printed covers were tacky. Ralf believed that there was little that we could do about it, though, as India was so far away from German jurisdiction. Anyway, how could you monitor such an enormous country, where bribery and corruption ruled?

In the middle of this wet week, our situation became even worse when the first of us became ill. Other cases of nausea and vomiting soon broke out among us and members of the crew, who were staying with us in the hotel. Oddly enough, though, I was fine, mainly because I was hardly eating anything.

Fortunately, I'd brought three packets of charcoal tablets with me in case any of us came down with a stomach infection, and I distributed them gradually to the sick, but it didn't help much – they'd eaten something that didn't agree with them. The situation was getting worse! The continuous alternation between deluge and heat spread within our bodies and penetrated our very souls. We were all becoming increasingly isolated, retreating to our bedrooms. It wasn't particularly comfortable there, either, because everything was damp. Even the bedclothes, which were changed daily, felt cold and clammy, and lying in a damp bed is disgusting. The only things to read were the days-old European newspapers that we found in the lobby, and we were sleeping late and doing everything slowly so that time would pass more quickly. I did enjoy writing letters to my father and friends at home in Germany, though.

Florian managed to explore the city, although the rest of us weren't able to because there just wasn't another dry day in the week, and some were suffering from diarrhoea. I optimistically gave out the remainder of my charcoal tablets to those that asked for them. On one morning, when I took my trousers out of the wardrobe, they were quite stiff and covered with greyish-white spots from the high humidity. I was disgusted, absolutely fed up with the constant dampness and just sitting around, waiting for the concert. I didn't even want to go into the city any more.

Saturday finally came. Both of our concerts were scheduled to take place in the evening, one straight after the other in the old hall, where they held traditional sitar concerts during the day. Florian had looked in there once. Apparently, the concert he'd seen there had lasted for the entire day, with individual musicians being replaced with others from time to time. This continuous rhythmical accompaniment was mesmerising. Members of the audience also left the hall on occasion, to be replaced by newcomers. The music didn't stop and start at the beginning again at any time but changed continually over the course of the day as other musicians joined the group. It was, in effect, a non-stop concert. It sounded interesting.

In the late afternoon, the roadies were finally able to build our stage and warm up the instruments, which was still necessary in order to obtain a stable pitch. Just before the tour, Ralf had acquired a new Polymoog synthesiser, along with a back-up in case there was a fault, but even these modern synths didn't have stable tuning yet. You could only rely on them to a certain extent, and they had to be left running for several hours.

During a short practice session, observed by many turbaned Indians, we realised that the roof above our stage wasn't watertight and that water was dripping through in many places, often directly above our synths and consoles. It was unbearable – the damned rain just never stopped! We were all under intense psychological pressure. The roadies quickly pulled plastic strips of foil over our equipment, and we tried slipping our hands underneath them and playing that way. Any other band would have left at that point, but our genetic musical heritage wouldn't allow us.

However, none of us wanted to stay in Bombay longer than necessary. Fortunately, we'd been able to change the booking of our return flight, and we just wanted to go immediately after the concerts, not a day longer – not to sweat and be sticky for an hour longer – so we'd booked a flight for immediately after the concert. Our crew would have to follow us later, on the flight that had been originally booked, as they had to dismantle everything during the night and pack it into the flight cases and get to the airport later. Still, we had seats on a flight home – what a relief! We were all glad – we just had to get away from there. Our digestive systems had suffered enough, but thanks to the tablets the others had been taking they'd been detoxified enough to get through that evening's performance relatively securely.

We had only one more problem: the plane was scheduled to depart very shortly after the end of our performance, so we wouldn't have enough time to drive to the hotel and fetch our things, and so we decided to check out immediately and take our luggage to the concert hall that evening and shoot off quickly afterwards. However, Florian and I had ordered some more trousers and shirts from the Indian tailor in the hotel bazaar, and he wanted to deliver them that evening. We had to have them, so we gave him the address of the venue and he promised to courier them promptly by bike. (We'd already paid him when he took

210

our measurements.) We travelled to the hall in crammed taxis and stacked everything that we wanted to take home with us ready at the rear entrance of the backstage area.

The concert itself was routine. Fortunately, very little rain was coming through the roof, and the roadies were able to remove the plastic from our instruments. The synths had been on since late that afternoon, and had warmed up properly. I think that, to begin with, the Indians found our songs quite puzzling, as the hall was utterly silent. The audience was exclusively comprised of men, clothed in white with white turbans and thick black moustaches. It was a crazy situation: a bunch of German technocrats from the elegant western city of Düsseldorf with an ultra-modern, electrifying stage show, electronic music and cool neon lights performing before a turbaned Indian audience. Somehow it seemed like Ali Baba and his 40 thieves listening to the musical story of the "Brothers Kraftwerk". I smiled to myself. We'd come so far. Nothing could surprise me now.

At the end of the performance, we walked off to thunderous applause. I hadn't expected so much energy. It was almost oppressive, the way the Indians lost control. The second concert, which began at about ten that evening, went just the same. Most of the turbaned Indians had stayed in the hall – they must have bought two tickets in advance. We didn't have enough time to play any encores after our last song; everything had been organised from that point. During the last song, 'It's More Fun To Compute', Ralf set the main sequencer to run continuously and we ran from the stage, following Emil to our dressing room, still hearing the thunderous tones of the sequencer and the roaring of the Indians. We quickly stripped our sweat-soaked stage clothes from our damp bodies and put on our day clothes, which were placed ready. There was no time to shower – everything had to be done as quickly as possible. Taxis were waiting for us at the exit with their engines running, and as we dressed Emil and the roadies threw our luggage into their boots, which then wouldn't shut because we had so much stuff to take back with us. Fortunately,

211

the hotel tailor had kept his word and had delivered the clothes we'd ordered to the backstage area during the show.

Freshly dressed, we threw ourselves into the taxis and set off at speed into the stillheavy evening traffic of Bombay. It was crazy. We had perhaps half an hour to reach the airport. Rush-hour traffic in Bombay is something that has to be seen to be believed. It's absolute chaos. People walk, drive, run, brake, crash and stumble around in a state of utter confusion. There's no order or traffic regulations, and hardly any traffic signs. If there are any, they are completely ignored.

The taxi drivers had already been informed of their important cargo. They'd obviously been given a large *baksheesh,* because the mad journey reminded me of a rollercoaster ride. The cabs drove in single file, hooting continually and overtaking dangerously, sometimes mounting the pavement and causing passing pedestrians to leap acrobatically out of the way. I'm still amazed that we didn't crash or hit anyone. I had a final glimpse of evening Bombay, but I wasn't really looking by that stage. We were genuinely escaping, and didn't look back again, only forwards, towards the airport and our flight home.

We reached the check-in desk at the airport at the very last minute and threw our luggage onto the conveyor belts while a stewardess accompanied us as we ran through the maze of corridors to the gate and ushered us over to the boarding personnel in person. As we embarked onto the plane, on which all of the other passengers had already belted up ready for take-off, all I wanted to do was kiss the carpet. The dry, cool air in the BA jumbo was the best thing I've ever tasted. It was a blissful relief after a week spent being perpetually soaked and surrounded by mould. Everything was clean, orderly and British. I loved the British then! The stewardess smiled because we were all chattering and gesticulating together so happily, laughing about our escape from India and our most extraordinary concert.

The woman could have had no idea what we'd just gone through. For her, Bombay was only a stopover. Soon, thankfully, the dreadful conditions, the dampness, the sultriness, the misery and the revulsion were forgotten as the majestic jumbo gently lifted away from this sticky monsoon area into a cloudless night sky scattered with clear, twinkling stars. It smelled so good. To cap it all, we were spoiled with a first-class European evening meal. Oh, how wonderful life can be when you can survive such adventures with your friends! We were going home. The end of the tour was near.

# 34 Electronic Lifestyle
## The First Cracks

DÜSSELDORF, 5 DECEMBER 1981

The German leg of the tour was accompanied by a mixture of success and sadness. Our solidarity began to crumble: faithful Emil left us quite unexpectedly, emigrating to the Bahamas. He was the first to change, no longer content with the band's range of themes and with they way we treated each other. He was just as disappointed by our general tendency to separate off from each other, and by the lack of attention with which his art and his intellectual importance were received.

December was also a rotten month for a tour, in any year. Admittedly, we had previously given a number of concerts in Germany in June, when it was warm, and they'd been triumphant. By this time, of course, the Germans had finally got used to synthesisers, to our music and to us as an international pop band, but we'd had to find success abroad first – especially in America – before they could love us at home. Now, though, the media were finally giving us the attention we deserved. The journalist Dankmar Isleib interviewed Ralf for the German publication *Musikexpress* under the title "Kraftwerk – Electronic Lifestyle", and among other things Ralf stated that "Kraftwerk stands for something quite straightforward, something that we have been doing for years. We're not really that flexible."

Looking back today, he hit the nail on the head with this statement. Although Ralf always spoke in the plural, in this he actually meant himself, because the rest of us were in fact very flexible. Today, I think that this admission indicated the main reason why there was less and less development in the group. A lack of flexibility is the greatest obstruction to progress and development. A lack of flexibility means refusing to acknowledge other points of view and ideas. Ralf had always had a very high opinion of himself, and it was almost impossible to convince him of other opinions, which is fatal for a music group. His behaviour undermined the rest of us because he just didn't pay us enough attention.

Apart from this, our lifestyle wasn't at all electronic. Although there was a lot of electronic equipment in the Kling Klang Studio, we lived quite natural lives when we weren't there. We loved nature, ate only vegetarian food, didn't smoke (I gave up after *Trans Europe Express*), would drink a glass of wine now and again to be social, and also rode our bikes a lot, some of us maybe too much. However, no one should think that our lives were boring. We found pleasure in making music on the stage, the applause of the crowd and, last but not least, love. It was the most natural thing in the world for us to go dancing, just like any other young people from our neighbourhood, and this form of recreation didn't need any artificial stimulants or electronic aids.

More and more reports about the Kraftwerk phenomenon were appearing in magazines and newspapers, and journalists were fighting to get to us. On 9 February 1982, Karl Schindler wrote a report for the *Kölner Express* announcing, "The Kraftwerk group is breaking into the charts." The report could just as well have announced, "The trade unions are breaking through the wage level," or, even better, "Crack tank brigade AG breaks into titanium safes!"

The music world had come to realise that we'd invented a

completely new musical genre: techno pop. With my amateur bands I'd copied English guitar groups and beat their rhythms out on old-fashioned drum skins. Now, we were the fathers of electro pop, or *robo pop*, as Ralf liked to call it. We had created something with millimetre precision, so to speak, with the instruments of our technology-hungry generation, constructed on the drawing board from the musical inheritance of minimalists and experimentalists such as Terry Riley, Karlheinz Stockhausen, Moondog and Oskar Scala. We were no longer playing in smoky caverns or dubious clubs, but mainly in large city venues like the Zirkus Krone, the Nibelungenhalle, the Alte Oper in Frankfurt, the Rheingoldhalle, and even the Westfalenhalle in Dortmund. Great venues were now being booked for us because our audience had grown and our music was becoming a cultural phenomenon. If we'd been a sweating, stamping rock band we never would have played at such elegant halls, although I think now that it might have been good for us if we'd left a little more "juice" behind after our concerts.

For concert organisers, our music was at least as important as jazz. Most of our themes had a philosophical content, and we didn't charge around the stage stupidly like metal bands, and we didn't drink, smoke dope or cause riots. Our image never gave fans the slightest reason to coalesce into cults, and there was no "frontman" for women to hurl themselves at.

Even so, our mood reached a low point during those winter concerts in Germany, after we'd been so enervated by the months of touring. That November and December saw the worst possible weather, which isn't pleasant during long journeys. On top of this, we had to leave our lovely flat in the Berger Allee, as the Mannesmann company, who owned the house, had secretly planned to build a new office building on the site and had asked all of the tenants to leave, without notice. Later, they would stage a dawn raid and brutally demolish six houses that were under a preservation order, against the will of a citizens' action group. This didn't bother Emil, because he had already fled to warmer climes far away. I felt bereft without him, and quickly sensed the first signs of disintegration. Because we'd been living in the Berger Allee for ten years, with a lawyer's help we obtained nine months' postponement of the notice to quit, and started looking for new flats.

This dispirited mood was made worse by the fact that our German management company, Lippmann Und Rau, sometimes chose venues that were a bit too large. When we played at the Westfalenhalle in Dortmund, for example, only some of the front rows were occupied. Of course, this was enormously frustrating when we'd previously been playing to consistently sold-out houses across the globe. However, we had many friends in our neighbourhood in Cologne – we knew this from our disco nights there. On 3 December 1981, we even played two concerts directly after each other in one evening at the Sartori-Saal, which was completely packed. The youth of Cologne went wild.

Later we appeared in the Philipshalle, in our home town of Düsseldorf, very nervous because this was our first local performance and because our families and friends would be there. Unfortunately, the hall was only half full, which told us that we weren't very popular in our own city. There was also a technical fault with the synchronisation of the synths during the concert, and applause was sporadic, but you have to live with this as an artist. Even so, we would have preferred to fly straight back to Japan or America, where we were so popular, but by now we were exhausted and all we wanted was peace and quiet. I would have loved to follow Emil to live in the sun, but we were obliged to complete the other concerts, which would be a torment.

When we played the Düsseldorf Philipshalle, I saw quite a few of my family in the front row, and I was glad at least that they had come to see me for once. It was the first time that my father had come to see what I did for a living. Afterwards, he invited me to an Italian restaurant with my brothers and some aunts and uncles, where he had reserved a large table for us. For the first time, I had the feeling that my father was proud of me, although I was unable to enjoy the feeling because I wasn't used to being loved by him – the concept was alien to me.

His rich sister, my godmother, sat to my right, and during the meal she suddenly rustled something to me under the table, elbowed me in the ribs gently and whispered to me that I should also put my hand under the table, where she pushed a crumpled piece of paper between my fingers. I surreptitiously manoeuvred it into my trouser pocket and unfolded it later in the toilet. It was a 500 DM note. I didn't know what to think of it; I just thought that it was a helpless gesture from my godmother. Perhaps she was moved by her conscience, because she hadn't shown any sign of interest in me after my mother's death – until now, of course, when she saw that her Wolfgang had become famous. Sadly, my mother was unable to see our concert in Düsseldorf. As I said, she had died several years previously, and I missed her a lot, but at least she'd been there for Kraftwerk's early successes, and had collected all the newspaper articles that she could find about me. I'd always enjoyed writing letters to my mother when I was on the road, and I know that she was proud of me.

We played two or three more concerts in Germany, and two more in Utrecht in the Netherlands and in Luxembourg, but we'd all been longing to get home, to get away from planes and long coach journeys, and just to be able to do what we wanted, free from the pressure of a timetable. I needed sleep, sleep and more sleep, in my own bed, which wouldn't be in the Berger Allee for much longer...

# 35 *Up And Away On A Bike*
## *I Am No Longer Saved*

DÜSSELDORF, MAY 1982

There wasn't a lot to do in the time after our world tour, as far as studio work was concerned. Florian and Ralf had bought two of the most expensive racing bikes on the market, and were seen increasingly often cycling around Düsseldorf and the lush Bergisch countryside. They became more and more competitive, and if you ask me they were almost as fanatic about their bikes as they were about music. When we met up in the Kling Klang Studio, they would prefer to study cycling catalogues produced by Campognolo, Shimano and other manufacturers of cycling accessories rather than think up new ideas for songs.

The bicycle seemed to have become an alternative to the synthesiser, particularly for Ralf. Like Florian, he nearly always wore black, skin-tight racing gear, and he'd shaved and oiled his legs to cut down on wind resistance, just like the professionals do. I have to admit, though, that he was becoming fitter from month to month; his skin always looked fresh, and he began to have that euphoric look that many racing cyclists have, like Rudi Thurau, if you know what I mean. I think that he achieved a completely new sense of his body at that time. He looked attractive, and said that he could feel his muscles growing.

219

I could understand his point of view. At that time, I too would have welcomed a new interest in my life. He was the leader in his cycling group, admired by everyone. Tyres lay around his flat in heaps. Over the course of the years, he fitted out several frames specifically designed for his body size and for the strict "criteria" that he demanded of himself in exaggerated asceticism. Sometimes, he would even travel to France with some of his sporting friends, and they would cycle through some of the more arduous stages of the Tour De France, in the Alps or the Pyrénées. They treated their tyres the same way that some people treat their wine – they had to be well matured, and he once explained to me that the quality of a tyre improved the longer it was stored.

In 1983, his enthusiasm reached its summit and he wrote a song describing the race, 'Tour De France', which was released on 5 July 1984. He'd acquired one of the first affordable samplers, the Emulator, and this piece of equipment was revolutionary in the field of electronic music. With this device, we were able to record all sounds, even natural ones, on electronic instruments and transmit them in all tempi and modes via the keyboard. This worked fantastically with the sound of his bike switching gears, for example, and the sound of the chain, which replaced the hi-hat in the song. Even Florian's laboured breathing and groaning was sampled and integrated into the song. This technique heralded the birth of techno, dance and remixing, which wouldn't have been possible without samplers and sequencers. 'Tour De France' was released in 1983, and was sometimes played when television companies broadcast stages of the race.

Of course, that meant that I had to get a bike, too, because we wanted to make a film for the single. I practised keeping my balance on this most unstable means of locomotion for several days before the shoot, because I wasn't very good at riding one. I'm still amazed that I didn't fall off during the filming, but if you look closely you can see that I was really wobbly. At any rate, riding racing bikes was a fleeting pleasure for me. When I'd mastered the machine to a certain extent, I often rode it to Krefeld to visit Ralf, taking a pleasant route through the flat Rhine meadows, through Kaiserswerth and Wittlaer, and then around Duisburg and across the Krefeld Rhine bridge into town.

I once had an accident there, on a cobbled high street in the town centre, very near Ralf's house, where tram rails ran down the middle of the road. Suddenly, a boy on his bike swept out of a side street from the right straight into my path, completely oblivious of me. I tried to get out of his way by pulling my handlebars sharply to the left, and landed on the tramlines. I fell onto the cobblestones with a thump and an awful pain stabbed into my right knee.

When I looked up, a huge army truck was rolling steadily towards me on its huge balloon tyres. That would have been the end of me, but the driver was able to bring his green truck to a standstill by the skin of his teeth, the front bumper only a metre from my bike. Although still alive, I was in shock, and my desire to cycle had disappeared completely. I hung the twisted wreck of my bike over my shoulders and hobbled to the tram stop, nursing my knee. I got onto the next tram to Düsseldorf and I bid a silent *adieu* to bicycles. After all, walking had never brought me into such a dangerous situation. To this day, I enjoy walking along the river, and I love being able to walk long stretches freely and without obstruction. It's a great opportunity to think, to dream and to whistle new melodies, which I record on my pocket recorder so that I don't forget them.

A year later, EMI released 'Computer Love', from the *Computer World* album, as a single in the UK. They had chosen that particular song because it sounded so melodic, and they put 'The Model' – a song from the older album *The Man Machine* – on the B-side. Oddly enough, the B-side became Number One in the British charts within a short time, and it stayed in this lucrative position for three weeks. Evidently, our fans now preferred our songs to have romantic melodies and human lyrics, and it showed that women were possibly buying our records, too. Women are normally less inclined towards electronic music or technical subjects, and our music was often too cold for them.

I was starting to feel the same way. I wasn't having as much fun with our themes about computers, robots and man machines any more. I preferred the romanticism of the early songs. For this reason, 'Neon Lights' and the really early 'Ananas Symphonie' are still my favourites. Such tunes are a part of me; they were in me even before Kraftwerk. I'm nothing but an incorrigible romantic, and this is evident in my music with Yamo today. With Kraftwerk, our creative periods were becoming less and less creative, and I found myself visiting the studio less frequently.

In 1982, I fell deeply in love with a girl called Constanze, and soon preferred to spend my evenings with her rather than sitting around in the studio waiting for the cyclists to turn up with Ralf. In the meantime, Karl had risen to become co-writer, and spent his time working on "beautiful things" in his home studio, which he then polished with Ralf and Florian in the Kling Klang Studio and integrated into the songs. He had more and more influence on the songs, while Florian continued to take care of the special effects and the gimmicks.

With the introduction of the sequencer, my tasks had been reduced to the extent that I needed to visit the studio only occasionally, to test out styles and rhythms and discuss the programming of potential new tracks. I retreated from the studio more and more, preferring to spend my time with my girlfriend and going on long trips with her through Italy, or to the isle of Ischia on Lake Garda, or to the Côte d'Azur, where we spent our holidays at Florian's parents' French farmhouse, near St Tropez. I'd missed out on hundreds of romantic dinners, city tours rich with experiences and making endless love on the long Tuscan and French evenings, and this need had to be requited desperately, so I promptly set about doing so. I often spent weekends hanging around with Constanze in Amsterdam, which we both loved because of its cultural cosmopolitanism.

I sometimes didn't see my colleagues for weeks on end, and we often took to meeting in discotheques in Cologne instead of at the studio. I was feeling increasingly superfluous. It became

222

more noticeable that I was in a period of great change myself. My emotional nature had shifted so much that I was unable to compromise with my friends' rational nature. I missed sincerity, warmth and humanity.

At the same time, I was also experiencing artistic difficulties with the band. The longer I participated, the less satisfied and more unrecognised I felt about my ideas and abilities. I persuaded myself that Ralf and Florian had taken me on because of my face and my love of invention. I was a passionate entertainer for them onstage, and behaved like a loyal robot. I'd dedicated my drumming and my heart to the group, but it was obvious that I no longer meant very much to them. I felt less and less occupied by my role, and began to fear greatly for my future. The band was no fun for me any more, because my friends had found pleasure in something else that was closed to me. It was plain to see that cycling was their new passion, and I didn't want to join in. The cycling group that they belonged to was full of new people and new machines, and I really didn't feel like becoming a competitive sportsman. Invention and music-making were no longer possible for me, and I had to consider my future. I sensed instinctively that I was no longer to be saved for Kraftwerk.

# 36 Cold Coffee

1985 was approaching, and we were recording new songs for an album that was originally planned to be called *Technicolor*, although we were searching for other titles because we knew we'd have trouble with the American film company that holds the international copyright for the name. We touched on *Technopop*, but when the album was finally released it was called *Electric Cafe*, although I thought that *Technopop* was a better title.

Ralf always found it difficult to let go of a work, and so this album became a long slog. A release date had already been agreed with EMI and catalogued, the dealers had received an official order number, and there was even a record sleeve in existence. Then, Ralf embarked on a complete reworking.

We were concerned about his health. He'd previously had a bad cycle accident on the Rhine Dam. Surrounded by his racing team, his bike had collided with another and he'd crashed, cracking his head on the asphalt track. He was seriously hurt, because he'd irresponsibly ridden without a helmet, and had suffered a fractured skull. He was unconscious for a long time in hospital, and we were deeply worried. He took weeks to recover, which of course put the release of the album back even further. Because of

224

this, there were later rumours that we'd recorded an album that was never released. However, *Electric Cafe* was the oft-reworked *Technopop* album.

We made a clip for 'The Telephone Call' (the only title that Karl ever sang with Kraftwerk) with Günter Fröhling, our resident film-maker. If you look at the short film now, it's easy to see how far we'd already distanced ourselves from each other. We appear disillusioned, solitary and afraid of strangers. It was just as Karl sang: "*Du bist mir nah und doch so fern*" ("You are so near to me, and yet so far"). How true. We were already so far from each other. There was only cold coffee left in the Electric Cafe.

# 37 Everything's Just Computers

That was what people often said about us. But then, people were unable to express anything bu unsophisticated ideas about our electronic music because they hadn't had a chance to get to know this new genre. How could they have done, when everything we were doing was still so fresh? But that was sometimes even the opinion of our fans and radio listeners in general. They couldn't understand what we were offering, musically, or indeed in terms of computer technology, let alone historically at all. In fact, even *we* had no idea of our achievements – but it should be noted without arrogance that we were certainly ahead of the pack. There were even some who were saying, "They can only do what they're doing because they have the cash. Everything's just computers."

If only they'd known how ignorant that was; if only they'd been able to imagine how stupid computers really are. In fact, you have to have music in your heart and rhythm in your blood, or at least nonsense in your head, or the computer or synthesiser can't do a thing. Ultimately, it needs to be fed something. If you haven't got anything to enter into the machine, you can hardly expect to have anything decent coming out of the cables at the back.

People actually thought – and I think there are still people like this today – that you need only buy a computer to land a hit. In fact, some guy grilled me about this just recently. "Wolfgang," he said, "What would I have to get in order to make music as beautiful as yours?"

And do you know what I answered? I advised him. "You don't have to get yourself anything in the first place. If you have to have anything at all, you must have the urge to express something. You just have to *feel* that you have something to say. The best thing is to go for a walk and whistle tunes, if you have any, even if, like me, you haven't got a musical instrument. If you like your tunes and it fills you with passion to do something like that, just buy a cheap Casio for using at home or a really small Roland first. If you then get enthusiastic about what you've keyed into your sequencer, even if it's just with a one-finger technique, you could eventually get yourself a computer with a simple program for composing music, such as Cubase or something just as simple. Everything is a matter of taste; it's a desire to be inventive and to get to know your machine. And if you can write stories and perhaps poems, too, that's a hell of an advantage. Just write a rhyme and sing it. The melody usually just comes automatically when you speak the rhyme."

We didn't just hear rubbish about the independent "computer hit machine" in our own city. No, the more famous and successful we became, the more grotesque were such assertions about us, in Düsseldorf and elsewhere.

In the end, we weren't scientists, as Ralf sometimes liked to pretend before journalists. Anyone who can play the piano or the organ – and, indeed, even those who can't play at all but feel like exploring the device, with its enormous possibilities – will have fun with such gear, just as we did.

Earlier, we just enjoyed making a lot of different sounds. Now, oscillators and filters are really what's special about electronic music, without having to analyse things too deeply. The world of the synthesiser unfolds only when you actually fiddle about with it while you're playing. And then only the mind that handles it is successful.

227

Ultimately, Kraftwerk started in just the same way. Most people probably don't know that there were no home computers in 1974. At that time, we really only had two synths – the Moog and the Arp – on which to experiment. We were electrified, to some extent, when we developed our drum padboard, becoming a sort of "electrio", until Karl joined us and we became an "electro quartet". There was no MIDI for a long time. Our Moog, in fact, was a MINI, and in any case we had a MAXI desire to invent the stuff that we wanted and needed. That's the most important thing of all – the desire and the enthusiasm for something you don't know but imagine. You really have to get involved in something, or you don't discover anything. If you don't have much, you have to invent out of necessity.

I think of our beginnings like that. We were really good at improvising like that. The thing was to think and to experiment. That kept our spirits up and buoyant. And when we accrued more fame and even more money, we could afford the expensive gear on offer in the display windows of music shops. The industry hadn't slept at all and quickly jumped onto the train of the electronic instruments and devices. The more equipment Ralf and Florian bought, the more they had o worry about the operating instructions. The sad result was that they seemed to read more than they made music.

Karl once told me that in 1996, after my departure, Ralf and Florian got themselves a Synclavier, the ultimate synthesiser at that time. He said that it had been outrageously expensive but had certainly saved them a lot of money on taxes. They had grappled with the operating instructions for months afterwards. That thing had brought them to a standstill.

However, if you don't have much equipment but the curious soul of a child, you'll find out the most astonishing, unscientific things. That was how it was with us – at first, in any case. Who doesn't like provoking a reaction and praise for his own actions?

Everything began in such a playful way; everything was enthusiasm with us, making discovering things that weren't available to buy and building them ourselves. That was just the glorious period when we had to improvise. It was certainly our most creative phase. Necessity is the mother of invention, as they say, and for this reason we also had that inspiring connection when four similar people meet accidentally. Now I know that we were never in need; instead, we had enormous luck in being together for all those years in the first place.

Now, I find myself in a similar situation. I hardly have any of my own equipment, preferring instead to go into a familiar studio with people whom I trust and are hopefully on the same wavelength. Of course, we do use technology at the same time, but everything's just computers? Rubbish!

# 38 Boing Boom Tschak *In Pixel Track*

Düsseldorf, 1986

We had the American film specialist Rebecca Allen flown in from the US to work on the absurd music video *Musique Non Stop – Techno Pop/Boing Boom Tschak*. A former art student, she now worked for the New York Institute of Technology, and had made her name working on computer-animated trailers and commercials for American TV networks. In the past, she had also worked for David Byrne. We spent entire afternoons in the Kling Klang Studio watching her videos of computer graphics. It was amazing what lavish and inventive animations were around then. It was possible to watch Rebecca's smooth, fluid animations for hours while falling into a psychedelic trance.

According to Ms Allen, computer animation was still an extremely costly medium. In the early '80s, animators had to work judiciously and imaginatively with low-memory computers and intractable software. Even so, we were very impressed by her creativity. She suggested ideas for a computer animation involving our four heads arranged in a lattice structure, which she suggested should transmit *"boing boom tschak"* while spinning around on their own axes.

After Rebecca had gone back to America, precise shots of our

230

heads were made in a video studio in accordance with to her instructions. For this, we were photographed by a video camera from all imaginable angles around our heads, image by image, centimetre by centimetre. The horizontal and vertical lines of our bodies, and the points at which they crossed, were marked with stickers at co-ordination points and scanned, and this formed the basis of the following computer animation that emerged from the computer screen's glistening, pixellated surface.

Rebecca Allen was actually the only woman who was ever allowed to enter the Kling Klang Studio, and only then for commercial and artistic reasons. Even our girlfriends weren't allowed in, let alone members of our families. Only a very close circle of male friends had the honour of being allowed to visit us, and even then no musicians from other bands.

# 39 *Cultural Vacuum*
## *The Others And "Afrika Bambus"*

Düsseldorf, 18 April 1999
When I listen to the world around me and compare the sounds of other groups with Kraftwerk, what I first notice is a difference in the instrumental line-up, as well as the sound. At the beginning of the '70s, when we were experimenting with the first Minimoog synthesisers and my own self-built electronic drum kit, the media saw this music as avant garde, and they made fun of it, labelling us as crazy button pushers. When Ralf and Florian were still in their experimental phase, I was much more flattering about them and their music. It's difficult for a visionary or a pioneer to bring new ideas and new sounds to the masses. Groups such as Tangerine Dream, Amon Düül, Guru Guru, Ash Ra Temple, Kraan, Embryo and Triumvirat also had to struggle with such problems at the beginning of the turbulent '70s, but in their own ways all of these groups added momentum to the whole genre.

Only when we began to structure our pieces according to the patterns of pop songs and allowed singing (even if it was rather German in pronunciation) on the conventional verse-and-chorus structure was Kraftwerk's music played on the radio, and as a result the group enjoyed international success and emerged from its experimental niche. People soon found it easier to get used

232

to the new sounds and the unfamiliar lyrics. Even so, our music was still dubbed as krautrock, pigeonholing us with many rock-orientated groups, which annoyed us considerably because there were no rock elements in our music.

Consider the period around 1973, which formed the breeding-ground for all of these events. It was the tail-end of a global revolution for young people, a generation conflict that could only begin to grow after the end of the worst of all wars. Our immediate past was haunted by the Second World War, a nightmare which brought incomprehensible suffering to the nations around us and to our own, provoked by the dreadful mass stupidity and repulsive military fanaticism of a generation submissive to orders. What did we young people have to be glad about when we thought about our country and about our parents, who had caused it all, participated in it or had at least looked away like cowards?

There was nothing for our generation to look back on; there was only the future. The future was a land of hope, heroes, security, music and fashion. It was, however, a future dominated by American consumerism and the sounds of England. We copied everything from these cultures that washed over us: music, fashion, hobbies, drinks, fast food, supermarkets, films, hairstyles, even showy chrome car designs.

But we had no adult role models from whom we could learn to take pride in our own culture. How could we comfortably feel German in a country where there had been book-burning, banned pictures, ruinous film criticism and "degenerate" art a short time ago? A time when many of our German poets, painters, composers, actors and the most ingenious engineers and inventors had been driven from the country and fled into exile, hunted and threatened with death in Germany because of their religion or their dissenting views and because they were threatened here with terrible new German discoveries – Zyklon-B and the "hygiene rooms" of the concentration camps, the death plants that the state had set up with the help of the German economy and the finance of the German banks?

Our fathers had first submitted to the Nazis and then to the Americans, and then had adopted the Anglo-American dream wholesale, implementing it of their free will and with the support of the Americans' Marshall Plan. The German economic miracle exploded, and in their desire for careers our parents entered into a new dependence on almost obscene consumerism and on the immigration of south-European workers, who were brought in to help us deal with menial work, supported by the local authorities and the "booming" economy. The accumulation of possessions and the desire to possess – this became the unexpressed axiom of a starved generation which, through its overwhelming desire to amass wealth, was becoming further and further distanced from its children, who frowned upon such greed. I find myself suffering even today from this heritage left to us by our greedy German ancestors, who bowed and scraped their way to prosperity.

We became hippies, full of romanticism, love and protest. We rejected the values of our parents and everything traditional. We no longer wanted to join in with the competitiveness and consumerism of our fathers. We protested against the Vietnam War on the streets, objected to military service, freed ourselves from the sterile, false orations of the bourgeois *diktat* and were generally against all violent conflict. The new slogan of young parents was "anti-authoritarian education", and those who wanted to be regarded as modern lived in communes. Children became sexually permissive and were brought up together. There were no stable relationships between the sexes. Everyone was getting off with everyone else, even men with men and women with women. "*Wer zweimal mit dem gleichen pennt gehört schon zum Establishment.*" ("Anyone who sleeps with the same person twice already belongs to the establishment.") You can see how much the English language had influenced us just by the word *establishment* in this phrase. In any case, the word sounded more modern than *bürgerliche* (bourgeois) *institution*, and the assertion that one should only sleep with the same person once expressed our rejection of stable, single-partner relationships. Of course, we also wanted to shock the bourgeois citizens, who often branded us with thinly concealed envy as drop-outs.

Many people of my generation began to take mind-altering drugs, and there was constant philosophising and discussion. We practised freedom of thought and of appearance. Young artists were best able to express this, and their message was often radical. We went to chaotic artistic events in empty factories and to loud rock concerts in parks, the air heavy with marijuana smoke. Young girls in the shortest possible mini-skirts hung around at parties in student digs and communes, free to be groped by anyone. When we were young, we felt that the most expressive medium was pop and rock music, but instead what we got to hear was exclusively written in imitation of American and British bands – the same singing, screaming guitars and pounding drums. We greedily sucked in anything that wasn't German and believed that everything that came from Britain or America was good, modern, honest. Our parents were unable to supply us with what we wanted, so we consumed the product of other countries.

In the middle of this identity-free cultural vacuum, the musical experimentalism of Kraftwerk suddenly appeared on the scene and did everything completely differently. We presented ourselves as German and fashionable, sang German lyrics and defiantly gave our group a German name. We played songs that sounded as technical and "calculatedly cool" as if they'd been written by scientists to chemical formulae, or to the German industry-standard DIN format. In our lyrics, we sang about autobahns, morning walks, neon lights and radio broadcasters – urban commentary about our environment. So what exactly did we expect to achieve with this technical image, these environmental themes and our ring-modulator noises? To break the habit of listening to guitar music and love songs within a few years? Hardly.

In any case, I'm convinced that the ability to recognise the sound of ancient stringed instruments has been passed down genetically, from generation to generation, over thousands of years of human development, just like language, feeling for shape, colour-recognition and other sensory abilities. Although the synthesiser is a good 30 years old now as a musical instrument, and is used equally with the guitar in almost every pop production, it's still a baby compared to the stringed instruments used in classical music. We're still at the beginning of the age of electronic sound, and we'll continue to develop the synthesiser for many decades to come, coaxing its tone generators to conjure up millions of new sounds. It's exactly this breadth of possibility that makes me so crazy about the instrument.

With Kraftwerk, we went through a hard time as pioneers, protagonists and propagandists, but in the end our obstinacy paid off and other bands became increasingly enthusiastic about synthesisers, putting their guitars (which always sounded the same) to one side and developing the individual sounds of electro pop, inspired by our rather philosophical themes and the unmistakably precise Kraftwerk sound. Ten years later, in England, there was a real synth epidemic, with artists such as Orchestral Manoeuvres In The Dark, The Human League, Depeche Mode, Gary Numan, Cabaret Voltaire and many others who took Kraftwerk as a model and began to create their own synthetic sounds.

We received more than enough proposals for collaborations from other artists, including David Bowie, who wanted to make a record and go on tour with us. David is a born chameleon, a characteristic that I admire greatly. He has amazed his fans and us again and again with a completely new sound and a change of image. When he contacted us, he wanted to adopt our style of minimalist electronic music. I wasn't present at his meeting with Ralf and Florian, although he was often in Düsseldorf to discuss the possibility of a co-operation. However, nothing came of this, even though he, Ralf and Florian shared a great mutual admiration. Bowie was certainly disappointed that nothing came of it, and it was no surprise that he later settled in Berlin and began working with Brian Eno.

Michael Jackson's management also contacted us, proposing a collaboration. In as early as 1975, on our very first American tour, the German caricaturist Heinz Edelmann even suggested a Kraftwerk soundtrack for a new cartoon film, to be produced in Chicago, the windy city. Edelmann had worked on The Beatles' film *Yellow Submarine*, and had invented the Blue Meanies. This project certainly had the potential to become something wonderful. (Now, of course, I would have some suitable songs of my own for such a project, such as 'DR.UG.LY' from *Time Pie*, for example, the story of a wicked seller of souls.) Also, in Italy, the science-fiction director Dario D'Argento wanted us to write some futuristic music for a film. All of these possibilities for international co-operation were rejected by my colleagues.

In his book about Rainer-Werner Faßbinder, Kurt Raab wrote that the cult director was one of our greatest admirers. On the set for his film *Querelle*, in addition to a constant supply of frankfurters, cognac and cocaine, he always needed a record player to play Kraftwerk songs, and even delegated a member of the crew to take care of this. And so it appears that the music of Kraftwerk seems to have been some kind of drug (a view which, incidentally, I've often heard echoed by other fans). Apparently, Faßbinder, too, would have liked us to have composed music for his films. I'm sure that this would have been an ideal collaboration, because we were the greatest fans of his films, but again Ralf and Florian decided against this and opted not to enter into any fusions with other styles, art forms or musical cultures. Kraftwerk was supposed to be as unique, individual, self-referential and self-contained as possible. However, Karl and I would have been very interested in occasionally working with other musicians. It would have been a ball to stand onstage with Bowie. I'd love to beat my electropads for him some time!

These days, I'm experiencing how refreshing it is to work with other, mainly younger musicians. If the chemistry is right between us, there's nothing more incredible. In the production of my new album, *Time Pie*, I worked with young people from the new Düsseldorf music scene, and also with Andi Thoma and Jane Werner from Mouse On Mars, who didn't consider themselves too good to work with me. I spent a delightful time with them, and I believe that the recording shows this. Jörg Burger (aka Bionaut), from Cologne, remixed the singles wonderfully, and Regina Janssen, the vocalist from The Donna Regina Project, sang better on this album than anyone else could have.

For my second Yamo album, *Serenity Supreme*, I'm working with Kurt Pyrolator Dahlke, who previously co-founded the group Der Plan and the ATA TAK label, and produced Fehlfarben, DAF and Andreas Dorau. He has found his mental and emotional centre through mystic contemplation and Buddhism, and I'm still moved by his unshakeable belief and his trust in me. Kurt always takes my ideas seriously, no matter how weird they are, and I really enjoy being around him. To sit by his side when he's writing music and to put the sounds together with him for my songs is a revelation. I also write my lyrics with Barbara Uhling-Stollwerck (yes, from the Cologne group Scholadenfabrik). Like me, she attaches great importance to the words she chooses, and sometimes we'll argue about a single word for weeks. We're always looking for the perfect meaning in the translation, or the right rhythm for the syllables, and Barbara – a tempestuous woman who is half English – is an indispensable adviser. She'll even ring me up at seven in the morning, just to tell me a word that she's thought of overnight. In spite of her three charming and yet draining children, she's always full of energy, and is the only person allowed to drag me from my sleep at that time of the day.

Even my talented niece made her debut on *Time Pie*, and my nephew Dominick often advises me and has even co-written some lyrics for Yamo. I find contributors for my projects everywhere, bringing them together and nurturing their talents through my songs. I learn from them and they learn from me.

This openness and co-operation is, for me, the ideal situation, working with artists who may not be permanently associated with me. For instance, in the winter of 1997, when Emil and I visited George Clinton backstage when he played at Cologne in order to film him for my video to 'Stereomatic', I felt an immediate connection. The man is just as crazy as me, possibly even more so, but you can usually tell at once if you have things in common. There's nothing wrong for a musician who wants to reach young people to be fanciful, natural and to have a good pinch of childish curiosity. George has a large helping of all three, and that night we resolved to work together, initially under the name Bone Connection, because George loves eating spare ribs, and when we met him he had really sticky fingers from eating delicious dips. He listened to my music through the "Stereomatic spacephones", and found them so great that he never gave them back. Well, I'm used to giving things up, and I gave them to him gladly. I'm eager to see what will come of our connection one day. I deeply regret that we didn't ever try anything like this with Kraftwerk. We could have had some wonderful experiences, and a lot more fun. Perhaps one day I'll be able to work with David Bowie, and with Karl, too, who means a lot to me. Whatever we do together will certainly be different, because I'm always crazy enough to try something new.

However, some other unusual things I like less. One such episode occurred in 1982 with a certain Afrika Bambaataa (whom I prefer to call "Bambus"), who released an album called *Planet Rock* with a gentleman by the name of Arthur Baker. The pair put together a hip-hop rap album on which they mixed parts of 'Numbers' and 'Trans Europe Express' for a single release, turning out an American-style piece of music. They didn't even ask in the first place whether Kraftwerk was in agreement with this, let alone pay for the use of the samples. This is the nastiest kind of theft!

Since the introduction of sampling technology, this has happened on a daily basis in the music industry. Artists are continually robbed of their intellectual property. It's impossible to take something like that lying down. In fact, the company that had released the single, Tommy Boy Records, had to fork out a lot of money after the event, but they just increased the price of the single (which was then selling by the cartload) by $1, and through this they quickly recouped their fine.

I have nothing against sampling in general, if the owner is asked before and acceptable conditions are negotiated. In October 1997, when I launched *Time Pie* in Japan, my label boss, Sadato, and I were invited to a party by the Tokyo show band Pizzicato Five, who had just returned from their first world tour and were playing their final date before their fanatical teenage fans in Tokyo. I thought back to our own performance in our home town of Düsseldorf, back in 1981, which hadn't been so great. In Tokyo, though, the audience was enthusiastic. The band's show was witty and tempo-driven, but I have to say that I was surprised at how many musical quotations and samples they used in their songs, taken from every conceivable genre. After that concert – which was completely sold out – we went downstairs to join a noisy party in the basement. As we entered the room, however, silence fell. Sadato is Iranian by birth and very tall, and he towered above everybody in the room by at least several heads, and at 1.72m I'm quite tall by Japanese standards. "Hello everyone," Sadato blared out above their heads. "This is Wolfgang Flür, once of Kraftwerk." Rapt silence. No one dared look at me. Everyone stared at the floor, and the mood disappeared. I was deeply embarrassed.

I asked Sadato where Konoshi Josuharu, the creative head, and Nomiya Maki, the singer of Pizzicato Five, might be. He pointed to two people milling about among garishly made-up and gaudily styled Tokyo scene freaks standing next to a delicate buffet stocked with remarkable Far Eastern canapés and large quantities of champagne. Pizzicato Five (although there were actually only two of them), it turned out, were very modest, almost shy. They didn't say much, and what they did say was very quiet, just like Ralf and Florian. Sadato also suspected that they were surprised to see me there.

"In that case, why did they invite me?" I asked him.

He thought for a second. "They probably wanted to calm you down and get your permission afterwards, because they've used sounds from 'Pocket Calculator' on one of their songs. Japanese fans see something godlike in you," he added. "They've got too much respect for you to party in your presence. Apart from that, I don't think they thought you'd actually turn up."

It was a pity that they didn't know how much I enjoy letting myself go, and how much I enjoy parties. However, I was deeply dismayed, even terrified, by Sadato's observation about our apparent "divinity". Even so, I thought, they should have reckoned on my presence. That sampling should really have been sanctioned in advance. As it happened, I wouldn't even have been able give them the right to use the sounds, because they lie with Ralf and Florian, and they would certainly react more angrily than I did. Nevertheless, I was glad to meet two such likeable people.

These situations are quite okay if there is a congenial relationship between the artists, if they've got together beforehand and if they've agreed on a way in which a new work can lead to an aesthetic result acceptable to both sides. However, such uses of other artists' musical property for these kinds of purposes are often tasteless and tend to damage the original. At that time, I could have had have no idea that the pair would actually sing one of my new songs, 'On The Beam', and in their own language, too. What an encounter! What an angle!

To my ears, the whole orgy of remixing and releasing cover versions that has spread like a plague throughout the entire music industry since 1982 is mostly detrimental rubbish. When I see a television advertisement accompanied by parts of George Gershwin's melody from 'An American In Paris' which has been disrespectfully cut and patched together, it makes my flesh creep. Unfortunately, such tasteless *faux pas* are endemic. As I write, remixes and cover versions of famous songs from every decade are polluting the airwaves.

The cover version of 'The Model' by the group Rammstein is the worst that I have heard recently – they should have listened to the earlier Snakefinger version. Unimaginative writers and unintelligent producers are supported by a greedy music industry which doesn't have any new ideas itself and is out for fast Deutschmarks and dollars with cover versions. Not only that but they're also neglecting to nurture innovative and talented musicians who genuinely have something new to offer. The music of Kraftwerk was so new, and for this reason our songs are still being copied mechanically, stolen and sampled throughout the world, because they're timeless and continue to be an inspiration to others.

"We have to master the inertia of people's hearts and the stubbornness of their minds."

– *Eric Kästner*

"You cannot achieve anything without love for humanity and for the things that you do."

– *Gérard Départieu*

# 40  *Last Telephone Call*
## *New Paths*

DÜSSELDORF, 1987
After our final work together on *Electric Cafe*, I hardly went back
to the studio. There were no more musical tasks for me to do, and
there was no tour, either, because none of the songs had got even
near to the Top Ten. Ralf and Florian had asked me to organise
the complete restructuring of the Kling Klang Studio, but that
didn't appeal to me any more because the whole thing had gone
flat. I didn't see any point in waiting endlessly for proper musical
activity to recommence. Instead, I occupied myself with designing
furniture at a friend's studio and travelled even further across
Europe with Constanze.

Then, in 1991, my world finally collapsed when she left me. It
wasn't that our love had grown cold, but she no longer wanted
to be bound to me and my insecure existence as a freelance artist.
At first it had been good to have her at my side when I decided,
with a heavy heart, not to go the Kling Klang Studio any more.
But then, when my lovely Aries girl left too, I felt completely
alone. The pain of her loss lasted for years, and compounded with
my separation from the group. Ralf and Florian never returned
my calls and made no attempt to contact me. They didn't even
answer my letters. What had happened? What had made them

stay so silent? I felt as lonely as Ringo Starr, who had been in a similar position to me, desperately waiting from a sign from his colleagues. His friends, however, had recognised his worth, and had dedicatedly called him back into their flowery studio, whereas I couldn't count on such a generous gesture. We just weren't as good friends as The Beatles had been; we didn't have the same amicable relationship.

In 1989, I was eventually able to reach Ralf on the telephone in his flat. "Hello Ralf," I said. "It's Wolfgang. Can we meet sometime and have a good long talk?"

Ralf answered, "Wolfgang? Which Wolfgang? I don't know any Wolfgang!" And then he cut me off. That hit me hard.

Much later, at the end of the summer of 1996, we made a final arrangement to meet for coffee and plum cake in one of our favourite cafés, the Restaurant Zur Rheinfähre, under the shade of chestnut trees in Düsseldorf-Kaiserswerth. I looked at Ralf's face for a long time and saw great changes. A transformation had taken place. I could no longer see the artist; instead, I saw the attractive, dynamic face of a sportsman. And how he talked about riding his bike! He couldn't talk about music with such passion and dedication any more. That was all in the past. Nevertheless, we chatted for a long time, and after almost ten years we finally told each other our opinions.

I reproached Ralf. "The way I see it, you disillusioned and divided the group with your overwhelming enthusiasm for bikes. You couldn't expect us to understand why we were always waiting around for new recordings and tours, particularly Karl and me. We had to earn a living, after all." I also explained to him that I didn't find their concept for *The Mix* so wonderful. "You could have commissioned anyone else to do that, rather than do it yourselves. If you ask me, you've done nothing more than destroy your own image and your credibility, in relation to the original and its vibe."

Understandably enough, Ralf's opinion was different, but he did say that these days he was able to see "the whole thing" more from my point of view. It really did me good to see that, for the first time, he was more open to my situation.

Encouraged by the fact that he was listening to me with such interest, I grabbed the bull by the horns and advised him to give our fans the so-called "golden goal", a "best of" album, if they were finding it so difficult to compose new songs in the meantime. The time for this was well overdue, and it would be a much more worthwhile endeavour than the tempo-obsessed *The Mix*. After all, it would demand hardly any work from them – all they had to do was select the songs. "But you should at least take the opportunity to include a bonus single, or a maxi, with some new pieces along with this release," I added. "That would be a sensation, and a great new beginning after such a long time. It would be a guaranteed golden album, and there'd be a lot of money in it for you. Our fans would no longer have to be satisfied with thousands of confusing rumours flying around, which in the end aren't so far from the truth any more."

In fact, I revealed to him, I'd heard that they were under a new contract with EMI London, and that they'd submitted new material there which had been sent back with the remark "not suitable for release". If that was true, for me that would have been a considerable shock because, even if it had been experimental music, for example, it would still have been Kraftwerk material, and ultimately Ralf and Florian first became famous with experimental music. Ralf played his cards close to his chest, however, refusing to either confirm or deny the rumour, which I suppose was answer in itself.

I also described to Ralf how I'd felt back in 1991, when I'd discovered his new robot on the advertising hoarding opposite my house. He paid great attention, and listened to me in silence, but said nothing and quickly changed the subject, suddenly enthusing about their new stage equipment and improved technology. "You'd be amazed, Wolfgang, how modern the Kling Klang Studio is these days – which, of course, you were unwilling to rebuild. The robots work perfectly with the songs, controlled digitally, and

245

at last they're completely movable. The studio is completely air conditioned. It looks just like NASA ground control."

"I just didn't want to be promoted to being the best-paid caretaker of the most famous sound laboratory in the world," I answered. "I'm an artist. I've always liked being onstage. I couldn't bear just waiting around on the off-chance that I was needed for a tour, or for recording songs or videos, just passing the time occasionally renovating or making things. You should have got more wealthy musicians in the first place. They would have been able to afford such a long lay-off. But inactivity apart, Kraftwerk also came to an end because we had insurmountable differences, socially and financially."

Ralf just went on describing their studio, and spoke of their robots in terms such as "bigger", "more perfect" and "even better", talking about them as if he was talking about a new Campagnolo derailleur. He didn't even notice how bored I was. I would have preferred to have heard news about cultural themes, or about his musical ideas, just as we used to talk about. For example, it would have interested me greatly to know whether he still saw a musical future for himself, and how he found working with Florian these days, or to have heard what his personal joys and fears were now. He did tell me that he had a new love in his life, and that they were thinking of marrying and having a child together, and for this I was glad for him. This was really something new, because Ralf had previously been passionately against marriage; he'd experienced too much marital suffering through his sister, just as I had witnessed my brothers' wrecked marriages.

And then Ralf actually said to me, "I can easily imagine standing onstage with you again."

That really threw me, and I could feel my anger rising. Why was he saying this now, after so many silent years?

Then, almost as an aside, he offered me money – actually, lots of money – if I'd play with him again. Once this would have impressed me, but Ralf was a few years too late. I was already deeply involved with Yamo, and was in the middle of recording

*Time Pie* with Andy and Jan, although I didn't tell him anything about that. This happiness couldn't have been compensated with any sum of money. Ralf knew me, and knew that I always did everything in my life out of pure passion. Money can't compare at all, although of course it is important, to a certain extent. However, I can get by with very little, as long as I'm happy and contented. I would have stayed with Kraftwerk even longer, and for a lot less than he was implying that I could make now, if the content and our relationships had been right, if Kraftwerk had been able to develop and accept new, contemporary themes.

It's not important whether I would have rejected this apparent offer because I was offended or out of regret that I had irredeemably left the band. At any rate, I paid dearly for this a short time ago. One of our German fans that I'm friendly with sent me the January 1998 edition of *Rock & Pop Sammlung*, which was completely dedicated to the subject of Kraftwerk, with the front cover and eleven pages featuring reports and interviews. Ralf commented within on mine and Karl's departures from the group in a way that really surprised me: "They were just some of our earlier collaborators. Florian and I have been working together for 23 years, always with different musicians. I really don't know how many." So that's the way it was.

I would love to meet these other collaborators at some time. Perhaps Ralf had actually built the secret robot army that he'd often talked about. However, from my perspective, I only ever saw Karl Bartos, Ralf Hütter, Florian Schneider and myself. Together with the visionary Emil Schult, for 16 successful years after 'Autobahn' we had worked together on the timeless themes expressed in the music, the shining stainless steel stage set and our unmistakable image, and had presented this to the world. Very few drummers at that time would have been crazy enough to go onstage with a percussion kit that looked like an ironing board and surf the wavefront of the drumming revolution. My desire for a private meeting with Ralf completely disappeared after reading his comments in *Rock & Pop Sammlung*. So that was all he could say about Karl and me, after 16 years of passion and collaboration. We were nothing more than disposable robots to him.

I also read in Pascal Bussy's book about Kraftwerk that Florian and Ralf were surprised by mine and Karl's impatience to try out new things. They said that it should have been enough for us just to belong, and that they didn't know what else we wanted. I can only guess at Karl's reaction and quote him freely: "We had a jumbo standing in the garden that only ever warmed up its engines. Now I have a small Messerschmitt, and I can fly freely and flexibly."

What did we actually want with the band, Kraftwerk, through which we'd found each other, made music, cut records and gave concerts? For Karl and me, there can be nothing more wonderful than that. However, the periods of waiting just became too long, and Ralf and Florian – who rang us up only once during this time – didn't make us very enthusiastic. Their priorities had changed, and by now they had other interests – the smell of chain oil, the *clunk* of a 24-gear derailleur, the feel of oiled biker's legs...

Nevertheless, Ralf's comments cut me to the quick, while on the other hand I still enjoy a great relationship with Karl, with whom I can talk to about anything. He didn't find it easy, either, when he threw in the towel in frustration in 1991, during the endless work on *The Mix*, after which he formed Electric Music. At that time, he called me often, still rather despairing, and we talked at length about what was happening and discussed our futures. I'd already experienced that stomachchurning sensation of feeling my existence threatened several years previously, after my own separation from Kraftwerk. At least I was now able to encourage him and bolster his confidence.

Karl, my most talented friend – a graduate with distinction from the Robert Schumann Music Conservatoire – really didn't know how things were going to turn out for him. By that time I was already a little calmer, and was keeping my head above water designing furniture. I'm like that – nothing gets me down. I urged Karl to go it alone. "You really should try it. You're such a good musician. God, I'd be so happy if I could play the piano as well as you! Then I'd write and record my own songs. Start your own band. It's got to be worth it, with your talent and experience. Do what you've always wanted to do. Kraftwerk will have to do without us now, and we'll have to do without them. They've lost us, and it doesn't seem to matter to them so they don't matter to us, either."

We've often supported each other in this way when either of us has been low, and I'm glad to have Karl – who, like me, saw things at such close quarters for so many years – as a friend. Who better could I exchange views with? In 1993, he wanted me to join Electric Music, but I hadn't gone far enough down my own road of selfdiscovery and still hadn't broken away sufficiently after the massively creative years with Kraftwerk to think about making music again. It was way beyond me, and I surprised myself when, in 1991, during the terrible war in Bosnia, I saw myself writing a children's song that would help me to cope with my sorrow and the horror I felt at the daily images that filled the media.

I later understood that 'Little Child' was a song for myself. I recognised myself as the abandoned child for whom I had composed it, writing the lyrics with Emil Schult. I became very proud of it, because it made me realise that I could compose songs without Kraftwerk. 'Little Child' was the spark that lit a small fire which quickly blazed in me, awakening my desire for a completely new music project. Thus Yamo was born, which helped my self-confidence no end.

I appeared under this new name for the first time in the late summer of 1993, when I drove with Emil to the Cologne Pop Komm. Completely unannounced, I sprayed the screens at the MTV stand with black paint while Emil directed a spirited speech about the victims of the war in Bosnia to the cameras. A video clip of Jimi Hendrix, my earlier hero, was running on the monitors at the time, but that didn't stop me at all – he just had to accept being covered with black paint and be the one to suffer for my social convictions. Steve Blame, who was then a presenter at MTV and who had interviewed us on an earlier occasion, was so impressed by our surprise attack that he let us carry on, and later reported our show of solidarity for the victims of the war as a lead story on the MTV news: "Former Kraftwerk member Wolfgang Flür, in collaboration with artist Emil Schult, released a benefit single, 'Little Child', under the name of Jamo for the orphans of the Bosnian war, with performance art and a message."

Our central message to the hip-hop generation at the gaudy consumer trade fair was basic: "Euro pop gets more and more, while genocide is at our front door." All the same, for a brief time we were able to broadcast our concern to a global audience, and we were able to demonstrate that we were still there, that we understood what was happening in the world and that, for once, we were becoming politically active.

Until the release of my first pop album, *Time Pie*, it was a rather exciting path full of surprising events and most affectionate encounters. But journeys are a particular pleasure and enjoyment for me, which the destination itself sometimes doesn't live up to.

# 41 Time Pie *For The World*
## *Affected By The 'Guiding Ray'*

COLOGNE, 17 APRIL 1997
EMI were going to release my first album, and I was ecstatic! With Yamo, I've been able to find my own sound. I often talk enthusiastically about the subjects and ideas that now interest me, quite independently of musical trends and short-lived fads. With Yamo, I can unleash my imagination without restrictions, as I never could before. I'm no longer just a performer, an actor and an inventor, but now I'm an author, a director and a producer, all in one person. I sometimes wonder in astonishment what's happened to me, because I can hardly grasp what my creative brain is constantly coming up with. Much of it lay ready inside me and had yet to be awakened because I lacked the support and self-confidence that I needed in order to express myself and be assertive in my youth. Now, though, I'm doing what I want to do, and I refuse to accept any kind of limits imposed on me.

Many people tell me how much I've changed. It feels like a door has opened for me, revealing a wide panorama of ideas, melodies and images. I feel just like I did when I planned radio dramas on my old TK17 tape recorder with my brothers. My pieces are put together with rather more effort and professionalism this time, however, and I'm also reaching a different audience than the Kraftwerk faithful.

251

When EMI heard the first Yamo album in autumn 1995, they immediately offered to release it, which I hadn't counted on at all, and I was of course delighted, but I wasn't sure if it was such a good idea to entrust my future to the company that also carried my former band in its catalogue. My sixth sense was warning me, and it later turned out to be right. And yet the various heads of departments that wanted to work with Yamo were so conciliatory, urging me to produce "a great work", and so, naïvely, I finally agreed, on 1 May 1996, still unsure whether this was the right thing to do, although EMI made great efforts to convince me that it was.

Initially, we released a limited edition of expensively printed CD covers with a hand-coloured drawing of my great-grandfather, an architect from Frankfurt. It showed a circular double cornucopia, demonstrating a cultural richness in colour, shape, imagination and nature. We also published our own newspaper, *The Yamo News*, which would accompany the CD and which contained information about the themes of *Time Pie* through sketches, graphics and stories. A rather expensive artist's portrait was made of me, and Emil Schult produced an accompanying video clip for the single 'Stereomatic'.

The promotion work began after the album's release in May 1997, and I told many journalists the story of my time with Kraftwerk, how I had changed and why I had sadly left the group. Then I went on to tell them about Yamo, explaining, "When, to my surprise, I became deeply interested again in pop music, after campaigning against the Bosnian war, I wanted to do something that took me further away from Kraftwerk and more towards themes of humanity and softer tones. I no longer wanted to describe the world of machines, but rather to say something about people. I needed a word that symbolised warmth and lightness, with no other meaning, no ambiguity. It had to be secretive and not necessarily German-sounding, because I see myself as a citizen of the world and want to be understood as such. The word 'Yamo' was constructed from the names of friends with whom I developed the very first ideas for a humane kind of electro pop. I liked it

252

straight away, because the sound of the word alone suited what I wanted, how my music was supposed to sound. It also had a positive 'Ya' at the beginning, which suits me fine. It was a good beginning, and our work is improving constantly."

I went on to tell the journalists, "Yamo describes the character of nature and the characteristics of the people with whom I live and work. You'll also find songs about comic situations found in everyday life, such as hunting for a mosquito, for example. It's all much freer and much happier than I remember from my time with Kraftwerk. Although I'm the one who thinks up the ideas and writes the stories, there's no hierarchy like there was in that band. I listen to the proposals and contributions of my colleagues carefully, accepting them gladly if they're appropriate to a piece or if they embellish it in any way. We have a lot of fun working together. We also try not to let ourselves sound too programmed and sequencer-heavy, although of course this depends on the theme. In Kraftwerk, when we were recording a song about robots, the music obviously had to sound like a constructivist world of machines. However, I'm simply no longer interested in those kinds of subjects, about the immortal man machine and computers. I want to record stories about people and their individuality, however absurd they may be. These days, I prefer to ask myself how does greed grunt? How does betrayal whisper? What melody comes from hope? And, above all, how does happiness chuckle, and how does sweet love murmur? In 'Speech Dancer', the artificial voice of the androgynous synth player, Kim – a new permanent member of Yamo – reveals why you can have such fun juggling with words, as long as you have the words to begin with."

## SPEECH DANCER

Words and voice we give and take
Our choice to cut the cake
Confirmation is the goal
Words show face, voice is our soul

Talk back – same track
Talk back – same track

A thoughtless word, how it hurts
Tender letter is even better
Words uplift, can defeat
Voices flatter – that's a different matter

Talk back – same track
Talk back – same track
Forming fast but changing slow
Meanings last, some come and go
Asking questions, giving answer
Juggling words with a speech dancer

© Wolfgang Flür

These are the kinds of themes with which I bake my "Rhineland specialities" in the melody kitchen of Yamo. With the help of my friends, I began to realise this in sound on my first album.

In 1998, while we were discussing the album, Tim Barr – who at the time was working for the British publication *Future Music* – asked me, "Does it sound like Kraftwerk?"

He promptly answered himself: "Well, imagine 'Radioactivity' or 'Trans-Europe Express' relocated far into the future, shot through with weird trip techno and a warm, sometimes whimsical delight in love, life and laughter, and you'll be pretty much on target. On tracks such as 'Mosquito', or the dreamy, liquid 'Aurora Borealis', it's obvious that Flür's partnership with Andi Thoma and Jan Werner is beautifully suited to the mix of fairy-tale storytelling, gorgeously crafted sounds and quirky grooves that make *Time Pie* the kind of album it's easy to fall in love with. Strange, charming and definitely worth tracking down…"

I often prescribe coaching for myself on the themes of my songs,

254

and if I am lacking in knowledge I research literature on the relevant subjects. On my album there are female vocalists who sing, whisper, laugh and kiss, and of course I'm there too, telling stories as if they were radio plays, stamping, singing, keening, crying out in anger or growling tenderly, sometimes allowing myself to be accompanied by the weird strains of a vocoder. I continue to rely heavily on this device in electronic pop music, along with our new Supernova synthesiser and modern Sirius sound generator. These simple instruments are just right for someone like me, who really doesn't want to plough through hundreds of pages of complicated operating instructions first. The arrays of buttons on their upper displays allow you to access all parameters, and you can start playing at once, so satisfying results can be achieved relatively quickly. Even so, the treatment of my own voice is the newest element that I have to offer, and what I like best about my new music. Just as my great-grandmother used to read to me from books, now I speak of my discoveries into the new AKG sound-absorbing Solitube microphone, which makes my voice sound so warm.

My intention with Yamo is to bring joy, humour and imagination to all of those who have eyes and ears open to their living environment. In the summer of 1997, after hearing *Time Pie*, Mick Garlic of the British magazine *Sequences* said, "You will dance to it or you will go mad." At any rate, Yamo is a new platform, which I'm currently using to develop a breed of pop that will show that electronic music doesn't always have to sound cold. This music is solely dependent upon the souls that bring it to life, and it will always be dedicated to those who travel towards joy and sound.

In concrete terms, I've been moved by the 'Guiding Ray' to undertake a new musical challenge, and the rest of the band have been perfectly trained for a nonexistent task that specifies no aim, apart from the joy of discovery and investigation, a challenge that we've undertaken without the vision of others, only our own. Music is the greatest restorative medium for feelings, and because I'm well aware of this I shall always arrange it delicately and tastefully. Anyone who would like to taste the pie of my own time will have to listen to the piquant "Rhineland specialities". Let your souls swing and enjoy the time. Delicious every minute.

Happy together at the Kling Klang Studio. This line-up formed in 1974.

The Beathovens play live in Düsseldorf, 1966.

Photo session in Hamburg, 1973.

Half of Kraftwerk. Hamburg, 1973.

Arriving in New York for our first US tour, spring 1975.

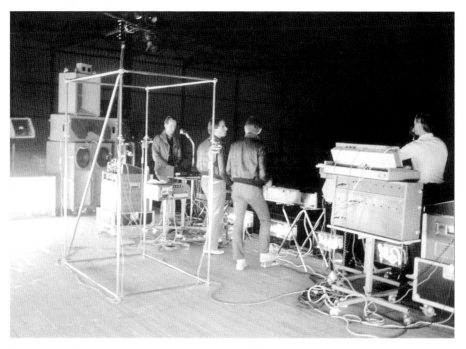

The percussion cage set up on stage. Lyon, 1975.

"Are we going on or what?" Waiting in the dressing room.

Wolfgang (far L) and Ira Blacker (R) at the Rumpelmayr café, New York, 1975.

Front cover of *Musikexpress* magazine, 1981.

The Synthetic Boys – a French caricature.

The vegetarian four – Japanese caricature from 1981.

The secret life of the robots.

1966 Mercedes 220S. Six cylinders, 110 hp, ivory steering wheel and extremely reliable.

On tour, 1981. Thank God we had beds on the bus!

Affected by the 'Guiding Ray'. New York, 1997.

*Time Pie* – delicious every minute!

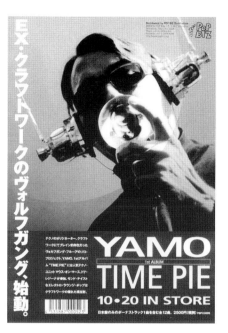

Japanese promotion for *Time Pie*,
October 1997.

Rhineland specialities: the cover of the Yamo album *Time Pie*.

Nomiya Maki of Pizzicato Five during a recording session for 'On The Beam'. This picture adorns the cover of the Japanese release.

Resting between sessions. L–R: Sam Leigh Brown, Wolfgang Flür, Nomiya Maki.

# 42 As The Dream Sneaks Away

DÜSSELDORF, 10 JUNE 1999, 7.45AM
What a morning! I return to consciousness once again, enriched by bewildering sensations from the paradoxical worlds of twilight and enjoying the vague muzziness of being half asleep on the sultry summer morning. My senses begin to organise themselves hesitantly, gathering rare impressions to ease my waking. Still sleepy, I embrace the sensual mood, hardly able to move. The quiet ticking of the green clock on the wall reaches my left ear, marking out the seconds for some minutes, until I resist it. "Rhythm, oh rhythm, texture of the time, why are you waking me?" The gently filtered morning light tickles me through the slits of my squinting eyes. A slight wind catches the curtain and lifts it, billowing in my room, whispering frivolously. Behind it the shadows of flies buzz past, fluttering, projected onto my bed like living shadows, flitting tentatively across my face. Their soft touch glides smoothly over my frame.

Suddenly, a magnificent erection bounces me out of this profound peace, urging for complete penetration. I roll over to the right. I don't want to have anything to do with physical lust at the moment. These minutes are too delightful, as the dream sneaks away. With burgeoning consciousness, the dream takes on the feel of a drifting party, garishly decorated with colourful fragments and outrageously cheeky grimaces. I hear the fly that has been flying in stoic ellipses around my lamp as she coughs. With her thousandfaceted eyes, can she not see that she will never reach her destination with circular flight? But perhaps she doesn't need a destination, and is just enjoying her flight. This is somehow familiar to me, and I dream of seeing myself through a magnifying glass, walking endless paths and climbing high mountains on the coarse carpet close to my head. "What a lot there is to discover here," I say to myself while I'm a fly. And then, full of doubt, "Who will praise me when I've traversed this hazardous land?" I shall do it myself. I feel full of inexhaustible energy, as delectable as a bar of chocolate greedily torn from the silver paper. My tumescence is already disappearing.

Suddenly, I'm an astronaut high above, looking down on the Earth from space. Where are the people? We don't exist. We have no influence. We are nothing but flies. There is crumpled silver paper everywhere.

What a great morning! I've finished working on Part I of this book. I could say a lot more, but then it would go on for ever. I've taken on something new. I see with my feeling hand, get to know the wind, taste the season early and listen to the day. I prepare myself clearly.

# II

# A Storm Brewing

# 43  *Having A Little Sleep*
## *The Scent Of Lena*

When the Vietnamese nurse in the respiratory department of the Florence Nightingale Hospital inserted an anaesthetic drip into the vein in my right arm, I hardly felt anything. I was lying on the examination table of a hospital in North Düsseldorf, my body completely satisfied but my mind confused. Barbara, my colleague in Yamo, had thoroughly recommended the facility to me, because she had given birth to her three children there and the conditions were most comfortable, and she knew a lot of people there.

An hour earlier, they'd injected me with something powerful so that the consultant could insert his bronchoscope through my nose, down through my larynx, past my narrow epiglottis and deep into my bronchial tubes to investigate a brachial irritation. If necessary, he would then take a small sample of the infected cells away for a pathological analysis.

Dr Kappes had decided to take such a radical investigation as a precaution after I'd spent weeks suffering from bouts of coughing at night. I'd already ducked out of two earlier appointments from sheer terror, even though the good doctor had already explained to me that I would be completely unconscious during the examination and wouldn't feel a thing. I had a terrible fear

260

of falling asleep in the presence of people I didn't know. In fact, this was the first time that I'd experienced such helplessness, and only did so in the interests of helping my ailing body. My mind was full of dreadful thoughts about what they could do to me in the meantime and, full of vanity, I couldn't help wondering what I would look like while I was lying there, powerless before them, unable to defend myself.

But the bouts of coughing, which kept me awake at night and left me weary during the day, had left me no other choice but to put myself in the hands of the doctor. He had been recommended to me by my family doctor, who told me that his colleague had the highest reputation in the field.

I was still conscious after the first injection, but my thoughts quickly became confused. An indescribably good feeling of contentment and warmth quickly suffused my being. My field of vision flickered and grew narrower, rather like having tunnel vision. I felt hazy and completely free as I sat, propped up in a wheelchair to stop me falling over, waiting for the examination.

At 6.30am that Monday morning, when I'd taken the tram out to Kaiserswerth, it had still been quite dark outside, with the cold and foggy dampness of January, and so I wasn't expecting amusement of any description, and certainly not in the way that events unfolded. To make the half-hour journey more enjoyable, I brought along a small copy of Albert Camus's *The Outsider*, but it was difficult for me to concentrate on the book because I was constantly worrying about being examined by people that I didn't know. I didn't want to have a hollow tube with a light, a lens and a small pair of tongs at the front pushed deep into the delicate mucous membranes of my lungs, and I had to push the image of it out of my mind again and again.

Then, sitting on the wheelchair in the day room next to a bunch of other patients, including a strikingly dressed woman, sedated and robbed of any inhibitions, I suddenly found myself developing a desire for any kind of sexual activity. Whatever they had injected into me had aroused me spontaneously, and my mind was suddenly full of a thousand things that would have satisfied my desire at that moment. At the same time, the people around me seemed to be completely unimportant.

All this happened as I was pushed unprotesting to the pre-op room by someone dressed in a green uniform. I was laid flat on my back on the table, and I saw lots of tubes and lights above me. As if from a distance, I heard the voices of the nurses as they were preparing, laughing about what they'd done over the weekend. One said something nice about my eyes to her colleague, which I hear clearly enough, and when the delicate Asian nurse rammed the IV into my arm I didn't mind a bit.

One of the nurses was a slender girl, her blonde hair knotted in a pert ponytail. The lower buttons of her crisply ironed gown were daringly agape. She was standing very close to the operating table, and I could smell the delicate scent of her freshly starched clothing, which – along with her lovely figure – excited me even more. She briskly put her hand under the neckline of my pullover and stuck something to my chest, then repeated the procedure at various other positions on my upper body, tickling me and making me laugh. I turned my head to the left and found myself looking directly at her thighs. They were beautiful, with skin like sheer velvet, slightly brown and slender and firm. I felt a great desire to bite into them. She was acting as if she didn't notice my desire and, as she bent further over me, she pushed her legs nearer to my face, until one finally touched my cheek. It felt very warm, and she must have been aware of my desire. There was something deeply erotic about her that reminded me of my earlier encounter with Lena, the pretty Hungarian girl. I think it was the smell of her young skin.

I could tell that the nurse had enjoyed our contact, too, because she just stood where she was, as if she was stuck to me. After over-meticulously linking the sticker pads on my breast to electric wires hanging over me leading from a monitor on my left, she switched on the ECG. I heard my pulse; so did she. "Just listen! Your pulse is so fast," she said, grinning with amazement. "It's almost as insistent as your album."

"You can believe that, with your lovely legs," I interjected. "You know *Time Pie*?"

"I was at the book-reading session you held recently, and you played something from it there, didn't you?" she answered as she worked, grinning and watching the monitor. "I really liked it, by the way. Honestly!"

"I'm just a drummer in an electronic band," I told her. "In my case, a raised pulse is something like an inherited illness." I'd hoped to be witty, and looked up at her, excited, hoping to see enjoyment in her face, but I found myself looking at her panties. That was too much. It excited me more that she was enjoying being looked at by me so unrestrainedly.

This room was where patients were injected with codeine before surgery, and the nurse knew its effects well. She bounced out of the room in her white orthopaedic shoes like a little bird, whistling and doing up her lower buttons, her ponytail swinging. Those legs...

She'd got what she'd wanted, just as I had, and she'd done what she was good at: electrifying patients. The cheeky girl knew only too well that she had great legs, and obviously enjoyed showing them off. I reacted immediately, just as I would have done to a musical prompt.

At that point, the specialist came in, looking even taller than he had before. From far above, he looked down on me, a routine case, his good-natured face rising from his white gown as he pulled out a large syringe filled with clear blue liquid, which he pushed into the aperture in the cannula stuck in my arm. I heard him say, "Now we shall have a short s-l-e—e———", and the word "sleep" stretched out longer and longer. His "we" amused me, and I wondered whether he was about to lie down next to me.

Before my eyes, the words of the doctor shaped themselves into a shining tube that became longer and longer, stretching to infinity. I can't remember hearing the *p* of "sleep". I was already under.

# 44  We Are The Robots, Mother!
## Dust In The Tyrol?

DÜSSELDORF, 10 JANUARY 2000
Someone pushed my leg. I started and opened my eyes. To my left
sat a dolled-up lady holding a manicured hand out to me, gold
bracelets jingling on her withered wrist. She was sitting upright in
her wheelchair, and she had a proud and aristocratic air about her.
Her lined mouth was sucking on an amber cigarette holder, inlaid
with glistening stones, holding a wrinkled, bent joint. It had already
been more than half smoked, and a long piece of ash depended from
it. The old lady sucked with great concentration, her eyes screwed
up to narrow slits as she pursed her lips so tightly that they went
white. As she sucked, deep furrows appeared in the downy edges
of her mouth, which was thick with lipstick. She blew thick, heavy
smoke directly at me, so I knew that she was addressing me, and I
coughed. She held a book up to me in a shaky hand and said, "You
dropped this, young man. Were you really once a robot?"

Without answering the grotesque woman's question, I reached
for the book, the cover of which had an image of plugs and
Polaroids and looked familiar. Then a familiar vocoder voice
to my left said, "We are the robots, Mother!", and then, in a
Rhineland accent, "Don't you recognise our Wolfgang any more?
Our drummer?"

264

Because of my coughing, my glasses had fallen onto the parquet floor, which was decorated with expensive-looking intarsia work, and I bent down to look for them awkwardly. This must have looked like I was bowing to the woman, because she said, "I am Mother Kraftwerk, young man – you do recognise me, don't you?" Lena wanted to look for my glasses, which lay somewhere under my chair. My good fairy, whom I had taken with me from a hot Budapest summer years ago and who always wore tight-cut white cotton blouses that always turned me on, had cared for me touchingly for many years, and had never left my side ever since we'd first loved each other back in her home country. For a long time she had been my reliable adviser and strength-giving muse. Sometimes, however, her constant care for me was almost too much. In the end, I wasn't yet so old that I had to have people bending down for me. I shooed her away curtly, and instantly regretted using the wrong tone with her.

I was able to manage this simple task – which I could normally do so easily – only by concentrating hard on co-ordinating my intractable body, which still hadn't recovered. When I tried to pick up my glasses, I missed them by a centimetre. Out of sheer vanity, because I didn't want to ask for any help, I just let them lie there and suffered the disadvantage. I couldn't decide what to look at first, the old woman or the book in my hand. Then the owner of the dry vocoder voice tore it out of my hands. Annoyed, I looked across at Florian, who was waiting in a comfortable wheelchair, as were Karl and Ralf a short distance away. We all looked equally wornout, and the whites of our eyes were bloodshot.

We were all sitting in the same position in the recovery room, right next to the transformer room and the beautiful half-timbered veranda of Dr Eberhard von Siemens's famous electro-convalescent home, a private clinic belonging to the famous engineer's brother. The home had been built during *la belle époque*, and had been designed by my great-grandfather, the same architect who had built the famous Berghof sanatorium featured in Thomas Mann's novel *The Magic Mountain*, on Davos. Through a magnificent feat of engineering, it had been built directly onto the rocks, and was only accessible by a narrow, serpentine access road, which had been carved out of the granite wall at a breathtakingly steep angle. An old-fashioned railway slowly and shakily clattered up the mountain four times a day on its curved narrow track, which was closely bordered by a low pine forest. The single wagon, which also housed the engine, was always packed full with suppliers, dealers and dustmen, who provided the clinic with all the necessary goods and services. The aromas in the wagon were correspondingly varied.

When it was winter and people wanted to get up the mountain, they had to wait at the post on time. At that time there was hardly anything going up into the mountain except the electric train, and its progress was slow and laborious because the rails had to be continually cleared of snow. This was no easy task for the local railway workers, and some of them suffered bad falls near the steep, rocky gorges while performing the difficult work.

Now, though, it was spring, the days were mild and the large limousines and the trendy sports cars of the more famous patients crept up and down the mountain. Seen from a distance, this trail of cars looked like a string of gaudy pearls, and the sunlight reflected from their chrome trims could dazzle from a distance, but like all stars we always wore classic Persol or the more fashionable Ray-Ban sunglasses to protect our eyes. With the assistance of our 24-gear, high-tech bikes we used to pedal up here leisurely, but now we couldn't manage that, and we would have been glad of a hydrolift or a cableway. However, the conservative director of the clinic – a truly stubborn man hailing from the lowlands, and a constant grumbler – was reluctant to provide these for nostalgic reasons.

The long wheelbase of our Mercedes 600 couldn't round the tight curves of the narrow road very well, and the driver often had to drive forward and back to negotiate the tight bends. Of course, this also disrupted the flow of traffic coming from the opposite direction, and the other patients were justifiably annoyed about this.

The staff had opened both doors of the veranda wide, and there was a fantastic view of the mountains and the lush green valleys of the Tyrol. The weather was lovely, the sky a steely blue, and a group of illustrious patients had been tempted outside into the fresh air. The resinous scent of needles and bark wafted into the room from the pine forest, blended with the heart-lifting twittering of birds which lightened the soul.

Helmut Berger, Rainer-Werner Faßbinder and our artist, Emil Schult, were sitting comfortably together at a small table bedecked with a checked tablecloth, holding hands affectionately. All three had met and become friends when Berger had accepted Faßbinder's offer to play the starring role in his film *Querelle*. Kraftwerk had brought them together when we managed to convince Faßbinder to let us write the soundtrack for the film, which later became a classic piece of cinema. We were supposed to receive 400,000 DM for the soundtrack, which made the commission a very attractive proposition. We were famous not only as being the discoverers of electro pop; we had also distinguished ourselves worldwide in the lucrative field of commercial music.

When Berger was hired, he recommended that Emil should also design the background paintings for the film, in the style of the inner poster for *Trans Europe Express*, which the thespian said that he had liked "extraordinarily", finding it artistic, delicate and dramatic. Faßbinder's film was intended to be a piece of pure theatre when it was finished. Through us, Emil – who had the same coloured eyes as Joseph Buyss, his model – had made a great name for himself abroad as being Germany's most capable designer, a painter of shimmering backdrops. Since the day they'd met, the three had been inseparable, and I remember thinking how good it was that Helmut now had a new mentor, and that they could all three take coke together, so that for once Emil got something else up his nose other than just the irritating smell of oils, acrylics and latex paints. (I remember that he'd loved the smell of Pattex back in 1973, when he'd helped me in my workshop.)

But, it appeared, I was completely wrong. Up here, Helmut and Faßbinder had no addictions, and their only indulgence was the Viennese Blend, topped with whipped cream. Emil, who was always healthy, poured a glass of cherry juice into his handsome curly head and belched twice quickly. I was completely bowled over by the trio, sitting there together so comfortably. Above all, I admired Helmut's elegant ankle boots. I would have loved a pair like that! They were just the kind of shoe I liked, and I dug Lena in the ribs, gesturing with my left hand that she should look too, but at that point a gust of wind rose from the valley and the curtains billowed out to the left and the right of the doors, obstructing her view of Helmut's footwear. Nevertheless, she nodded vigorously, although she usually did this, because she nearly always agreed with me.

Helmut then turned towards me, as if realising that I was thinking about him. He looked sensational, just as he had in his prime, and his red cheeks showed the effect of the good air up here. He seemed completely relaxed. Laughing sweetly, he blew me a kiss. "If you only knew what you missed with me in Rome, Wolferl," he said, adding in a lecherous undertone, "I just wanted to do something good to you, you little coward. You wanted it yourself. Admit it! But now it's too late – now I have Rainer-Werner. He's not as damned coy as you were then. This evening, perhaps, at your song recital. I'm looking forward to it already." Then he patted the famous film-maker, who was pouring a cup of coffee down his throat with relish – in one gulp, of course. "And we'll go for a shower afterwards, right?" giggled Emil, and at the same time his face became a unique shade of pink that he could never have mixed on his painter's palette.

Lena, who had been rearranging one of the huge bunches of gladioli that had been decoratively placed by the staff at strategic positions in the room, asked jealously, "And just what did he mean by doing something good?"

"Forget it, my love," I said soothingly. "It's a long time ago. It's a completely different story."

"But I'd really like to know," she persisted.

"It's nothing to do with you," I said abruptly, ending the discussion. It was my own responsibility, after all. Perhaps I was glad that all of these people – the great and the famous from the art world – were with us today. However, I couldn't make any sense of Helmut's insinuation about a song recital.

My old father, who was fanatical about the benefits to be obtained from fresh air, was also sitting out on the terrace on a wooden bench in a corner protected from the wind, dreamily playing a soft melody on his accordion – *"Muss I denn, muss I denn..."* – and was driving me crazy with it. "For God's sake, Father, can't you play something modern for once, instead of this tasteless old stuff all the time? Play one of our songs. Play something like 'Autobahn', or 'Neon Lights'," I ordered him, but he didn't hear. He hardly heard anything these days. Lena reproached me, saying that I shouldn't speak to my father so coldly, but I waved her aside irritably.

Father had first learned to play the accordion to please Mother Kraftwerk, because she usually went for men of an artistic and cultural bent, but otherwise only young men attracted her. My old man was perhaps an exception, because he had taken very good care of himself, but he really annoyed us with his tootling. Years ago, we offered him a job in the Kling Klang Studio so that he could supplement his pension a little and so that he wouldn't be sitting around at home alone after the death of his wife, Hilde. As pedantic as any civil servant, Father exchanged burned-out faded neon lights in the studio, working to a precise timetable, and he loved to sign the autograph cards for us. In fact, the old rogue could imitate our signatures perfectly!

However, that had been several years ago. Now he had grown too shaky for this kind of work, and we'd had an automatic signature-maker built for him. He now had even more leisure time, and would continually annoy us with his amateurish musicmaking, always hanging around, hoping to be recorded. And now he'd followed us to the Tyrol. We'd assumed for a long time that something was going on with him and Mother Kraftwerk. What else could he be after up here, apart from the great air and the brilliant view? He hadn't gone on any walks for years.

## 45  Recharging Our Batteries
### Transforming The Cleanest Power In The World

DÜSSELDORF, 10 JANUARY 2000

We were robots showing slight signs of wear, all with our red shirts on and black ties on which LEDs blinked in a row from top to bottom – our power-loading indicators. When the diodes stopped blinking, that meant that we were fully charged again. However, we already knew that we couldn't continue to be revived for ever. Our time had long passed, but left us unmoved. Defiantly, we rolled up our right sleeves, as we always did when we were recharging. Again, all four of us had these awkward IV tubes stuck into the arm veins inside our polyurethane elbows, while a tangle of wires hanging from the supply channel on the marble wall behind us allowed electrical energy to flow into our bodies. We were recharging our batteries, transforming what the reservoirs in the healthiest mountain region in Europe were able to supply, the cleanest power in the world, and we were doing it wonderfully. Only the privileged and the richest could afford it, which was no problem for us. This was the prerequisite for good German functioning. How often we had been here before, and how well we always functioned again afterwards!

Florian leafed through my book cheerfully and lingered at the pages illustrated with colour pictures of us. Ralf and Karl also wanted to see the pictures again, and they squabbled over the copy of the book. "Watch out for your charging cables, and don't quarrel," I warned them. "You can have one each. I've left a signed copy for each of you in the Kling Klang Studio so that you'll have a good reminder of our best Kraftwerk years." Father had put the heavy accordion on the floor outside after suffering from a bout of coughing. Lena hurried towards him, supporting him while they walked back in. As she moved, she knocked over one of the splendid Venetian flower vases and it crashed onto the parquet floor, spilling its floral contents everywhere. Father was startled and complained that he'd breathed in a speck of dust, and ringing laughter broke out on the veranda. Nobody on the terrace bought that from him. Dust in the Tyrol? In this clear mountain air? Father's coughing actually did sound rather artificial, and he'd never been a particularly good actor. Of course, he was looking for a pretext to meet Mother Kraftwerk one more time. Once inside, he tried to convince us that what he'd breathed in was probably some pollen from one of the many bouquets, but this was another foolish excuse. Even so, he didn't look bad at Lena's side – they looked like father and daughter. How he had taken the sweet girl to his heart! She had restored his youth. To me, too, she had been like an elixir of youth. She embellished me, and I loved her more than anything else.

Karl and Ralf didn't want to wait to receive their books. Electrified, they crowded over my Polaroids while the LED signs indicating their power supplies on the marble wall behind them raced upward, dangerously high. They chattered and laughed in high, young voices, as if they were overdosing or on helium.

Florian had grown very hot, pulsating strongly, although I couldn't tell whether this was because he was charged up with energy or not. With stiff joints, he moved his wheelchair nearer to me, and I could smell his Weleda aftershave, which I'd always liked. Then, looking down for my glasses once more, I had a terrible shock. I didn't have a lap any more! None of us had lower bodies, only long, thin metal legs sticking out from under our red shirts. We had no sexual organs, either! Something had gone tragically wrong during our construction.

Mother Kraftwerk swore angrily to herself when a nurse in a green overall took away her joint. We were glad, though, because her puffing had really been getting on our nerves. "Okay, boys," she said resolutely, spitting crumbs of tobacco onto the parquet floor, prompting Lena to look away in disgust. Mother Kraftwerk glanced briefly across to Father, as if searching for his approval of what she had to say to us. "We've brought you vain prima donnas together again up here to freshen you up. Now you'll do us and the world a favour and crown your re-unification this evening with a concert in the pavilion in the park, as a kind of payment."

The room fell silent. Rainer-Werner and Helmut looked at us expectantly, astonished by the mood, which had suddenly become serious. Emil leaned over the railing, embarrassed, gazing spellbound into the depths. Dumbfounded and firmly tethered, we looked across at Mother Kraftwerk, who was leaning back in her wheelchair with satisfaction, calmly scraping the undersides of her long, mother-ofpearl- varnished fingernails with a silver nail-cleaner, then submitting them to strict examination. "You heard right, you vain band of singers," she went on, without taking her eyes from her bony claws. "You'll do it just as I say, and that's the end of it!" Father gave a doubtful cough.

After a pause which felt like an age, she continued, "I've also invited David Bowie, Rainer-Werner, Rosa von Praunheim and the wonderful Iglesias. They've all taken suites here in the health farm, and they're all looking forward to seeing you peacocks perform. Life has become *soooo* difficult for you, and I have such sympathy for you, having to shoulder the heavy burden of discovering electro blues. Just look what you've done to people, and yourselves! You made people addicted to your music drug, and then you fell out and left people high and dry. Stupid children!"

Lena was just about to protest against her use of the term "music drug", but I held my finger to her mouth, curious about what would come next.

"You're just a bunch of prima donnas, nothing more," Mother Kraftwerk's poisonous lecture continued. "I feel very sorry for you. And do you know what? You make me sick! You could have been so famous and made millions of fans happy all over the world. I can't find the words for such stupidity. Your friends love you – you, Karl; you, Ralf; and you, my Flori; and, of course, Wolfgang as well. Do what you think is right. But let me tell you, as someone with experience: you completely destroyed something. You didn't get any advice from an old lady. This world needs wise people – people just like me." And then she laughed out loud.

That was giving it to us straight! Abashed, all four of us looked at the floor and then across to my father, as he continued, in the same sharp tone of Mother Kraftwerk, "Everything has been organised as much as possible, don't worry. We'll be alone together this evening, and only the high-society guests that have been invited will be allowed into the park. You must promise to get on with each other and be nice to each other. By the way, I've brought you some Bittner chocolates from Düsseldorf. Perhaps it would be better to give them to the guests, hey? In any case, we're not expecting any embarrassing situations this evening. Agreed? David has also told me in confidence that he wants to come onstage with you to sing 'Computer Love', do you understand? Faßbinder will record the whole thing on 35 millimetre for a pop operetta in his new film, *Tanz Am Lido*, and tonight your show will be broadcast live across the globe. That'll give you an audience of about 700 million. Good, no? Show them what you can do – if you still can."

Florian wanted to rebel against the uncharacteristic harshness of my father and Mother Kraftwerk, because we all knew that he hated being addressed in any kind of peremptory tone. His arm twitched violently, and his charging cable was torn from the wall. He slumped over dramatically and fell sideways on top of me, and his plastic hands slapped hard against my face. The noise rang out loudly, and it felt as if he'd just boxed my ears.

Just then, the door opened and Ian Dury came limping into the room, supporting himself on a fine little stick with a silver-covered handle. He was looking for my father, with whom he'd arranged to have a small glass of Almdudler. Ian had also given up alcohol long ago, and they both loved this Austrian herb speciality. It looked like a whisky soda but it tasted like a mixture of ginger ale and champagne.

When Dury saw what had happened, he tried to manhandle Florian back into his wheelchair, but he couldn't manage him. Emil and Lena rushed to his assistance, and together they held the robot – whose head was already hanging mournfully to the side – firmly in an upright position. Emil reached across me and plugged Florian's cable back into the charging point behind him. As he did this, some round shining metal plates spilled out of his jacket pocket and fell clattering onto me and onto the floor. It was impossible to ignore the noise.

Everyone looked him. "Oh, yes. I'd completely forgotten." He reddened again, as if he'd been found out. "I got them from a Düsseldorf scrap-merchant as a replacement for your electro-pads," he said. "You can screw them on later, if you need to." *Strange*, I thought. *He must have stashed them away back in 1973, when he helped me build my board in our workshop in the Berger Allee. What could that mean?* Bewildered, I thanked him for his precaution, although I hadn't asked him for anything.

Ian grinned at me artfully and bent down to collect the fallen discs with Lena, handing them up to me. Florian was slowly reviving; he had sat up straight again and they were able to let go of him. Softly, almost tenderly, Ian whispered in my ear, "Would like me to dance with you again, Wulfgaaang Robbiiiee?" and at the same time he trod hard on the completely bewildered Florian's foot with his bootheel. It looked like he wanted to take revenge for something on my behalf.

I was horrified. "Hey, man, what are you doing to my friend?"

"That was for the bump he kicked in your car door once, remember?" Ian answered.

I couldn't remember anything of the sort, and said, "Keep out of it. Too long ago, that stupid story. I'm not angry, anyway!"

"I never liked this polished guy," Ian continued. "Not even in Venice. Remember, Wulfgaaang?"

Flattered by his unexpected partisanship, and by his offer to dance, I politely answered, "I can defend myself if necessary, Ian, but thank you for the offer. Maybe tonight, after the concert. We'll be able to do anything down in the Kurpark after that."

Lena didn't like hearing anything like that. Ian grinned at her triumphantly, turned conspiratorially toward me and answered quickly, "So we shall!"

Suddenly the Englishman took his fine little stick, pushed it together like a telescope and lifted his arm. It seemed that he wanted to conduct us in a song: "*Wir sind die Roboter, Mutter – doo-dee-dee-doo-di-di-ditt.*" Instead, however, he struck my right shoulder with his rhythm stick, as if he wanted to knight me – or was he trying to cast a spell on me? Perhaps I was shedding sparks!

# 46 Catching On

Somebody was striking me on the shoulder again and again and a familiar voice was calling out to me. "Herr Flür! Herr Flür! Listen! Do you know where you are? Why are you waving your arms about? Wake up, now. Do you recognise me? I'm the doctor treating you."

I woke up reluctantly, thinking that "Herr Flür" meant my father. I noticed the *we* in "We'll wake up now", though. There was this doctor who'd wanted to lay down next to me. Had he or hadn't he? I was deeply confused.

The wrinkled woman in the wheelchair next to me with all the bracelets and bangles said that I'd slept for a whole hour and that towards the end I'd been making some really strange defensive movements. "You looked insane. Were you fighting with someone?" Without waiting for an answer, she continued, "Yes, yes, I know already. You just want to resist the examination, don't you?"

When I'd woken up, I'd wondered how much longer it would be until it was finally my turn. I was utterly convinced that nothing had happened to me yet, and that the test was still to come, but then the doctor explained to me, "We've finished with you. You can go home again soon."

I remembered everything: the specialist, the injection, and his invitation – "We shall now have a little…" I had to smile at his words, which the man probably used to his patients a dozen times a day, and I asked myself how many of them he would actually like to sleep with, the rogue! I could have screamed out about my mad dream, about the meeting with Florian, Ralf and Karl in the electro-convalescent home in the Tyrol. Above all, I had to smile to myself about the undeclared love affair between my father and Mother Kraftwerk. I couldn't forget it. You can't imagine what an interesting encounter I had recently with the woman whom I'd long referred to by that name, accompanied by Martin and Markus, two friends of mine. It was fantastic – but I'll have to leave it until later.

I stayed in my comfortable chair for another hour or so after the thorough investigation of my inner life, and I wasn't in any hurry to go home. I was still in a state of dazed deafness, but the codeine was making me feel relaxed and content and I dozed off several times, jolting awake immediately. My brain was continually waking up and going to sleep, like a light going on and off. It was fascinating how well it worked: consciousness on/consciousness off, light/dark, on/off. I always had the same picture in my mind when I woke up, like a postcard. It was the picture of Ralf, Karl, Florian and me sitting in wheelchairs, with rolled-up sleeves and IV tubes in our right arms, recharging. Then I thought about drug dependency and its victims, and I suddenly understood a lot more about it. On *Time Pie*, I had recorded an absurd song on the same subject, dependency, to which Andy Thoma supplied some suitably weird sounds:

*DR.UG.LY.*

---

(More than slim)

He's the one to be faithful and true
Dr the ugly is dealing with you

278

Promises healing from daily fears
Consulting the doctor – drops against tears
DR.UG.LY. – he's a snake,
DR.UG.LY. is a fake

But the truth you won't believe
Dr the ugly laughs up his sleeve
He will keep you addicted to him,
Offering pills that make you slim
Needing help, needing help
DR.UG.LY. – he's a snake,
DR.UG.LY. is a fake
Needing help, needing help
DR.UG.LY. – he's a snake,
Needing help, needing help

© Wolfgang Flür 1996

I didn't have the foggiest idea what they'd done to me then, and at that I really didn't care. That was the great thing about it: I didn't perceive any peripheral phenomena; I didn't care about anything – only the centre was interesting. Now, I'm in two minds about it. I understand why life is just too difficult for some people, and why they have to resort to finding themselves clumsy means of deadening the pain from day to day. It must be terrible!

I wasn't hoarse from the metal probe penetrating through my larynx, and neither was I suffering any brain damage from the anaesthetic. It was as if nothing had happened. At the same time, though, I'd had a deeply strange experience. It was bizarre to think that the doctors had been messing about within my body while I'd been taking part in one of my craziest ever flights of fancy. I hadn't felt a thing when they'd delved deep inside me, prodding with that long tube.

Then Dr Kappes called me into his consulting room. I reeled in on rather unsteady legs and collapsed into a rococo chair. He told me that the tests had come back negative, and that he was quite satisfied with my lungs, although there was a slight inflammation of my larynx. That was a result of my coughing, though, which in turn had to be caused by something else, possibly an allergy. My ear, nose and throat doctor had already assumed as much.

Later, I was sitting in the tram again on my way home, basking in the sun while it was still cold outside, enjoying a view of Kaiserswerth, with its rectangular fields covered in hoarfrost, glistening as they flew by. They reminded me of the large white tablecloths that had covered the Christmas presents we'd received as children, which had moulded themselves to the shapes of the gifts beneath them.

In 1965, when I was an 18-year-old boy playing with my amateur band The Beathovens, this same tram journey had always been my favourite. Then, on Saturday afternoons, I would travel on Line 11 to Kaiserswerth to pick up Brigitte, my first girlfriend, from the Theodor Fliedner Gymnasium. I remembered how excited I'd always been, and how much I'd looked forward to seeing her. Waiting at the school gate, my eyes would search expectantly for a sight of her shock of blonde hair, trying to pick her out from the hundreds of pupils, who would always surge out of the old building together after the obligatory three strokes of the gong. I would always find her immediately, and would run towards her, crazy with happiness. Then we would usually go to the meadows by the Rhine to kiss and cuddle, although not without first making a diversion to the Café Bovers in the Stifts Gasse, where we would suck on a Capri lemon ice cream together.

Now, though, I was just glad to be myself again, none the worse for my ordeal other than suffering from shaky limbs, a side-effect of the anaesthetic. Thank goodness my memory hadn't been affected! In the tram's extra car, I took the Camus novel out of my jacket pocket, put on my reading glasses and read on, this time concentrating completely. I'd become used to the short sentences that the writer used: "I took the bus at two. It was very hot. I ate in the Restaurant de Céleste. They were all sorry for me." It seemed to me that Camus had taken on the same simple spoken style of the man in his novel to make him seem more authentic. I also had the impression that the author had combined the story of his own life along with the one he'd invented. If this was the case, it was a great idea. I knew that, after his mother had been buried, Mersault had associated with people who meant something to him, from whom he'd drawn something that excited him, although he hadn't recognised this initially. He later discovered that he'd gone too far, and that he didn't really want this any more. However, he made a fatal mistake and was unable to save himself.

I discovered a parallel in this with my own story, although I'd managed to save myself. I had also once leapt onto a running-board and had taken part in an idea – an ingenious idea, I thought for a long time, but a discovery that wasn't my own. In the beginning I'd been completely convinced of it – utterly enthusiastic about it, in fact. Then, in later years, as I matured and was able to understand things better, I discovered its emptiness and the inhuman coldness of it. Even then, I'd almost been unable to escape from the relationship, which had become frosty, with a dictatorial quality that in the end proved counter-productive.

When I stopped going to the Kling Klang Studio in 1987, I had no idea how good this decision would be for me and how warm I would feel once again. It was a difficult decision to withdraw from my "teachers", to discharge myself from something that was no longer good for me because it no longer offered a future or any fun. I'd had to do this twice in my life: when I left my parents' house and when I disowned Kraftwerk.

Inspired by *The Outsider*, I thought about the previous year and all of the excitement that it had brought. My book had been published in Germany, and although the reviews had been rather contradictory my fans loved it. Although I'd wanted to write the book for myself, like an exercise in aversion therapy, I dedicated it to our friends. Later, Ralf and Florian took out an injunction to prevent its publication – as even Emil did, later – and if I hadn't observed this I could have ended up in prison.

281

What had got into them? No one I spoke with could understand the reaction of my three "exes". In my book, I'd wanted to draw a line underneath a long chapter in my life. The only solution seemed to be to break away entirely, to give myself a genuine fresh start, but I found myself having more to do with my past than I wanted. The precious artists felt attacked, and they didn't have the magnanimity to allow my achievements with the band to be recognised and to accept a little criticism. All this was accompanied by a pungent smell of sour grapes which wafted from the written statements of their lawyer.

These days, I'm no longer prepared to submit to their *diktat*. While I was on the tram that day, I decided to go public and tell our fans what was happening, encouraged by their letters. I'd received a much warmer and more human response – some really affectionate letters – from those for whom we'd ultimately made our music than from those with whom I'd previously performed this music so passionately. That had really opened my eyes. For the second edition of the book, I wanted to write a new section which I would dedicate especially to those willing to understand and prepared to judge realistically and occasionally to take the so-called Kraftwerk myth a little less seriously. I also decided no longer to bow to the titans that once led me: Kraftwerk and EMI Electrola.

When I'd almost finished writing my manuscript, I started to look around for a suitable publisher. I had a lot of rejections, with the stupid clichés that I could have done without, such as, "We read your manuscript with great interest, but we have to inform you with regret that we don't see any space in our company strategy for a publication in such a subject area at the moment." I was also told that the market for music books was at rock bottom. Nevertheless, they wished me success in my search for a publisher, blah blah blah.

I had particularly high hopes of one publisher, the reputable Mosel-Schirmer publishing company in Munich, having once heard that the boss had been a Kraftwerk fan himself. Apart from this, his company also specialised in publishing biographies of world-famous artists. His books were expensively designed, and I found them in stock in every German bookshop I visited. I wrote Herr Schirmer a letter, enclosing part of my manuscript to give him a rough impression of the contents and what my personal writing style was like. I also wrote that it wasn't a "book of reckoning" about my previous group, but more a report about my own search for my own destiny, and that I'd dedicated a long and honest chapter to Kraftwerk, as my "trainers".

After several months with no reply, I wrote to Schirmer again, pushing for a decision, which I promptly received. Schirmer wrote that he had read my sample with great interest, and thought that it was good. Nevertheless, for various reasons – including the fact that it was too close to another project – he was obliged to refrain from taking it on. "Nevertheless, I wish you…" and so on.

That was rather interesting! Of course, I had an idea what this coded message meant. I remember that Ralf and Florian had often spoken of publishing a book about Kraftwerk, which they'd intended to design with our resident artist, Emil Schult, and I think that I remember them saying that they wanted to publish it with just this company. When I rang Karl in Hamburg, he confirmed my supposition immediately. "Yes. Have you forgotten? They always wanted to write a book themselves. When I was still in the group, they talked about it a lot, and I was going to contribute. I know that they'd made quite a lot of progress, and I think they'd already discussed details with Mosel-Schirmer. When I left in 1991, I withdrew all my undertakings to contribute to the book because we'd quarrelled about something and couldn't see eye to eye. At that point, Ralf and Florian shelved their publishing plans, and Schirmer found himself unable to do business with them. He's probably still saving himself for their book and didn't have the courage to take on yours because, if he did, Ralf and Florian would pull out. It's just the same as it was with your music at EMI." Since then, of course, the situation had become explosive. This made me somewhat insecure.

Of course, I now had to look for another publisher, although I had an idea who to try. In early summer 1999, I phoned the journalist Albert Koch of *Musikexpress*, who'd been at the back of my mind for a while as a reliable contact, and I asked his advice. He was delighted about my book, and he immediately told me, "You need to speak to Robert Adzerball in Austria. Ring him up, Wolfgang. He's the boss of Hannibal Verlag, and he's the right person to take your book because he only publishes books about music. In the meantime, I'll encourage his interest."

Koch's words were very encouraging, and it wasn't long before Adzerball called me on my mobile when I was on my way down the Kö to go for an ice cream with my nephew during his lunch break. He was a pleasant man, and quickly made some sensible proposals, and we came to an agreement in July to publish my book in Germany, Austria and Switzerland in the autumn. After this, we had to move fast. The publisher wanted to present my report to the media at Pop Komm in August, the IFA in September and at the Frankfurt Book Fair in October. However, there was still a lot of work to be done on it – it still needed to be edited, proof-read and, most importantly, designed and given a title.

An acquaintance introduced me to a young man called Martin Hausen, who was working with her in Düsseldorf Derendorf. "He's a charming man," she said, "and he'd be delighted to meet a genuine member of Kraftwerk." My curiosity aroused, I consented, and met him a few days later in a café under the Landesgalerie at Grabbeplatz.

Martin was accompanied by his girlfriend and another friend, Markus Schmitz. To start with, we were all rather awkward around each other, but as time passed the atmosphere thawed and we relaxed and launched into a discussion rich in ideas and full of humour, which was not without its consequences. In fact, I learned that the two men were students at the graphics and design department at the Düsseldorf Academy, and that they were about to take their finals. Suddenly, I had the idea that they might be able to design my book. They were fans of my music, they loved good design and they were familiar with the history of Kraftwerk, so they were as highly motivated a team of designers as I could hope to find. In fact, I couldn't have asked for better credentials. Some time later, I gave them my gold aluminium case, which I had once bought in the fashionable New York... Well, you know that already.

I wanted the design of the book to be something very special, and I couldn't have found anyone better than Martin Hausen and Markus Schmitz, who turned it into a miniature jewel with evident affection and dedication (although I prefer to call it radiation or human magnetism). Since then, their tasteful work has been constantly praised, even by specialists who have read the book and have examined it carefully.

## 47 An Unexpected Encounter
### Mother Kraftwerk

DÜSSELDORF, 14 AUGUST 1999

After spending the whole afternoon sitting together in Martin's digs, rejoicing at receiving the first author copies of our book, which had just been printed and which we must have leafed through 100 times already, Markus and Martin had the idea of dining out that evening in a lovely bar in the Altstadt to celebrate our work together.

We drove into the city, and Martin parked his car in an underground car park at Karlplatz. The night was mild, and we strolled through the streets of the Altstadt, smelling its many pizza stalls, falafel palaces and huge steakhouses. Our path took us through the Mata Hari Passage (where else?) and later to Karlplatz, Düsseldorf's weekly market. I wanted to go to a bar there called Marktwirtschaft, on one of the corners of the market, because a friend of mine worked there. When we entered the bistro, Lothar recognised me immediately and greeted me warmly. He asked where I wanted to sit, and I indicated Martin and Markus and told him, "There are three of us. We'll have a quiet table where we can be by ourselves." I'd hardly finished speaking when any chance of being by ourselves was lost.

Someone pulled my sleeve. Annoyed, I looked down into the face of an elegantly dressed woman sitting at the table next to where we were standing. "Aren't you Herr Wolfgang, the Kraftwerk drummer?" asked the woman. "I am Mother Kraftwerk. Don't you recognise me?"

At first, I found it difficult to wrest a name from my brain to fit the face, but after a few milliseconds it supplied me with an image that I had stored as "Mother Kraftwerk". At any rate, she had occupied this position for a long time, and I'd never revised it. I was astounded to see her there, and answered that yes, I was, and introduced Markus and Martin as if we were about to start negotiations. "These are my friends. They've designed a book I've just written about my life. It's just been published, today. We were hoping to have a small celebration," I added in the hope that she would leave us alone. I was rather shocked by the way that she'd aged – she used to be so stylish – but I supposed that it's always like that if you haven't seen someone for a long time.

Nevertheless, Mother Kraftwerk still had an aristocratic air that couldn't be ignored. "Why don't the three of you sit with me and we'll eat together?" And so, with the hesitant agreement of my two friends, our astonished trio sat down at Mother Kraftwerk's table.

After the waiter had handed us the menu and we were all looking at the menus, Mother Kraftwerk asked me, "So what sort of a book have you written, then?"

"I've already said – it deals with my life, and Florian Schneider, and other people from Kraftwerk play a role in it, too. In fact, it's also a book about my time in Kraftwerk."

She was curious, and wanted to have a look at it, so I passed it to her and she put on a pair of elegant gold-rimmed glasses and leafed through the pages. She lingered over the coloured pictures in the middle and said, "It was good between you then, wasn't it?"

"That's true," I said.

"Oh, yes. Those parties! I think of them often, of how we always listened to music and ate chocolates, and the joints that we'd pass around. Hee-hee-hee!" she giggled, full of memories.

287

My companions looked at me in amazement, their eyes full of questions. "Yes," I answered the old woman hypocritically, "but I didn't join you, in those days. I didn't enjoy drugs, Mother Kraftwerk. That must have been before my time, when you had parties with the boys earlier."

"Oh, come on. Don't give me that story, young man. We all enjoyed things like that then. Don't be so coy. And don't behave as if you were above everything. We're not small children any more, and we don't need to be ashamed about it, do we?" She was trying to make me her accomplice! "My word," she went on, "this is a very attractive book that your friends have made. Very nice. Can I have one, too?"

"Of course," I answered, "but not this one. This is the only one I've got at the moment. I'll be getting more from my publisher in the next few days and I'll send one to your house, I promise. Where are you living now?"

Meanwhile, we had received our Italian *hors d'oeuvres*, and we began to eat. Mother Kraftwerk and I drank a glass of dark Düsseldorf beer, and I'd also ordered an aquavit, which she was sipping now and again. During the course of the evening, the atmosphere became more and more cheerful, and I thought to myself what a pity it was that I'd lost contact with Mother Kraftwerk over the last few years. I was always able to talk to her.

She then told us that she had also discovered writing, and that she had published a small volume of her poems. That I had to see! "Come over and see me sometime, just like you used to. We'll drink some tea together and talk shop as young writers." I pointed out that she hadn't given me her address yet, and when she gave it to me I was flabbergasted. "If you really don't have the time, just send the book across to me, like you said. I'd love to read it." I promised to her that I'd keep my word. We politely bid her goodbye, at which point she asked us to accompany her to her taxi, because she was loaded down with bags, a purse and a large bunch of flowers from a shopping trip. In accordance with her social status, she requested our company and porterage to her chauffeur, who was waiting for her very near the taxi rank.

Later, Martin and Markus confessed that it had been an interesting encounter, and observed how nice Mother Kraftwerk was. "That thing with the joints was really impressive. And that was the mother of your famous robots?"

"So?" I said. "She's still a person, Eva-Maria!"

## Pop Komm, Cologne, 20 August 1999

My German publisher had a stand at the colourful Pop Komm music fair, loaded up with his books, and I arranged to meet him so that we could present my book – which had just been announced in the press – to the trade people there. Journalists from music magazines and radio and fans who had learned of my appearance from advertisements and on the internet also turned up, as did my niece Jeannine and her boyfriend. The head of Hannibal and his charming wife – who was, like me, born in Sachsenhausen in Frankfurt – had brought with them a supply of sparkling wine from their home in Austria. In the dry, hot halls of the trade fair, it was a refreshing drink for the "reverent" fans, who crowded closely around us.

We showed a 15-minute video of my artistic activities and the short but previously missing film of my previous group's appearance on *Aspekte* in 1973. Afterwards, I got hold of a microphone and spoke to those present about my reasons for writing the book and signed copies for them on the spot. We'd planned to hold a similar event that evening in the Popdom in Cologne, to which the publisher had officially invited me, which turned out to be held in a room full of enthusiasts and reporters. My favourite colleague from Kraftwerk, Karl Bartos, also turned up, and was even asked to sign his own name in my book. I was proud of him, and glad that he hadn't forgotten me.

The evening was a complete success, for myself and for all of those present. The radio station Bayerische Rundfunk had sent along two alert young reporters from the south, and we later recorded a long interview for an extended radio report. This turned out to be the best and most comprehensive piece of journalism I have ever heard about Kraftwerk, Karl and me. There were similar events over the next few weeks.

# 48 How Time Changes Everything!

Much too early in the morning, the ARD recorded a short
interview with me for breakfast television about my appearance
at the IFA international radio exhibition – I was supposed to
give commentaries and my thoughts on the future concerning the
most recent developments in entertainment technology and their
products, which I enjoyed.

The author George Lindt also filmed a comprehensive piece
with me about my book, commissioned by the ZDF. This took
all afternoon, and was filmed both inside and outside the huge
trade fair. His report was scheduled to be broadcast the following
evening, once again on *Aspekte*.

The following day, interviews and reports for local newspapers
and the daily press followed in quick succession. Paying hundreds
of marks for taxis, I rushed from appointment to appointment
and from west to east and back again in the now-unified Berlin,
past endless ugly pre-fabricated buildings of the GDR and elegant
suburbs populated by villas with green lawns. I wouldn't have been
able to cope without Vera Seehausen, a sensitive and astonishingly
energetic woman possessed of the finest management skills, who
was working along with my publisher for her own operation.

I was unable to appreciate what people found so wonderful about the imposing new buildings that had sprung up in the rebuilt government quarter around Brandenburg Gate and Alexanderplatz. I found them all so pretentious and inhuman – so imperial! I was also horrified that they continued to call the historic government building the Reichstag. This had been the "promulgation building" since the year dot, which the Nazis had set fire to in a surprise attack, and which had now been renovated with millions of marks and fitted with a spyhole in the roof (apparently so that the citizens could better monitor the legislating of their leaders down below).

What a scandal! The name must have sent cold shivers down the spines of older visitors to Berlin, conjuring up past images of the bureaucratic sarcophagus. It would have been better to pack the stone relic in tinfoil, like in a shroud, as the visionary Christo pair did in 1995. In my opinion, that would have been an honourable Holocaust memorial, a plea for pardon, and it would have avoided years spent discussing what would be an honourable memorial to the victims of the Nazi regime at an historical site in Berlin. Also, *Bundeshaus* (federal house) would be a more suitable, more modest and, above all, more human name for this crate of politicians, who should have had a less grand structure built for themselves after the legacy of the war.

I thought that back in 1946 we'd decided on the formation of a humane Federal Republic, that we wanted to give up this imperial concept of the Reich. Or was I mistaken? Of course, Germans aren't renowned for their modesty. What's the world supposed to think of us, now that this expensive lump has been built for the politicians, bankers and industrial giants of Berlin? Or of those who crossed to the other side and turned away when asked to pay restitution to their former slaves?

My days in the federal capital – and after all, it isn't called the imperial capital – were immensely tiring, and I gradually came to understand what I'd done with my book. With some surprise, I experienced the momentarily awakened interest of the media.

When *Aspekte* was being recorded, something unexpected happened: the show's producer confessed to me that he'd also invited Ralf and Florian to Berlin, although he'd only been able to reach their answer machine in the Kling Klang Studio. He suggested to my former colleagues that they should also appear so that they could give their views on my book and respond to the critical remarks that had appeared in the press about their spectacular deal for Expo 2000 in Hanover. Although the producer had thought it through, I said to him, "Don't hold your breath. I know them both well. They won't come. I'd put money on it." To start with, the idea of being confronted by them in a contemporary TV show irritated me, and I didn't know what to make of it, but the more I thought about it the more it appealed to me. I'm sure it would have been great for our fans to see us together again, especially on the same programme which we'd first appeared on 26 years before, presenting the drumboard to the world for the first time, when the sparks of electricity had first flown between us. I would have liked to have signed a copy of my book for Ralf and Florian and shaken their hands in front of the cameras and thanked them for the great times we'd had together.

However, I hadn't been mistaken. That afternoon, a lawyer phoned the producer's office and told him that, as the legal adviser of Herr Hütter and Herr Schneider-Esleben, it was his duty to inform the producer that his clients weren't coming to Berlin. (As it turned out, legal steps had already been taken against my book, and I would hear from them myself soon enough.)

How time changes everything! Before, they couldn't get me into their world fast enough; now, they were rushing to get my recollections silenced even faster. But the book was already out! Just as the music press had predicted, it had put the new Kraftwerk under some pressure. But to what, exactly, were they objecting? What were they so afraid of? Why had they reacted so sensitively? I didn't know the answers to these questions, and neither did anybody else that I talked to about it, but a rough idea slowly began to take shape in my mind.

## BERLIN, 3 SEPTEMBER 1999, EVENING

That evening in my hotel room, I phoned a friend in Düsseldorf. If I'd had any remaining respect for my former colleagues, his shocking news robbed me of it completely. Suddenly, I no longer believed in the justification of their so-called world fame. In my eyes, in the light of their recent crass behaviour this was no longer deserved. It appears that Martin, my designer friend, had been faxed a page which, on my return, we recognised as being the copy of a US patent document. I didn't want to believe my eyes. It actually concerned the registration of "the ornamental design for an electronic percussion musical instrument, substantially as shown".

According to this document, on 14 July 1977, at a point in time when Karl and I had already been playing the thing for four years and it had already become an everyday instrument for us, Ralf Hütter and Florian Schneider had patented the drumpad board with the United States authorities under their own names. I had no idea that they'd done this, and the pair hadn't informed me about it at the time.

Klaus Zäppke, who had leaked the document to us, didn't want to name his source, but he had wanted to do me a favour, and had actually thought that I might be able to make good use of the information. It was also outrageous that Ralf, of all people, was listed as the originator! Ralf, who really had no talent for making things, not even a training in any kind of craft, claimed that he had thought out the design of the first drumpad board with Florian. They weren't even drummers.

The page also included an amateur sketch of my board, complete with metal discs, that I had made myself and played on the *Aspekte* programme of 1973, right down to the small brass corners I'd fitted to protect the edges and the small, curved, celluloid labels that I used to indicate the descriptions of the different drum sounds. My board had just been drawn completely, although rather amateurishly.

It's impossible for me to prove whether the two founders of

Kraftwerk have ever made any money from their US patent – from potential sales to industry, for example – and I'm not interested. For me, the important thing was their barefaced betrayal. It was like being robbed by a friend! I suddenly understood why they had taken out their temporary injunction on my book, which after all claimed that I had devised and built the electric drumboard back in 1973, when I'd become a member of their group.

Since the phone call in Berlin, I'd sworn that I was completely through with Ralf and Florian, and I no longer had any respect for the men from whom I had once learnt so much, both musically and artistically. While travelling home on the train, I found myself with time on my hands to think, and brandy helped me to keep my composure. I began to wonder if they'd been lying to Karl and me from the beginning. For example, they'd told us for years that Kraftwerk wasn't "profitable" when we negotiated our wages, and told us that they couldn't pay a high salary because we were doing "pioneering work", that we were constantly pushing the boundaries of experimental music and there wasn't a great deal of money that could be made in Germany in this field. Nevertheless, Karl and I had often enough seen our tour managers in the USA, Great Britain and Japan and everywhere in Europe disappearing after the concerts with suitcases full of cash. It didn't look like little money, but according to Ralf, "Everything costs so much that there isn't much left over." How often Karl and I heard those words while renegotiating our salaries!

Today, after seeing the documentation that has now been leaked to me, I don't believe the "electro brothers" at all any more. Everything comes out in the end, even if no ones takes account of these things – it's guaranteed to come out! Even my "friend" Emil is now getting involved in such behaviour.

# 49  All Too Human?
## Headlines Speak For Themselves

Later, many newspapers, magazines and radio channels focused on my book, and there were some very exciting reviews. There were also some that were extremely controversial, however, and I sensed confusion in the air. Yet the headlines speak for themselves:

"Intimate Insight Into German Musical History"
(Amazon Online)
"Inside The Robots" (*TAZ*)
"After Book Revelations: Kraftwerk Row" (*Express*)
"And When Will The Music Start?" (*FAZ*)
"Wolfgang Flür Writes – As It Was" (*Überblick*)
"Kraftdwarf" (*Kölner Stadt-Anzeiger*)
"A Robot Gives Information" (*Cash*, Switzerland)
"Wolfgang Flür Acts Humanely" (*WAZ*)
"A Myth Loses Its Magic" (*Berliner Morgenpost*)
"Of Man-Machines And Robots With Soul" (*NRZ*)
"Kraftwerk: War Of The Robots" (*Hamburger Morgenpost*)
"Whatever Kraftwerk Brings To The Boil" (*WZ*)
"The Intimate Kling Klang" (*Musikexpress*)
"Kraftwerk As A Complex Roadblock"
(*Hannoveraner Nachrichten*)

"A Relaxed Taste Of *Joie De Vivre*" (*Keyboards*)
"Thought Is Free" (*Süderländer Tageblatt*)
"Number Four Lives!" (*Prinz*)
"Musical Ex-Colleagues In Legal Dispute" (*Rheinische Post*)
"Machines, All Too Human" (*Stadtzeitung Wien*)

"All Too Human" – that was probably what was such a shock to many journalists and even to some fans. As I'd written, what annoyed my former bandmates most of all was too much humanity. Apparently, humanity was exploding the Kraftwerk myth, which had long been shrouded in rumour. After all, there hadn't been anything like this around when I left the band in 1987. The myth didn't finally die until a short time later, when Karl left, and since then there hasn't been a single Kraftwerk album with new songs released.

Today, now that I've broken away, many people find it difficult to see me just as Wolfgang Flür. I still find myself connected with Kraftwerk, and our fans really don't want to let me go. They expect everything from me, a former "electrician", but they didn't expect me to write about one of the most human of themes: how I'd been soldered onto a robot for half of my life, and how I'd slowly and laboriously freed myself from the chilled amplitude and muffled vibration of my mainframe and become independent in a new cult of the synthesiser. Apparently, no one expected such open and honest attitudes from someone who was once a gleaming chrome mechanical android, let alone a transformation into something like Yamo.

But why should they? After all, EMI made sure that this new Wolfgang couldn't even be approached. I had to understand how little the world knew of us, how little Kraftwerk itself knew of me. I didn't have the faintest idea how infamous we'd become in the meantime, and how completely unwilling some people were to realise that humans were operating the machines behind which we hid our humanity so effectively. After all, we were human, with quite normal, natural needs and characteristics. One such characteristic was injured pride, and I would soon be confronted with this.

# 50 The Oath

DÜSSELDORF, OCTOBER 1999
Not long after the release of my book in Germany I received a preliminary injunction, sent via a law summoner from the county court in Hamburg, from clients Hütter/Schneider-Esleben. As I studied the thick document in detail, it was impossible to hold back fits of rage but also benign smiles. In a narrow-minded, hair-splitting dissection of my words, a ban was being imposed upon me regarding various statements, along with prohibition of further distribution in the future. With reference to the damage of their business and reputation, Ralf and Florian were threatening me, in the event of any violation, with a penalty payment of half a million German marks, or alternatively imprisonment.

It was all to do with a few photos over which I had no copyright, ones I could easily exchange for others – for example, with photos that we had taken ourselves, or which our fans or the press had provided. It was also to do with three Polaroid prints taken in our younger days, portraying us in Florian's garden under the shower, with bare torsos and flowers in our hair. Flowers in our hair...

Furthermore, it was about some statements which, according to Ralf, were not true but to my mind were. And above all, it was about my statement that I had invented and built the electric

298

percussion board in 1973. Florian, on the other hand, was claiming that they already had the thing in 1972. In addition, Kraftwerk was claiming that I was not the drummer on the recording of 'Autobahn' – they had supposedly staged this by themselves!

What I read was outrageous. Had they entirely blown their fuses? After all, I was well aware of what I had experienced. What right did they have to forbid me to express my memories and my opinion? I would be lying if I now claimed the opposite according to their wishes, and I was not in the least bit willing to be exhibited as a liar. So, in agreement with my lawyer, I refrained from signing anything and put up with the ban of the book for the moment. For outsiders it must sound childish. Using the power of their money and the most expensive lawyers, Ralf and Florian were obviously serious about having my book banned. I, on the other hand, was just about ready to let myself be sued for the sake of proving in an official court, with full access for the public, that my memories were correct, and to put straight that my book was written in a sincere, honest and fair-minded way. A clarification was absolutely necessary.

The point for me was simply that our fans, who had been faithful to us for over a quarter of a century, should hear what had really happened behind the scenes of the Kling Klang Studio, and what had finally led Karl and me to leave our band of our own accord.

I couldn't bear to be stuck in a perpetual state of inactivity and ignorance any longer. I had changed so much and, just like Karl, I did, after all, love working with music. Apart from that, I needed to do something that my record label had disgracefully failed to do for the past couple of years: I had to publicise my *Time Pie* album. In the summer of 1997, EMI had released it, but had hardly told anyone anything about it and had done no perceivable advertising for it. There had merely been one day of promotion in their private rooms in the presence of three or four local newspapers, to whom I had given interviews. How strange!

It made me furious when I thought about all that valuable work, and I had to admit to myself that the "deadbeat music label shack" not far from Cologne cathedral was just not worthy of our "Rhineland specialities", and that they had brazenly lied to me. Recently an EMI office junior had confessed to me that my album had become a political issue in their corporate group. Shortly after its release in 1997, the discontinuation of my debut had been determined at top level, and a great many of the employees working in the gigantic concern, whom I knew personally, were appalled. It was probable that private enterprise or so-called in-house interests lay behind all of this, and it appeared not to have been considered by anyone in the company beforehand and in all probability had not been considered by any other person either.

In a discussion in October 1997, my top boss, Helmut Fest – an important man in the German branch of the label in those days – sat stiffly in front of me in his leather armchair. Suddenly he lifted both hands as if he were making an oath: "Wolfgang, I assure you, it has nothing to do with a Kraftwerk conspiracy!" Excuse me? Pardon? What had I just heard? The man had uttered this of his own accord, without being asked! His indication was a revelation to me, especially since during our entire conversation I had never once touched on the subject. Such a possibility had never even occurred to me.

He had revealed something with his oath. It indicated that there had been some agreement made against my project. As I struggled to straighten things out in my mind, all at once I understood the frightfulness of the entire panorama. I had certainly known prior to our talk how awkward it would be for the sports-car driving executive. His secretary had postponed our meeting three times, always commenting evasively on the immense strain her boss was under and referring to his constant business travel. Today the corpulent man was sitting at his desk in a distinctly hostile manner. He was irritatingly playing with a large bunch of keys hanging on a Porsche tag, and hardly looked at me while speaking. He appeared to be embarrassed, and kept staring at his huge, highly polished walnut desktop, performing one activity of displacement after another. For example, he kept sliding his bunch of keys over the desk with a noisy rattle, hindering my inquiries, only to grab hold of the keys again a moment later. It spoke volumes; it was disruptive! He could not have been more disrespectful towards me and my questions.

Again and again his keys flew over his "negotiation barrier" in a casual gesture. Once, when he was actually listening, I asked him candidly why nothing was being done for Yamo anymore. So soon after the release of the *Time Pie* album, all I was hearing were excuses every time I made marketing suggestions or had any ideas for promotion. Only the most cursory steps had been taken, and not one of his members of staff had shown any commitment, even though they had previously been enthusiastic to help. Next, the man even asked me which of his colleagues had been present at the signing, since he had not really heard anything about my project. Now that really bowled me over. Was he effectively saying he did not know anything about a new project by an ex-Kraftwerker on one of his own labels? I was not prepared to believe this and listed the names of all his subordinates who had urged me to sign the contract. These included the head of the record label, Spin, the marketing chief, the chief of representation abroad, the press manager, plus the department head of my Odeon label, which I had especially re-started for Yamo and of which I was so proud, since it had in the past released music by The Beatles. The big boss then promised to catch up extensively on the matter and to let me know at once what had happened. It was already clear to me that this was just drivel.

All at once his face lit up. It appeared that he had thought of a way of niftily getting out of the subject. "One of your former colleagues was sitting here four weeks ago on the very same chair as you are," he revealed. It wasn't clear to me at first what he meant by this, although I did have a faint notion that he was conveying a further message, even if it was, in all likelihood, not done consciously. A Kraftwerker at EMI in Cologne? A former colleague had come in person? What was behind this? Someone who, for many years, had never come to see anyone working for the record label, had neither been available by telephone nor ever let himself be ordered to come, had appeared personally to see his boss, and they had concocted something?

This, to me, was implied by the unconscious message this man conveyed. It must have had something to do with the recent release of my debut album by the same firm, and likely as not also with the big boss's expectations of, at long last, new product from Kraftwerk, and his rubbing my music under their noses. I quite simply believe – and this is my firm conviction – that Ralf (or Florian?) had dictated their conditions – Kraftwerk's conditions – for further co-operation with the firm at the time, and that these could not occur in parallel with my project. My former band would not be able to grant such a thing to me – I know the lads! To have an "ex" looming large alongside their project at the very same firm – what a pain! This would not be in the interests of Kraftwerk.

After this sudden awakening of Helmut Fest and his vague evidence, he went on to enquire about other perplexing things. "Have you heard about your 'exes' losing all their dosh in America? Wasn't there some lawyer involved in it, or something? Cat – or mouse. He's supposed to have embezzled all their fortune, and done the same with other famous artists."

In fact I had heard about it, and if it was true, it was surely a disaster for Ralf and Florian. If you place a great fortune a long distance away and leave it to others to manage and grow, then you have to either be mad or playing a game of chance, and should expect anything to happen. I really did not want to believe it – but it would explain why they were so keen on selling advertising jingles these days.

It was in Japan of all places, at a later date, that I was enlightened, learning that there had indeed been a conspiracy against my new album. I was in Tokyo in October 1997 for a week to promote *Time Pie*. The record label Pop Biz had released it. My local manager – a large Iranian named Sadato, who was fluent in German, English and Japanese, among other languages –

escorted me daily to radio stations and magazine publishers and translated the interviews I gave. At one of the tiniest radio stations in Tokyo I got to know the presenter, who interviewed me briefly about my life. Afterwards we went off to a similarly tiny Tokyo bar, where we drank beer and whisky. After a while, the Japanese man told me that he actually came from London and had recently worked for EMI there. As such, he was in the know pertaining to certain information.

"Your album has become a political issue within EMI, Wolfgang," he told me. "It wasn't allowed to be promoted. The president of European EMI was a Kraftwerk fan. When he found out that an ex-Kraftwerker would be launching a new album through EMI in Cologne that he hadn't yet heard about, he thought it best to add on the name Kraftwerk and then promote this modern-sounding music properly. But it's not a Kraftwerk album, it's only an ex-Kraftwerker. And it's the former drummer boy, of all people, from whom no one had expected anything like this. Presumably the order had then gone out to Helmut Fest not to promote either the *Time Pie* album or Wolfgang Flür any more. The European EMI president must have thrown a tantrum when he found out about a campaign in Cologne he hadn't been informed about. There was a huge argument about it between the two bosses, one of whom lost. Helmut Fest then disappeared from the executive suite – apparently there had been other cases of factionalism as well. Nobody knows if he left voluntarily or involuntarily. In any case, off to Switzerland. Your record was locked away by EMI."

By the time I heard all this I was at the end of my tether. From then on, I was determined never to have anything to do with the cowardly "ramshackle hut" EMI again – indeed, nothing more to do with radio, magazines or any media at all in Germany. I said to myself back in 1997, if I ever do again, it will only be in the UK.

# 51 Number Four Lives!

The German magazine *Keyboards* published a review of my book in its December edition. It was more of a description than an assessment, and I liked the final passage particularly: "What does it feel like to be part of a trend-setting pop band, one of the most significant of our century? In around 300 pages, decorated with many pictures (some previously unpublished), the superstar Wolfgang Flür allows us to take part in his experiences. In this autobiography, Flür opens his Pandora's box and reveals his first contacts with rock music and accompanies us through his Kraftwerk period, entertainingly and richly interwoven with anecdotes, closing with a chapter about his current project, Yamo.

"The chapters about Kraftwerk will be of particular interest to fans. Flür presents his view of the Man Machine, from first contact and sessions in the Kling Klang Studio to his departure, with all of its highs and lows. He makes a piece of pop history accessible to the reader from a backstage view. He relates how the legendary electronic drumpad was made from a beatbox, in a period when synthesisers were an extraordinarily expensive means of production and were still very rare. He supplies information about the circumstances under which the Kraftwerk albums were made, and tells us about the fun and stresses of the tours. Meanwhile, the reader learns that *Radioactivity*, one of the best Kraftwerk albums, took no more than six weeks to produce, on the heels of a wearing but inspiring tour of America. Some myths are also finally abolished, for example that 'Autobahn' is definitely not to be regarded as a gentle satire on 'Fun, Fun, Fun' by The Beach Boys.

"Flür reflects on the group's significant decision to consciously detach itself (musically and also in terms of appearance) from what was then primarily an English-speaking mainstream, and how the band's unique secondary artistic products were developed, the perfected style typical of Kraftwerk on photos, album covers and videos, to which respected artists often contributed.

"Finally, with rich humour, the romantic Flür describes the lifestyle of a star and the characteristics of the 'electric quartet', and he makes no secret of his opinions: 'The cover version of "The Model" by the group Rammstein is the worst that I've heard recently,' he writes. We learn about a persistent Helmut Berger and many adventures with female fans from all over the world, but also about the circumstances that finally led to his break with Kraftwerk. Meanwhile, Hannibal Verlag has been served with a temporary injunction against this book, so anyone who wants to be sure of finding an unabridged edition should grab it fast. The book has a relaxed feel of *joie de vivre*, and is unfortunately much too quickly read."

*Jan Szulerecki*

DÜSSELDORF, 5 DECEMBER 1999
Although there had already been advertisements and features in the fashion publications and in the daily press drawing attention to my forthcoming presentation at the Zakk, I devised a campaign with the help of Markus Schmitz, which we prepared at his house on the weekend before that of 7 December. Markus designed two different flyers on his Macintosh, both printed with text that I'd

written combined with two pictures from the German edition of my book.

Early on the Monday before the presentation at the Zakk, I copied this flyer at a copy shop and also had it punched out in CD format. Then, on 6 December, we went around the record shops of Cologne and Düsseldorf in Markus's car and slipped the flyer into Kraftwerk's newly delivered 'Expo 2000' maxi singles. We didn't even have to be surreptitious because the branch managers of Saturn and WOM and the shops in Cologne loved the idea. They already knew of my book, and they supported us in our do-it-yourself ad campaign. That evening, I distributed the other flyers to those bars and cafés in the Düsseldorf Altstadt that the members of Kraftwerk used to frequent. I didn't receive a refusal anywhere; on the contrary, in most cases I received the complete support of the manager.

## DÜSSELDORF, 7 DECEMBER 1999, 8PM

This started out as a non-descript Tuesday. The town was enveloped in cold and damp, washing away any desire to go out in the evening. The drains were already overflowing with the downpour. Every sense compelled one to spend a comfortable, candle-lit evening at home in the warm with lebkuchen and a loved one.

I was overcome by an urge to stay at home. I thought that there'd be hardly anyone at the Zakk that night, which I would have completely understood. Also, I still remembered my previous appearance in the Philipshalle, which had been a bad evening as far as audience numbers were concerned, and so I had no expectations for that night.

I drove to the club that night with mixed feelings. When I got there, I stuck some notices that I'd made myself on the entrance door and next to the cash table (entrance fee: 10 DM) informing the audience that tape and video recordings were forbidden. I didn't want Ralf and Florian's spies mingling with the audience and recording my presentation in order to check it for possible breaches of their temporary injunction, which was actually preventing me from reading out certain passages from my book.

As it turned out, around 200 people came to the event, which was held in a room furnished with groups of chairs around small tables, so that there was something like a club atmosphere. When I came onto the stage (a little late, as planned), I was still wearing my wet raincoat and holding my blue plexiglas neon display. I also had a small briefcase containing my book, my reading glasses and letters from my fans, and was holding the letter describing the terms of Ralf and Florian's injunction in my hand.

Calmly, I took off my coat and hung it next to me above the stage parapet, then spent rather a long time looking for a good place to put the neon light on the floor in front of my lectern, and then plugged it in. My name suddenly illuminated the whole area beautifully in blue, and I bid my guests welcome. Firstly, I told them something about how the neon display had been wonderfully recreated, and then read a letter that I'd just received from a man called André in a small town near Zurich, which had affected me deeply. (This letter appears in Chapter 57, "Letters".) After I had reported briefly and concisely (but nevertheless with a lump in my throat) that my book had been written in self-defence, so to speak, I continued with that evening's programme.

That weekend, I'd written down the plan of events, after some adjustments, just as we would always compile a set-list for our concerts in Kraftwerk. I intended the presentation to be colourful and entertaining, so I had to mix together the old and the new, tales of our great time with Kraftwerk and absurd stories about Yamo. I showed videos and to loosen the atmosphere between my readings the private dancer CindY danced to 'Speech Dancer' in a breathtaking black patent catsuit, which clung to her sculpted body like a thin foil, as if it had been ironed on. Later that evening, she danced to 'Aurora Borealis', surrounded by masses of billowing blue tulle, shrouded in dry ice and pursued by the mystic blue spotlight.

The guests were enthralled by CindY's erotic performance and clapped and shouted their approval. After a short interlude, while *Time Pie* played in the background, I read out the choicest excerpts from Ralf and Florian's lawyer's injunction and, like the audience, I could hardly stop myself from laughing. This was actually the funniest part of the evening. However, the reasons behind the injunction were more serious than the words and images contained in my book could ever be. A Kraftwerk insider from Cologne by the name of Ralph Schmidt put this very well. For this reason, I'd invited him to come along that night, and urged him to present his own, self-penned analysis at point ten of the programme of events. As he spoke, a fresh downpour hammered on the tin roof of the hall and we were hardly able to hear him.

"Kraftwerk has always been more than a band, in the usual sense. Its members dedicated themselves to innovation, and were always at the cutting edge of multimedia. The band's music and its concept were constantly re-orientated towards the future, but to many this was disturbing. They had already experienced great interest at an early stage because of this, and yet at the time their whole image was the subject of some controversial discussion. Theirs was a band that seemed to plan every step in advance, leaving nothing to chance.

"One unavoidable question, however, is this: did Kraftwerk choose this image themselves, or was it imposed upon them from outside – by the press, for example or by the fans – and did they then take it on as their own? In the meantime, are they so self-absorbed that they're at the mercy of their own image?

"Have they lost humanity, the characteristic that defines a person, over the course of the years? Have they actually become robots, or are they hiding behind this façade to conceal their own human frailties? Why are they now reacting so oversensitively to a book written by an associate of many years, about his own life both with and without Kraftwerk? Sixteen years is a long time, during which you experience a lot in a group. Was it purely a working group or, after all the tours and studio work, has something that can be described as a friendship arisen? During the 16 years when

Wolfgang Flür was a member of Kraftwerk, it always appeared to be a closed formation, as is reflected on all their album covers and in their concerts.

"Of course, interests can develop separately, and different views can emerge through aims and ideas in any relationship. This has also been the case in Kraftwerk, where the founding members, Ralf Hütter and Florian Schneider, dedicated themselves more to sporting interests. With this in mind, it becomes understandable that Wolfgang Flür and Karl Bartos decided to leave Kraftwerk. Were Ralf and Florian unable to cope with this departure because more than a purely working relationship had arisen over the years? Could it be they had to admit that they lost two important and creative personalities with Wolfgang and Karl's departure?

"The question has arisen concerning how things continued after this. Wolfgang Flür and Karl Bartos have founded new projects with open concepts, which would have been absurd with Kraftwerk. Perhaps Ralf and Florian actually envy Wolfgang and Karl's courage and openness. It is an openness that they couldn't grant themselves and couldn't have not wanted.

"When Wolfgang and Karl gave interviews, it was a novelty. Previously, Ralf had usually felt that he was the mouthpiece of the band. Suddenly, the other 50% of Kraftwerk was expressing itself, and for the first time the public had the opportunity to take a peek behind the façade. For fans, however, it seems as if Kraftwerk feel dazzled by the light that is being shone into their darkness. If they imagined that they were safe and protected behind their façade, now they've been dragged from their selfimposed passivity.

"The press and many fans have accepted Wolfgang's project positively, and some have even dared to say that Kraftwerk should now follow suit. From this, it's possible to observe that, from an early stage, Florian and Ralf developed a negative feeling towards Wolfgang, who had freed himself from Kraftwerk in order to retain his humanity. It seems as if Ralf and Florian don't want to grant him the recognition that Yamo, his new project, deserves.

"This could also result from the fact that Wolfgang Flür is still regarded as a member of Kraftwerk, even as an 'ex', and for this reason a connection is always drawn between him and his previous group. Even so, this in no way justifies their present behaviour. A new period of life has begun for Wolfgang with Yamo, and he is looking to the future positively, searching for new ideas. He has found this path after a long process of breaking away, and has discovered the need to write a book about his life up until now. This book contains anecdotes and stories from the life of Wolfgang Flür, who has discovered the storyteller in himself. Following his separation from Kraftwerk, at no time has he expressed anything negative about his previous group, and has even paid them respect and recognition, which is not to be regarded as a matter of course, if you look at the way that Ralf Hütter, for example, talks to the media concerning Wolfgang and Karl: 'They were some employees… We've worked with so many people. I don't know how many any more!' I find this statement more wounding than Wolfgang Flür's book could ever be.

"Why did Ralf and Florian react so over-sensitively, even before the book had been published? Is it perhaps because they couldn't come to terms with the separation of their long-term comrade-in-arms, or with the realisation that there could be life after Kraftwerk for Wolfgang and Karl Bartos? Or was Ralf simply not thinking about what he was saying? This is hard to accept, however, because we know that Ralf is highly intelligent and very educated, and so his bitterness must be more based in emotion. In any case, it's a sad and unfair comment by him and fails to indicate any self-confidence or intelligence.

"Perhaps these reactions to the book are more deeply rooted than we can imagine. Perhaps they are related less to a criticism of the book than to their own principles, as I believe is clearly illustrated in the temporary injunction filed through the Hamburg land court. In fact, Kraftwerk should be glad that someone else has written the book; they haven't been in a position to do it until now because of their principles. Now, an ex-colleague has come along and gone against Kraftwerk's old principles, and perhaps their attitude to the book is so negative because of this. In my opinion, they lost their sense of humour a long time ago, if they ever had one."

During Ralph's speech, the rain gradually stopped and another noise grew rapidly. This time, the noise didn't come from the roof but instead from inside the hall. The audience was applauding the speaker. They understood him completely.

A photographer and a journalist were present that night on behalf of the radio station WDR 1-Life, home to the Unger brothers, the only ones permitted to record the passages from the lawyer's letter. They recorded everything on DAT tape for an item in a special programme several days later. On that broadcast, the whole stupid business sounded like a slapstick scene from a Cologne comedy.

Towards the end of the evening at the Zakk, I played the fans two new songs from the second Yamo album, 'Greed' and 'On The Beam', and many there told me afterwards how much they liked them. As I was taking my CD to the DJ at the back of the hall, someone else at the front was busying himself with malicious intent – the swine took down my old Europe Endless tour poster from the lectern and slipped it to his bag. I didn't notice until later, and was shocked by such impudence. Apparently there were even people like that among my fans!

At the book signing, I saw my ex-girlfriend Constanze with her younger sister, Jule, waiting in the passageway outside, smiling sweetly at me in such a familiar way. I was astonished that they'd both come. She'd never seen me as a working artist, and it must have been an astonishing experience for her, as I could see from her face. Now she was standing before me in a stylish short fur jacket and muff, and I thought to myself, *You don't like women like this at all. They belong on the fashionable Königsallee.* It was really strange to meet the girl who had fascinated me for such a long time. She had changed so much! Or was she still the same, and I was just seeing her with different eyes? Was it the same with Kraftwerk? It had to be.

Question marks condensed in the air above us, and they weren't about to disappear. We exchanged a few non-committal words, and she blushed just like she used to when we first met. I could hardly believe it. I was especially glad to see her more lively and humorous sister. Jule had previously seemed to be too young for certain things, and yet she'd been the one who had first wanted me, back in 1982. Now, the girl who once had giggled so girlishly had become an adult beauty, and I could only gaze at her and pay her compliments. She was still able to giggle, thank goodness! The pair of them grabbed me like a pasha, and I took one on my left arm and one on my right and accompanied them to the exit, where their taxi was waiting.

There were other sensational women who courted my attention at the book signing. A beautiful girl with a number of body piercings and a cheeky bob aroused me with gestures that had me immediately thinking of mischief. It was just like it had been in my days on tour, although these days I've become much more careful about casual sex. Apart from that, my drive isn't as irresistible as it used to be, thank God – an advantage of growing older, I suppose. I wrote my name around the plug that appears on the front cover of the German edition of my book, and I did so veeerrrryyy ssssslooooooowwlyyy, the way that women always like, as if the plug was her pierced belly-button. At the same time, I looked deeply into her blue eyes for several long seconds, and the girl didn't avoid my gaze at all; she breathed quickly and held my gaze without batting an eyelid. I'm sure she would have loved it even more if I'd taken her somewhere else to flutter her eyelids at me. She was signalling that she wanted me with all her being. Our penetrating eye contact was like sex. Nothing else needed to happen.

I had another surprise that night when I saw that my first amateur band, The Beathovens, had also come. You can't imagine how glad I was to see them. That night, I also learned something else – perhaps the most important thing: I found that I still had enormous fun being onstage. I'd forgotten it that felt like. This

312

time, though, the feeling was much more intense, because I no longer saw myself as part of a group, which gave me some security onstage. I'd stood up there quite alone and spoken to the audience, holding their attention for two hours and even making them laugh. I'd also suffered from intense stagefright beforehand, just like I always used to, but my butterflies quickly disappeared during the presentation and as I became more and more confident. Of course, my motivation this time was also quite different. Now I was reading my own words, whereas previously I'd been presenting Kraftwerk's themes.

Something had begun to take shape in me. In the future, an evening with Yamo could look something like this, once I was no longer being brushed under the carpet by the recording industry and I could present my own music and its absurd stories freely, perhaps as a kind of electronic wandering circus, full of dancing, acting, bewildering projections and misty veils, excerpts from old films and new stories in decorative guises. I'd actually become a kind of actor, slipping into roles, ambiguous once more, out on the stage again. These evenings would be vividly colourful, startlingly varied and full of surprises and laughter – just Yamo!

For now, though, I had become a teller of stories, a presenter and commentator for the first time, and I was happy to realise that people enjoyed listening to me. My ex-girlfriend said as much, after the show: "What an entertaining evening, Wolfgang! You've become very wise." Wow! That really moved me!

My dear nephew Dominick was also there, and afterwards he also praised me: "Wolfgang, I was really proud of you tonight. But why didn't you pass one of those lovely women onto me after the book signing? You could have thought of me, you old egoist!"

I smiled and replied, "You have to do that yourself. You're old enough now, and good-looking enough too." And I was proud of him. He really enjoyed visiting me, and I'd taken to him long ago.

After the event I was tired and hungry, but I still found time to be interviewed by Manuel Unger. In fact, this went so well that we promised to meet again for more private "word play".

DÜSSELDORF, 14 DECEMBER 1999
Contributions and programmes about my book were growing,
coming now from a wide range of radio stations, including WDR
1-Life, WDR 5, Bayerischer Rundfunk and the cultural station
Deutschlandradio. In these programmes, journalists, producers
and fans alike learned about my music for the first time. Meanwhile,
there were many reports in the media about Kraftwerk's hostility
to my biography and analyses of what it meant. I must confess
that I found this encouraging, because the content of almost all of
the reports tended to indicate that the media were quite aware of
what was going on and that they supported my view. The WDR
writer Thomas Ebern even judged that some anecdotes from my
book would be suitable for a film that would fill an evening.

Of course, this idea appealed to me a great deal, and I began to
think of how I could actually approach the film industry and find
a scriptwriter. I thought that the film could start with my dream up
there in the electro-convalescent home in the Tyrol and then, after
a fade-out, cut back to my small workshop in the Berger Allee
in order to cover the later development of the "electric quartet".
We could find good doubles for the way we looked at that age in
England, where it would be a lot easier to interest a producer than
in Germany.

Astonishingly, Maximilian Schoenherr of Deutschlandradio
predicted that Kraftwerk wouldn't have got their Expo commission
at all if my book had been published earlier, which irritated me,
I must confess. You see, we'd been unable to take the release of a
new Kraftwerk single – for Expo 2000, of all things – into account
when my book was published. (Incidentally, I found the easy-going
radio version completely typical of the band.) I knew nothing
about the service contract that they'd signed, but this wouldn't
have been jeopardised by the media attention surrounding my
book because reporters now had something with which to gain a
better insight into their years of silence. Also, whenever my book
was discussed, they played the Kraftwerk jingle. Many asked
themselves why Ralf and Florian were fighting it so ardently,

and wondered what this implied. The journalists couldn't find anything injurious or commercially damaging in my accounts. I imagine that my former colleagues were probably put out that it was generally so well accepted! But there are so many things that they don't like these days.

OBERHAUSEN, 14 DECEMBER 1999

The *Neue Rhein Zeitung* (*NRZ*) published a review of my presentation in the Druckluft Arts Centre in Oberhausen under the title "Of Man Machines And Robots With Soul: Ex-Kraftwerker Reads At *Textverarbeitung*".

The article went on: "For a long time, Wolfgang Flür was the drummer of Kraftwerk, one of the most innovative and forward-looking bands in recent German musical history. On Saturday evening, in the context of the *Textverarbeitung* in the Druckluft Arts Centre, Flür read from his autobiographical tale *Kraftwerk: Ich War Ein Roboter*, which was published in the summer, while he also talked about the first years and the development of Kraftwerk in a personal retrospective.

"The band had always consisted of musicians who were flesh and blood but who were far removed from all human emotions. The electronic pioneers produced the consistent music of machines, to the extent that they employed robots to represent them onstage. This was the furthest extreme of the calculated image that they cultivated in public.

"In his presentation, and with the anecdotes that he wove into it, Flür gave the robots thoroughly human characteristics without putting the uniqueness of the project or its members into question. The description of Flür's first meeting with Kraftwerk's founder members, Ralf Hütter and Florian Schneider, in the Mata Hari Passage in Düsseldorf, and their legendary first TV appearance on *Aspekte* in 1973, were well worth hearing. Flür even illustrated the latter with clips of the original television recording.

"His description of wild partying and everyday touring experiences – which even includes a dance with Ian Dury and the

315

occupation of Julio Iglesias's dressing room – is also interesting. Again, none of this really damages the myth of Kraftwerk, although it does tend to perpetuate the clichéd ideas of a musician's wild existence. The only thing that's new is the realisation that this was even true of such users of electronic instruments.

"During his reading, Flür stood on the tiny stage of the Druckluft with a worldfamous relic: the neon letters of his first name, such as all members of Kraftwerk positioned next to them at live performances, a memento, along with many supereight recordings and oxidised aluminium drumsticks. With these, he played his electronic percussion, which he had built himself, the first drumpad in musical history. However, Ralf Hütter and Florian Schneider had the bround-breaking invention patented and earned a lot of money with it, just as they did from the band, Flür was pushed into the role of being almost a session musician. On the other hand, he finds a tenor that stretches through the whole biography and the evening in Yamo, his new musical project.

"On the whole, he left a slightly bitter impression. Was this because of the temporary injunction served on him by Hütter and Schneider and the ban on his book, and the human disappointment associated with it? Hardly. The first was preprogrammed in typical Kraftwerk fashion, and the second was an everyday occurrence with life in a band, in which he was already rendered superfluous, in any case, by the eventual introduction of the sequencer. Finally, the question remains whether Flür was entitled to take on his former comrades-in-arms, or whether he has done so out of wounded vanity. The answer probably lies somewhere in between."

# 52 *Spies Among Us!*

I was right again. There was no reply from Ralf and Florian. As always. Why did I still bother writing to them? Instead, I received another letter from their lawyer. She had got into the habit of sending all correspondence to me with normal postage and then additionally by registered post so that her protest had every chance of getting through. A third letter was also sent to Rüdiger Plegge, my lawyer and long-term adviser. This must have become really good business for her, all this constant correspondence and prohibition on Ralf and Florian's behalf. For me, she'd become a permanent part of Kraftwerk, and by now I knew her name, Hundt-Neumann, well.

I imagined that maybe she was really nice, and that I might enjoy meeting her one day. She always signed her sternest letters and, more importantly, her hefty invoices in a friendly way, always "kind regards". This most recent letter demanded payment of 2,000 DM for something that hadn't even been proved! "We expect the settlement of our above invoice by 24 January at the latest. Yours sincerely..."

That was in just ten days, and I had hardly any cash! I read through the letter again. This was just too much. She wrote that

317

she was in possession of a tape recording of my presentation in Oberhausen, which I'd given on 11 December at the Druckluft Arts Centre. I remembered that, for obvious reasons, I'd hung a notice warning that "tape and video recordings are forbidden". The notice was visible from every point in the room, but somebody there had ignored it and made secret recordings anyway, probably on Ralf and Florian's behalf. Now, Frau Hundt-Neumann was forbidding me to read out the personal letter from André, the Swiss fan who'd written to me earlier. In addition, she also forbade me to show the video of our early appearance on *Aspekte* in 1973, which I'd shown to the fans in Oberhausen, just as I had in all of the other towns in which I'd held presentations. It was the main visual attraction. People liked it, because earlier we still appeared so human. Earlier. Precisely.

Well, I thought, now they've run out of sensible arguments so I'm getting rather dubious legal orders like this. Now surely they would get to the point. It was clear, even to a layman like me, that no one could forbid me to read a letter addressed to me personally in public, even if a third person's opinion is expressed in it. This was precisely the point that was grating with Kraftwerk.

In fact, in his letter, André had written of his own personal idea of Kraftwerk, that "Kraftwerk definitely no longer exists now. For me, Kraftwerk was Ralf, Florian, Karl and Wolfgang." The letter expressed his own, deeply personal view of a now "faded" band, which he had once loved passionately and fervently, and he had to be permitted this view (which, incidentally, is a view shared by many other fans).

The lawyer implied that André's letter wasn't genuine, in that she wrote of the "alleged" correspondent in her communication. She simply assumed that I'd written it myself! If that had been the case, it would have been a great compliment to my creative abilities, and this amused me, I have to admit.

I still wanted to clarify the matter of the video of our 1973 performance on *Aspekte*. I even wrote to Dr Ferdinand, ZDF's chief lawyer, asking if I could use it. I couldn't imagine that they wouldn't let me show a four-minute clip in public, and I very much doubted that Ralf and Florian could have acquired the rights. Ultimately, ZDF is owned by the state, and we'd flown to Berlin on their invitation. They had paid for our hotel, our flight and our fee. Ralf and Florian hadn't forced them to allow us to appear. For this reason, they had to have exclusive rights to their own video material.

As I said, the clip is actually an extremely rare piece of footage. It shows the very first demonstration of the prototype of the drumpad board, and it also shows how unsure I was about playing the unfamiliar instrument at that time – proof, in my view, that it was new. In fact, there is no earlier record of it, as a photograph or in any other form. Crucially, the founders of Kraftwerk are claiming that they'd developed the instrument with Emil in the year before that broadcast. This must be the reason why it was so important to them that I didn't play the video before my fans.

Gradually, the whole thing had become farcical, and I decided that their lawyer could write to me as much as she liked. In the meantime, I'd also learnt how to write, and while Kraftwerk's lawyer hit me with more and more prohibitions, served by court officials "in the presence of a witness", she was supplying me with more and more material for the English edition of my book. In terms of free speech, Britain is much more liberal than my home country. Unfortunately, in Germany they muzzle you at the earliest opportunity. This is something that's just typically German, as is the following chapter.

# 53 The Issue Of Materials

I didn't want to believe what I heard on the radio. During the eleven
o'clock news, the newsreader said that the German government
was considering changing the Basic Law in the way that it regulates
the export of defence technology, and reported that it could no
longer be sanctioned to supply weapons to countries where there
were human rights issues at stake. I didn't like the use of the word
*supply*. It sounded like the legitimate distribution of tools through
the issue of materials in a factory. They were referring to Turkey,
which had been trying to enter the European Union for years but
had been continually denied access because human rights are still
being abused there. However, during the winter, our chancellor
had supplied them with German Leopard tanks on his own
initiative, independently and in the face of strong public protests.
Perhaps he wanted to test exactly how much human rights could
be abused with the most precise German machines, operated by
*mensch maschines* – by soldiers. By robots.

As a precaution, the Turkish government had already ordered
1,000 of them. What madness! The newsreader's words incensed
me: "Where human rights have been abused…" What was that
supposed to mean? The way I understand it, weapons of whatever

calibre are constructed and manufactured for the specific purpose of taking the most important human right of all: the unrestricted right to life.

I'm a committed humanist, and I break out in a rash if I think of weapons, even at the back of my mind, and I cried out in protest. Could it be that my country had forgotten again what it had done to the world 60 years ago, when it had applied its ingenious engineering skills in the production of "defence technology"? I've often wondered about this reassuring phrase, and more importantly about the lack of public criticism in the face of the arms trade. Meanwhile, the manufacture of ultimately lethal products is rationalised by concepts such as the preservation of employment or the retaining of industrial locations. I've been waiting for a penetrating exposé of this subject for a long time. Can weapons, of whatever type and size, be regarded as material suitable for trade at all? In my opinion, absolutely not. In recent times, Turkey has already attacked the small Kurdish state in the north of the country with "legally acquired" tanks and has devastated the population, taking their basic right to life and their own culture and bringing death in its place, and this was done with German "defence technology", a traditional technology, which the Rheinmetall company, for example, freely advertises on huge posters opposite my house:

DEVELOPING SELF-CONFIDENCE THROUGH RELIANCE IN QUALITY. RHEINMETALL DEFENCE TECHNOLOGY IS OUR BASE. GROWING WITH THE APPLICATION OF AUTOMOBILE TECHNOLOGY AND ELECTRONICS. THE WORLD MARKET IS OUR BUSINESS: A SYMBOL OF OUR COMMON INTEREST. THIS YEAR, 30,000 PEOPLE WILL ACHIEVE A TURNOVER OF NINE BILLION MARKS.

This poster advertises a "militarily historical" production site, where their administrative building, which was built in the '30s, has just been newly renovated and linked up to a glass-covered extension of the factory where they'd previously made tank turrets for the Nazis. Now, whenever I wait there for the tram, I have to look at the blatant implication of their stupid advert, and ever time I feel like I've been soiled by war.

The fact that they're "growing with the application of automobile technology and electronics" is only a diversion from their actual passion: defence technology. It's well known that they used to produce it with forced labour, which their customers had ripped away from countries that they had overrun and flattened with tanks produced by this very defence technology. The perversity of this apparently innocuous phrase has no limits. They're trying to make it sound positive and harmless for the simple citizen, to associate it with advanced technology.

Technology for defence. What do we Germans have to defend ourselves against? Wasn't it everyone else who had to defend themselves against us, against our ingenious "defence technology" and those who played at being tough guys with it? Or did I misunderstand my history lessons at school? "Brothers of the world, defend yourself against the attacks of your enemies" – that was the propaganda that was issued, but the only thing created by the distributing of weapons is a potential for aggression. Is this a symbol of our community interest? What's the message that Rheinmetall are trying to put across? Their only concern is the world market, not Turkey. The hypocritical message emblazoned on the company's poster supports this. Ultimately, they're only concerned about their nine billion marks, but there are so many others who also want a slice of the huge global market.

The duplicitous morality and the sickening contradiction shown on the eleven o'clock news was unbearable, and made me think again of moving away from here, and soon. Away from Germany, where things were becoming more and more strange; a country where my music was locked away because it tarnished the image of another, highly profitable product; a country where it was so easy to have the publication of my own memories banned by public courts; a country that was unashamed of its falseness and greed;

a humanitarian society that has accepted without embarrassment that its reputation abroad has been ruined by the public trade of weapons of war.

Recently, the repugnant corruption practised by almost all leading politicians – who are quite happy for themselves and their parties to be supported by arms dealers – has been getting more and more on my nerves. Of course, the chancellor – and, more importantly, the sale of weapons to foreign countries, which are soothingly justified by claims that we're actually supplying our allies – irritates me anyway. Moreover, I think that it's impossible to determine the government's intentions after the event. For example, what on Earth did the impoverished Turks want with 1,000 Leopard tanks, the most accurate in the world, so I'm told? The country has a permanent deficit, and the most devastated regions in the world of the last few years, and its government will never be able to provide enough money for reconstruction efforts. So how did this poor country plan to raise the obscene sum of money to buy the tanks in the first place?

Once again, Germany is coolly besmirching itself with guilt from committing war crimes and abusing human rights, albeit from a distance. As arms dealers, we're participating in a disgusting trade. In doing so, our country has committed a violation of human rights. Could no one see what a bad decision this was for our leadership? People are so blind. The chancellor has got into bed with any Tom, Dick or Harry with enough money to buy such material. My song 'Greed' is dedicated to people like him.

# 54 Pages Of Frost

DÜSSELDORF, 20 JANUARY 2000
I felt a chill when I recently read an interview with Ralf Hütter
by Oliver Creutz in the German weekly magazine *Stern*, in which
he said that he felt like a robot. I'd seen this development coming
for a long time, that Ralf would no longer be able to escape
from the same role that we all used to play. This admission was
long overdue. As I see it today, the subject of the man machine –
which he'd chosen himself – was just too broad. It had become
overpowering, and would no longer release him. The world of
the robots could no longer be contained. It was like Goethe's
sorcerer's apprentice: "Come here, you old brush. You've been a
slave for a long time!"

He and Florian still recorded material based around the theme
of the slave, the worker, the robot and the master, if they allowed
themselves time for it. They even lived it somehow. As Ralf says in
this interview, he doesn't feel like Ralf Hütter but as Ralf Kraftwerk,
and "I feel like I'm a robot!" Although he's expressing something
he thinks our fans want to hear, there's also a grain of truth. He
has already admitted to his own inflexibility in the past, and so
it would be difficult for him now to adopt a new, contemporary
vision after grappling with this complex knot of themes back in

the '80s. In fact, artists always embody what they have – or, more accurately, once had. If not, they would be implausible. Believe me, our fans are clever. They instantly recognise what's credible and what isn't. In our case, *The Man Machine* album once embodied the most wonderful idea of four people becoming involved with each other and creating something and feeling extremely at ease with each other. Now, I can't imagine that Kraftwerk will ever exceed the content of the original theme for the Man Machine. In as far back as 1975, the posters for our first US tour were already proclaiming "Kraftwerk: The Man Machine", and we had built on this concept until it became a matter of course.

When I'd first heard Kraftwerk playing, in the girls' gymnasium at Düsseldorf-Golzheim at the beginning of the '70s, they'd played the sound of Stukka air raids, which I and many other people had found frightening. In this interview, the reporter asked Ralf which song he thought would most frighten people these days. "Perhaps 'Computer Bombs'," Ralf replied. "Blanket bombing can be carried out by computers these days. The technique is the same as the one we use for making music."

I was disgusted by his cold, intellectual approach, and upset that he could make such a comparison. He could just as easily have given positive examples of the application of computer technology, such as graphics programs, household technology and digital communications. These are all humane applications of technology used by everyday people, as are computer-generated art and music. Ralf could even have answered that they didn't want to frighten people with their music, but had instead chosen to devote themselves to constructivist themes.

Instead, however, he chose 'Computer Bombs', even though he'd never formally announced that he wanted to write such a song. Or had he? Had he inadvertently betrayed what they were currently working on? It sent shivers down my spine, and I was glad that I didn't have to perform anything like that any more.

In the same interview, Ralf said something honest about himself. When the reporter asked him whether he was lonely in his work, he said, "It's good to be lonely." In fact, after my experiences with him, I can't imagine that Ralf has many friends these days, and I don't get the impression that he has that much fun with his old mate Florian any more. Reading between the lines of his interview, there's enough cold there to fill pages of frost, if I were to analyse all of the remarks and glaring details. I remember only too well how he replied when I asked him how Florian was doing the last time that we met for pancakes in the Rheinfähre in North Düsseldorf back in 1997...

I imagined him going to the Kling Klang Studio, apprehensive of meeting Florian, and there would be no one else there that he enjoyed meeting. How could such a situation foster happy music? And, if any music emerged at all, how would it sound? Perhaps like computer bombs? They haven't released anything since 'Expo 2000', but I get the feeling that something is going on there.

Ralf's Kafkaesque conversion into a computer-controlled leisure robot, a rhythmic unit with all the kinetic energy of the 24 gears supplied by his chrome bike, who finds inner peace in hearing the regular hum of the bike's serpentine chain, moved me deeply, and his admission somehow also reminded me of Allal, Paul Bowles's small snake boy. The snake boy lived lonely and alone outside the settlement. He had little contact with society, no real friends and no experience of genuine love. Then he fell so thoroughly for a poisonous snake that he allowed her to bite him, after which he became a poisonous viper himself. If Ralf is criticised these days, he bites those around him, however gentle the criticism.

# III

# The Cradle Of
# The Kraftwerk Sound

# 55 *The Wind Sang Me A Song*
## *Plank's Stone*

"Back... back... stop! I saw it! I don't believe it. I've found it!" I shouted to Markus. Once again it had proved necessary to travel an unusual route (by car this time) in the pursuit of a hidden goal: the cradle of the Kraftwerk sound.

On an unusually mild and dry February day in the new year, we'd started out from Düsseldorf in Markus's car at about 4.30pm and had driven south down the old A3, leaving the autobahn at the Lohmar/Troisdorf exit – still just in the Bergische Land, but almost in the Westerwald – and driving along Bundesstraße 484 towards Lohmar. Just after this spot, we turned right onto the 507 and reached Neunkirchen a few minutes later. I'd already been to Conny Plank's studio with Ralf and Florian once before, back in 1974, when we'd been making the recordings for 'Autobahn', the song that had made Kraftwerk world famous overnight.

A few days earlier, I'd heard a new single by Nina Hagen, 'Der Wind Hat Mir Ein Lied Erzählt' ('The Wind Sang Me A Song'), which the DJ said had been recorded and mixed in the late cult producer's studio. Originally sung by Zarah Leander, it's a very beautiful song, and Nina's new version of it sounded fantastic. It inspired me to look for the legendary studio's phone number in

328

my business address book and phone the people currently there, who had created it.

Again, it was no coincidence that I got straight through to the sound workshop. I was looking for a studio myself where I could mix my own songs, which I'd just recorded with the ATA TAK label's Kurt Pyrolator Dahlke in Düsseldorf. During the radio broadcast, an exciting idea had been planted in my head: to attempt something similar with other mixes in the same studio that we'd worked in so many years ago, when Conny had first developed the famous Kraftwerk sound.

Calling the studio so that they could remind me of the route, I was put through immediately to Christa Fast, Conny's widow. We agreed to meet that evening, and I was really looking forward to seeing her again. I had little confidence that I'd still be able to remember the location, as I'd only been to the studio twice, and I'd been very new to Kraftwerk then. Even so, I remembered something unforgettably picturesque.

I had a vague recollection of a farmhouse lying on high ground on a village street in a rural area. As we drove past the scattered rows of houses in the tidy village, the image that had been lurking at the back of my mind suddenly returned to me. It just popped up. I'd seen it pass by me, but only for a fraction of a second, and yet this was enough to prompt Markus to brake immediately. He turned the car around in the road and we drove back four houses. Yes, that was it! I recognised it exactly. This had to be it. Apart from the reddish-brown framed walls, I recognised the now-plastered and steeply rising entrance to the inner courtyard behind the housing complex on the Hennefer Straße. And there – number 19. I was amazed that I could remember it so clearly after 26 years!

As Markus parked in the inner courtyard, a large stone immediately caught my eye, an enormous rock from the Rhine set into the corner of the house. In 1974, there had been heaps of stones in the same place, ready to be built into the property, which was still under construction at that time, and I'd enjoyed sitting on them and basking in the sun while Conny worked on our songs.

I had a charming image of myself in my mind: a young man with long, straight hair sitting on stones, watching the sun and leaning on the house wall. It's a lovely picture, isn't it? Great for a kitsch postcard! But that picture had been reality at that time. I'd felt at home there and dreamed. That spot with the stone stimulated my memory, and a whole gamut of feelings then opened up, as if I'd been there only yesterday. I could even smell the sourness of the plastic seats in Ralf's Volkswagen, in which we'd travelled there, and I remembered the relaxed and friendly atmosphere of the place.

We entered through one of the many doors that led from the inner courtyard, and stood in the Plank family's comfortable kitchen-cum-living room. Christa Fast, a warm-hearted woman of my own generation and the long-term life partner of the former producer, received us warmly. She invited us to sit on a comfortable corner seat next to the six-ringed gas stove, which was surrounded with cooking equipment hanging from the ceiling and resting on racks, arranged according to size and purpose. There was green tea and a big bowl of the most delicious oriental crackers.

After watching Christa's face for a few seconds, I knew that she'd experienced a lot in her life. She seemed clear, clever, emotional and serious all at once. I'd also experienced my fair share, so we must have had a lot in common. I told her a little about my new Yamo project, and asked about the time when we recorded *Autobahn*. I wanted to know more about her husband's meeting with Ralf and Florian, because I'd only been there twice, back in 1974. I wanted to know why we hadn't spent more time recording and mixing there later, especially since it was so comfortable there.

"At that time it wasn't at all comfortable for Plank with either of them," said Christa, beginning to relay another facet of Kraftwerk's development. This was a story that I hardly knew, because Ralf and Florian had never talked about it, and yet it was the crucial developmental phase that would later lead to what became the Kraftwerk sound – pure electronic pop, discerned and encouraged at an early stage by Plank's visionary talents, back when the band had still been called Organisation.

Christa enjoyed talking about her husband, who had died in 1987. "Plank came from K-Town, which is what the American GIs called Kaiserslautern in the '50s and '60s. The high standards of the stars of American jazz and rock 'n' roll shaped Conny's instinct for music from his very youth, as these 'musical gods' were flown in directly from America to perform for the boys of the American army in K-Town. At the time, I was studying English and French at the University of the Saarland, where I met Conny in 1966, who was working at Saarländische Rundfunk as a sound technician. That was just before I disappeared for three years to the drama department of the Folkwang Schule to study and train to be an actress. Kraftwerk met my husband in the late '60s, while he was working as a freelance sound engineer in Cologne, Munich, Hamburg and Berlin. He worked with them on their music during this period, more or less from the beginning. They hired various studios – also in the Cologne area – on a daily or nightly basis."

Conny had realised at the same time as Ralf and Florian that, through their mutual love of electronic music, he could build up an independent German image for the two young musicians, independent of the influence of the omnipresent American music. In any case, Conny always said that Americans do their own music best.

"Why did you build your studio here?" I asked Christa.

"Well," she began thoughtfully, "the media gradually began to talk about Kraftwerk, and Conny wanted peace from constant visits from journalists, so he set up his sound studio out of the way here in the old farmhouse. It was a pretty precarious situation at that time, however," she recalled. "All of a sudden, Conny came across a great obstacle. During the production of *Autobahn*, Plank relied on old verbal agreements with your two friends. Then, we suddenly found ourselves having to make additional credit arrangements with the bank, and to begin with we had to

331

tell them what a sound studio was. We couldn't speak of securities that we didn't have."

At that point, I was about to say that they weren't my friends any longer, and that they were taking me to court, when her son – a strong young man with red hair and alert eyes – came into the kitchen, and Christa introduced us. "This is Stephan, Plank's son. He's been managing Conny's studio for two years now. He actually wants to become a producer. He also has his own publishing company, and he produces young groups."

"I see. Is he also your son, then?"

"Of course," she said, laughing. "What do you think?"

It was immediately obvious that Christa was very proud of her son. I was glad to see the pair of them looking so good together. Stephan sat down with us for a while and asked his mother for a cup of tea.

While Christa filled our cups, I asked them if I could record our conversation with Markus's MiniDisc recorder, just so that I'd be able to remember details of her account afterwards. I immediately got the feeling that I'd be hearing something important, something that the music world didn't already know. I asked her what sort of agreements had brought her and her husband into difficulties at that time while I stuffed several giant crackers into my mouth.

Christa took a deep breath. "Oh, Wolfgang, you weren't here often. Konrad had his mobile equipment as well, and he was often with you in Düsseldorf. You know how things were then. Everything that's now signed in stone with comprehensive written contracts and expensive lawyers was at that time sealed with a handshake. Conny relied heavily on his contribution to *Autobahn* as a producer, just as he had in the case of the first three albums. We built on it, and got a lot of money from the bank to improve the studio. After the work was done, though, Ralf and Florian didn't want to acknowledge their agreement fitting the facts. They didn't even credit Plank as their producer on the record. When he had served his purpose, he was simply discarded."

I had to know more about the circumstances at that time,

because I was gradually piecing together an image of Ralf and Florian's personalities, stone by stone, like a mosaic.

Then Markus interrupted us and pointed out that the batteries in his MiniDisc recorder had run out. He asked whether Stephan and Christa had a couple more lying around. Stephan left the kitchen with his mother, and Christa returned quickly and gave Markus two fresh batteries. I put the microphone back in front of her and asked, "Did you know that now they're not even printing mine and Karl's names on the new pressings of the CDs? And that there's not even a hint that the recording was made in Conny's studio."

"Oh, Wolfgang," she sighed. "What did you expect? I've always marvelled at the effort they put into adopting 'smart' poses. They seemed to me like exhibits in a Kienholz exhibition, with poses copied from Warhol. I always felt that they were copies, not originals. The paralysis due to the discreet charm of the bourgeoisie always seemed to me to be the essential ingredient of their aura. Apart from this, at that timein some artistic circles it was fashionable to present oneself as a work of art, like advertising. Kraftwerk were essentially German, which is to say continental European, but their intellectual attitude, their image, their affected, blasé behaviour had been adopted from a trend that had swept over from America.

"Of course, this was justified in a way, because a band needs to adopt a sensational image and produce sensational music, and it's important for them to be taken seriously, not just by the audience but also, more importantly, by the media. Kraftwerk were masters at this. They've followed a direct path, from the image they invented for themselves to the building of the robots. The visual design was wonderfully appropriate for the time, and they were years ahead of their time. Remarkable. The way they always spoke softly was also part of their image, too, which was a particular problem on the telephone. They were works of art themselves, and they felt that it was an imposition to have to speak to 'ordinary people'. It always seemed to me as if they were practising the way they appeared to the media on the people that they had to work with every day.

"I always found it silly. For example, Brian Eno was completely different. He was capable of behaving quite normally in private with Conny, Möbius, Rodelius and Devo when he was working here in the studio, and yet he instantly became the cult figure as soon as a journalist turned up. It was fascinating, witnessing the switch. For him, it was part of his job to play this game, but his personality remained unaffected, uncontaminated by the image that he presented to the media world. I remember a session with Ralf, Florian and Conny in a studio in Cologne. This was before 1973, before Conny's studio existed. For a long time nothing happened. There was silence, absolute silence. Then Plank played a phrase on a synthesiser. Florian said, 'Do that again!' Conny repeated the phrase. Silence again. Then Florian said to Ralf, 'What do you think of that?' Ralf said, 'Hmmm... good!' Silence. Then Florian again: 'We'll take that.' No, I haven't forgotten this scene, Wolfgang, and there are others just like it."

Christa paused briefly to gather her thoughts, then continued. "Conny made his musical contributions, made offers, filtered and linked things together. Conny was very good at creating an atmosphere that gave the musicians free rein of their musicality, and they must have valued this quality or they wouldn't have worked with him for so long. But, as he told me years later, he's astonished that they've got stuck artistically, and that their music hasn't developed significantly."

"Didn't you have any contracts then?" I persisted.

"No, nothing significant. I think there are some contracts or other with the record company that were used at the time about the sharing of the production costs – in which Konrad also participated, to a certain extent – and licences. He actually worked on the first records 'at his own risk', but, as I said, that was the way it was then. Konrad despised everything that stood between free musical workers, as he always liked to describe himself, and the musicians more than anything. 1968 wasn't that long ago. He looked down on lawyers, contracts, and so on."

That gave me a start. There, that phrase *musical worker*, which Christa had said precisely in Conny's extended drawl, without knowing how much it gave me the creeps. I'd heard this description so often from Ralf in connection with the concept and the philosophy of Kraftwerk, our personal man machine. Ralf had continually used the phrase in interviews, spouting the words again and again to journalists. He'd even hijacked Conny's phrase *musical worker* (which I never liked personally, because I never felt that I was a worker), because it fitted so well with his own rubbish. And so it seemed that the ironic concept that had impressed Ralf so much had come from Conny Plank. I suddenly understood the group's pre-history, with all the misappropriations, adoptions and the fuss that surrounded them. (Ralf had previously played his Hammond B3 like a Farfisa organ, and we know that Florian played the flute and the violin a little.)

"Plank believed that you can't eat the cake until it's been taken out of the oven and everybody who helped make it has sat around the table and had a slice," Christa confirmed. "Other bands employed solutions that would have been worthy of Solomon. They would reach an agreement, even if things got a bit noisy, but an acceptable solution was nonetheless found for all participants. The concept of 'work in progress' didn't actually appear until later, when the creative contribution of the engineers became increasingly recognised, and when it became clear that songs were actually being created in the studio, particularly in the case of electronic music.

"Ralf and Florian, however, were in a quite different camp, and the veneer disappeared very suddenly. Today, people would say that it was foolishness, or that it defies description. Well, you learn when you have to. Plank never submitted to it, though; he never accepted it, and always despised things like that. There was a meeting, where the fundamental relationship between the musicians and him was agreed on, the work was done, and then the division, the sharing, was made after the work was finished.

"The fact is, Conny actually produced the sound of the first Kraftwerk records. He didn't just sit there and take orders to record and mix it; he produced it. He was something like the midwife of their sound. You what I mean, Wolfgang?"

"Of course I know what you mean," I affirmed. "I've just made an album myself, *Time Pie*, and Andy Thoma and Jan Werner played a huge part in being midwives for that. And both of them are listed in the credits as co-producers, too, just as they should be. Apart from that, I like talking with them about our experiences together during the recording sessions."

"Yes, that's the way it should be. But that's not the way it is with Ralf and Florian. They're hiding the creative help that Plank gave them in their early years. Without him, Kraftwerk would probably never have found their sound. Without Plank it would have been a different sound."

I also wanted to know more about the financial side of things, and I asked Christa how much Plank had received for *Autobahn*. "They paid him 5,000 DM for the use of the studio. Nothing else." She glanced sideways through her kitchen window to the distant Westerwald, which has already made a great contribution to contemporary history. She still seemed shaken. Then Stephan came back into the kitchen and silently joined us in the corner seat.

Christa's account upset me greatly. "That was a pretty much standard sum from them at that time," I said. "A while later, Karl and I were offered about the same amount for the month-long US tour. We hadn't made any contracts at that time, either, because we just trusted them implicitly."

"You were working for next to nothing," said Stephan.

I still wanted to defend myself, to say that 5,000 DM was actually worth more in 1974, but I remember that Karl and I had felt belittled when we were given the money in the hallway of our flat in the Berger Allee, shortly before the tour, after they had been teasing us for weeks with the idea of a wonderful trip to the USA. We accepted it out of necessity, because we wanted to go. In fact, thinking back, this wasn't a far cry from blackmail, although I kept this to myself, saying only, "You could be right there, as far as 'next to nothing' is concerned. You'd be amazed how long I carried on with it, naïve as I was. Now, it's embarrassing to tell anyone."

I asked Christa where her toilet was, and she showed me the way through the large hallway. When I walked through the doorway, I just stared. The lavatory was lined with gold. Gold records were everywhere, decorating every wall, reflected in the ceiling, which had gold foil stretched across it. I read only famous names there, artists that Conny Plank had produced and whose sound he had developed: Ultravox, Gianna Nannini, The Eurythmics, Ideal, Rita Mitsouko. There were also names of bands that had found success with other producers in Conny's studio after his death, Die Fantastischen Vier and Fury In The Slaughterhouse, who had even given the studio a gold record as an acknowledgement of their work there. There wasn't a gold record for *Autobahn*. A disgrace! A surge of humiliation made me feel weak. How could I show my face again to the wife of Conny Plank? Ultimately, I was an ex-Kraftwerker, and now I was responsible for the things that my former colleagues had neglected to do, or so I felt.

When Christa rang me up again a few days later, it was to read me a letter from her dead husband, the last one that he'd dictated to his lawyer, Alfred Schacht, on 7 February 1974. In it, he wrote: "I refuse in principle to work with these two men in the future if... formerly discussed agreements that have applied to previous productions, and have not been rescinded during this production, should suddenly fail to be observed after the production has been finished."

On the original cover of *Autobahn*, Ralf and Florian had demoted Conny to the role of engineer, and had only printed the words "Recorded In Conny's Studio And Mobile Equipment" instead of acknowledging that he had co-produced the record.

There is a tremendous difference between the two. His role was properly credited on the first three records, but on Kraftwerk's most successful releases they didn't give their mentor the status he deserved. That suited them; they were unable to be generous. They never give sufficient recognition to the achievements of others. In fact, they obscure them totally, just as they've done by dropping mine and Karl's names from their material.

There are actually many people who have helped them to achieve something special, and without whose huge contributions Kraftwerk would never have become as big as they were. This is exactly what I meant when I spoke of their lack of social skills and empathy at the beginning of this book, their inability to praise others for their performance or work, even if only occasionally. Their parents hadn't taught them anything like that.

To me, the fact that they hadn't even paid their producer properly was the culmination of their meanness. I mean, 5,000 DM for a world-wide hit. It's grotesque! Immoral. Any decent person would come back after such great success, even if there had been no profit-sharing agreement, and would have rewarded the ingenious sound man for his contribution to their success.

Ralf once told me that Plank had received a share in the profits of the recording. I'd been at his place with the others twice, and had met him when he was working on our material. I had asked Ralf what Conny received for his valuable contribution to our work. "A share," he had replied. After all, Conny was their producer, or at least co-producer. So perhaps they actually had wanted to give him something and only decided differently later. I remember how I felt when I told myself then that there was no such thing as profit-sharing for musicians. I actually believed that there was only such a thing for producers and for those who held the recording contract, and that this was written in stone. My own contribution to the recording is again part of the injunction which Ralf and Florian have served against me.

"What other German groups was Conny producing at the same time?" I asked Christa.

"Neu!, La Düsseldorf, Cluster, Möbius, Rodelius, Harmonia, DAF, IDEAL, Rheingold, Michael Rother and Arno Steffen, among others – many of the more interesting bands in the new German pop music élite."

"So things turned out well for you in the end?"

"*Toujours flottant, pas submergeant*," she answered, smiling sweetly. Then, because my French is not good, she explained, "That means we're keeping our heads above water, basically. Yes, we managed. Yes, we survived. You can't make a fantastic living from a studio, or at least not from the philosophy that Plank had and that we still practise here. Today, people call it the human touch. But you can live in a studio if it's in such a beautiful location.

"We have to buy new equipment all the time, of course, and it becomes obsolete quickly. Plank had one of the first Emulator samplers in Europe, for instance, which cost him 20,000 DM then. Now that technology has been completely superseded, and the device has value only as a collector's item. It's not even vintage equipment now. He also had one of the first MCI automated mixing consoles on the continent. Of course, this is completely out of date, replaced by new technology. We've just bought a new 24-track Radar machine so that we can still link up our analogue machines with the digital standard. Of course, we couldn't have done this without Peter Lang, our engineer, who used to work with Conny. He's very committed and very ingenious, and without him it would have been impossible to maintain Plank Studios' profile after Conny's death and to continue to install the most up-to-date technology. It's a good team, and it's still fun because of that."

So now I saw why we never drove to Neunkirchen to record. Ralf and Florian had earned so much money with *Autobahn* that they could afford to build their own studio, the Kling Klang Studio, with equipment supplied and installed by the Hamburg company Barth in the following year. Ralf and Florian had obviously been closely examining Plank's studio for years, learning from it, but I can't condemn them for that. Now they were able to make their own recordings, completely undisturbed by the outside world.

Later, even really highly paid mixers, such as François Kervorkian, were flown in from America, at great expense. Money was apparently no object. But they never again named Conny Plank, to whom they owed so much, and in so doing they conceal the cradle of their sound. In their place, I would have been proud to have worked with a man like him, and I would have enjoyed talking about it in interviews.

There may well be something inspired in Ralf and Florian – I don't want to dispute that – but for me no one is great until they've achieved personal greatness as well. Only when they've achieved this will I admire them. Genius and talent have never counted with me.

It had grown late, and I really wanted to go over to the studio to talk to the sound engineer. He was the guy who had recently mixed Nina Hagen's song, and I thought I'd introduce myself, seeing as I was there. Christa and I walked across the courtyard together and knocked on the studio door. The three men inside welcomed us warmly. Christa introduced Ingo Krauss. "This is the man you want to speak to. He makes the sounds here now." Ingo shook my hand and I told him that I thought Nina Hagen's single was great. I also told him that I was looking for a mixing studio. "What have you done recently? Do you have anything you could play me?"

"Yes, I've got a few things. It's best if I play them for you. Just sit down on the control seat. There's the volume control, if you want to change it." Ingo took a CD out and put it in the player in the rack next to me, and I heard new tracks from Melotronic, Terra Nova, Fetisch and Thomas-D, one after the other. Ingo's mixes sounded great – I really liked the outstanding panorama effects and the tasteful sound he'd achieved. I gazed reverently at Conny's console, which he'd had custommade by engineers Michael Zähl and Peter Lang to his own personal requirements. All of the channels were lined with high-quality wood veneer. I'd only ever seen anything like it once before, in Bodo Staiger's Rheinklang Studio. Mike Otte was the ingenious carpenter of the team at that time. Even so, that console was slightly smaller, and Bodo had told me at the time that it had once been part of Conny's mobile equipment, and that he'd bought it from the master. Everything fitted together so well, and I was convinced that the wind had actually sung me a song, telling me exactly why I'd travelled precisely here. No, why I was guided here, by fate and by Markus – there are no coincidences. I feel that they are both linked to me, because they've both stood beside me.

In July 2000, work began on the mix of one of my new songs, 'On The Beam', once again with engineers Ingo Krauss and Stefan Lindlahr, from Conny's studio. That was a great experience. Those days in Neunkirchen did me the world of good, and the mix couldn't have turned out better. Instead of a cumbersome two-track tape machine we were now using the fantastic OTARI-Radar hard-disk recording system and the new Roland VF-9000 Variphrase voice processor, which Stefan Lindlahr – who occasionally writes reviews of new recording equipment for the German paper *Keys* – had already tried out. The gear was perfect for creating the sugary-sweet sound of the female choir – quite an exciting idea.

"Kraftwerk meets The Andrews Sisters," said Christa, smiling as she listened to the mix in the studio one evening. What a combination! But it was excellent for my warm style of electro pop and the ironic humour of Yamo. We were all enthralled, as were the others when they heard the finished version.

The days we spent recording in Neunkirchen, surrounded by good company and good food, really spoiled us. There was even the occasional refreshing shower of rain, which reminded me of my time in Bombay during the monsoon season. The most violent summer thunder storms raged over the farm. Sometimes, for safety's sake, we had to switch off all of the equipment and wait until the storm was over in order to avoid power surges and getting electric shocks. So much energy hung over the farm – it penetrated our very minds. Not that I enjoyed such incidents!

Once again, it was the 'Guiding Ray' that showed us the way.

I found my new address, and we resolved to work together more often in the future. However, this happened much sooner than I had expected, on 28 August.

# 56 Sweet Encounter

## Far East Meets Near West – Pizzicato Five And Yamo

NEUNKIRCHEN, 28 AUGUST 2000

I met Pizzicato Five (which actually comprised only two people) in Tokyo in 1997. On their European tour, they played quite near me in Cologne and Düsseldorf. (There's no such thing as coincidence.) For some time, I'd had the idea of translating my song 'On The Beam' into Japanese and having it sung by an Asian singer, as the start of the song features a teaser from a piece by composer Hiroaki Ide. We got the idea from Tokyo's central subway station, Shinjuku, where I heard the melody every day when I took the train to the offices of Pop Boz, my record company. I'd been living very comfortably in a lovely part of Sedagaya with Sadato, the head of my label, while promoting *Time Pie* and travelling to and from the record company's offices for interviews.

This short melody had inspired something in me, the whole Asian feel, which seemed to me so companionable, positive and lovely, but I had no idea then that I'd end up using it so effectively. But now I began to have an idea which could incorporate this positive vibe. I see with my feeling hand...

I had the wild idea to play 'On The Beam' to Nomiya Maki from P5, and to suggest that she should sing the song in Japanese.

My manager approached her manager, who promptly agreed. Yes, Ms Maki was interested.

I attended the Pop Komm music fair, held at the Prime Club in Cologne, with the singer Sam Leigh Brown and engineers Ingo Krauss and Stephan Lindlahr. The band were performing there, and were greeted enthusiastically by their German fans. A few days later, they had a similar reception in Düsseldorf. While they were in town, my manager arranged the deal.

We arranged to meet on 28 August. When we picked up the singer and her manager from their hotel, the genuine warmth with which they both greeted us completely won me over. I was using the shopping bag that the band had given me in Tokyo back in 1997 to carry around my studio things. Ms Maki and her manager remembered it and were amazed to see it in such good condition. "Yes, but that's Japanese quality for you," I said. "I even use it for my daily supermarket shop."

Ms Maki was charming. Her clothing was international and stylish, and the elegance of her shoes was a revelation! She knew the startling effect that could be obtained by combining international chic with Asian charm, and I think that we were all affected by her gentle, unassuming manner during those few days at Conny Plank's place in the sunlit mountainous countryside.

Professional as Maki is, we finished the takes in three or four hours, and she had even personally translated the English text into Japanese, which proved to me how much she liked my song. She seemed so delicate, and yet she had an energy that belied her outward appearance. And I thought she looked fantastic – divine! She was a delight to the eyes and ears, and had a voice that was as beautiful as a lotus blossom opening. To me, she was a perfect distillation of the chic of Audrey Hepburn and the irresistible charm of Mereille d'Arc, international and quite unique. I can see what her fans see in her – she's a star, with some indefinable quality that can move an admirer into a kind of erotic trance. Such modest beauty, coupled with suggestive charm, is seldom seen in an entertainer. I was in heaven. As Maki sang the first three or four lines into her microphone, I said to her manager, "I knew it! I knew it! I was sure that her voice would suit my song." Ms Makiko was of the same opinion, overjoyed with her artist as we looked on and listened.

Afterwards, Christa Fast treated us all – including the numerous journalists and photographers, whom my manager had invited – to a delicate Italian lunch that she cooked herself. We all set off for Düsseldorf, leaving the two engineers with the complicated task of mixing Maki's singing onto the backing track of my song and finishing the final mix.

After the meal, we arranged to meet up again in the middle of October in Tokyo, her beloved home town. I now saw Yamo as a transmitter between worlds – Far East meets Near West – with emotional ties between people transcending geographical distance, something that was impossible with Kraftwerk. Today, I'm happy to be free to go on such journeys.

I've written this book as a passionate retrospective view of my artistic past. Writing doesn't always come easily to me; my memory is sometimes too full. The excellent time that I had with Kraftwerk was one of the most important stages of my life-long search for pleasure and sound. To find melodies and stories, and to arrange songs which are often extraordinary – that's what I enjoy, my desire. I have a lot to thank Kraftwerk for, in furthering my artistic development. The band was far and away my most important mentor. In terms of human traits, however, I think that its founder members need training. I can't warm to either of them now, and I even feel sorry for them. What I've heard about them, and what I can still sense, leaves me cold. I much prefer to write about the people that I've worked with since leaving Kraftwerk (see Chapter 41), about real people, artists and friends – Karl, for example – who have stuck by me and have given me the courage to do my own thing.

It was only because Ralf and Florian chased me into the courts and consequently set their legal snowball rolling that I had to search for witnesses to defend myself. The more witnesses I found,

345

and the more we scratched at the surface of the things that we had in common, the more I learned about Ralf and Florian. They began this cycle of persecution. My book should have been an account of my personal artistic discovery, and as such should have stood as a tribute to Kraftwerk, but they never understood this.

When I stood on Plank's stone once again, 26 years on, I swore that I would do everything I could to make sure that my music was never locked away again, and that I wouldn't allow Kraftwerk to silence me. With what I've learned and experienced, I can no longer support them. It pains me to see how the passion I have for the group in the early chapters ebbs away as the story unfolds, and how my account eventually picks away at the group's very ethos, which we all shared and to which I subscribed, as their drummer. It really does hurt, believe me. But to gloss over something artistic would be dishonest; it would be "not my style", as Christa so succinctly puts it.

My rejection of what Kraftwerk has become is the direct result of the behaviour of two artists who became too robotic. I'd much rather remember them with the energy and enthusiasm of the early years. Although the end of my Kraftwerk days sadly came sooner than I might have liked, it was also very important for me to try something new. I've always known instinctively when to let go, but because I helped create what Kraftwerk became I'm proud to have spent a few exciting years as a member of such an innovative band, to have contributed something to the greatest electro pop group in the world. I simply wish that the music of today's Kraftwerk still surprised people.

If I'd stayed in the group, things would have ended even worse for me. I would have gone down in the history of electronic music as being a world champion in waiting, as a talented participant. I would never have been appreciated in my own right, and I would never have baked my "Rhineland specialities". I would have had no self-respect if I hadn't at least tried. I'm very glad that I restrained myself artistically during my years with Kraftwerk – now I have a wealth of ideas and melodies at my disposal for

Yamo. I can understand how some people are surprised – my friend Michael, for instance, who put it so bluntly in his letter: "Suddenly this album appears – Mr Flür is not only credited with the composition of each title but also in the production. Astonishing! I have honestly enjoyed [*Time Pie*] more than *The Mix*. But how did it come about?"

I also learned during my admittedly long training with Kraftwerk exactly what Ralf and Florian saw in Konrad Plank's vision as a producer. As the Japanese reporter Yasumichi Noma rightly noted in a review of my debut in Tokyo's *Music* magazine, "It's good that you have quit your robot duty, isn't it, Wolfgang?" I can only agree. I was simply no longer in tune with their cold themes. But when one beloved thing turns cold, new hope and new passion usually emerge. For me, that passion is Yamo.

# 56  *Current View*

The evening of the 11th of November in the Jurys Inn Hotel in Birmingham was not a good one to begin with. I was getting ready for an appearance at The Flapper club that night, but the colour of my hair was not right. At the age of 69, I need a bit of black colour at the temples from time to time. I am vain! The English colour didn't suit me; it didn't go with the original and I was annoyed that I had left my German product at home. I jumped in the shower and washed it all out. At least I have hair on my head.

Afterwards we cruised with our host through the Brindleyplace quarter. A district burred with the narrow, navigable waterways of the Birmingham Canal, these days it is a bistro/club/shopping/tourist spot. It was here, in industrial times, that iron was "cooked" into steel. Birmingham had prospered and many citizens of foreign nationality had gained a foothold. The city had become international: Brummies, Kashmiris, Rastafari, Pakistanis, Indians, the English – all lived happily here with one another. Heavy metal had originated here – not in the USA, as I had wrongly assumed, but it was invented here by the youth of this city, whose fathers had struggled daily at noisy furnaces filled with bubbling iron. The noise made by the industry was rackety, it sounded warlike. (One of the first and most renowned groups in this musical genre was Black Sabbath, who formed in Aston within the city.) Our "cooking" district back home is the Ruhr area – similarly long gone. My friend Peter Duggal, a composer and music producer with Indian parents, was born in Birmingham. At the moment I am working with him on a song about the city, which includes the line "Cooking iron into steel, sounds like battle, this is the birth of heavy metal". It is composed in the style of electro – danceable electro, that is the plan, not like the sound of a heavy metal song – so that it will later be suitable for my shows.

My "*Musiksoldat*" ("musical soldier") programme, which I was to perform that night and the following had been advertised on social media for months and was therefore sold out. As a result, I was looking forward to a good show, which it turned out to be. An assembly of dancers, fans, music lovers and drunks was present. The Flapper is small, refined, steeped in tradition and situated only five minutes on foot from the Symphony Hall, where my former group Kraftwerk (mark III) would be appearing in July 2017.

The next day, a Saturday, I was invited to give a reading from my book at the Seventh Wave Festival at the Midland Institute. When I arrived at about 11am, I entered a hall filled with interested citizens, journalists and music colleagues. I met Andy McCluskey from OMD; Mark Fordyce, formerly of The Mood; Rüdiger Esch from Die Krupps, as well as both the creators of *Electronic Sound* magazine, Mark and Push, plus Richard Barbieri from Japan and Rusty Egan, formerly of Visage. It really was a very strange feeling to be standing at the centre of a hall, in an auditorium with balconies ascending high up above me like those of a lecture theatre at a university, presenting the chapter "America Endless: Too Fast On Broadway" from my autobiography and subsequently answering audience questions on it. I nervously asked myself: "What has happened to you, to be standing here today?" Hadn't I just wanted to do a bit of drumming? My extraordinary story is written down in this book – a book that has became so successful that, after its German publication, it was translated into seven different languages, including Japanese.

The latest news: my story is to be filmed as well! A German film production recently secured the rights and the film is on its way to the Berlinale 2017, where they are hoping to find a suitable director. Wim Wenders is the favoured choice; he comes from Düsseldorf, after all. Let's see if that works out. Four young actors, who are supposed to look like we did then, are to be selected in casting sessions. It would be best, of course, if they were musical and played instruments too. I can immediately think of a candidate who could represent Florian: Lucas Croon. Lucas is a member of the Düsseldorf group Stabil Elite and has a lot in common with Florian. He is similarly talented and likewise droll in his manner of dressing and with his ideas on the synthesiser. To my mind, Lucas is the only one who, with his band and talent, could continue the tradition of the "Düsseldorf school" of music for the synthesiser in this day and age. He would be a phenomenon in the film – if he wanted to be...

My reading that day went very well. My English is not perfect, but people seemed to like my German accent and they often laughed. After that, I went for lunch and prepared for the second evening of my versatile performance with the sound-and-video check, which had to be done in the evening and was followed by a wait in my hotel until just before 1am. This is always the worst for me – waiting for long hours in the hotel. I often fall asleep and have to set an alarm so as not to oversleep and miss the pick-up service for the event. But my partner is usually there and makes sure that we arrive at the backstage entrance on time, especially since she wants to film everything right from the beginning. We often arrive to find a gathering of fans waiting there, wanting to have various things signed or to have selfies taken with me.

13 NOVEMBER 2016

"Are you going to your ex-colleagues' concert when the Tour de France starts in Düsseldorf?" a fan asked me while I was signing books in the Directors' room at Manchester's Principal Hotel (formerly the offices of Refuge Assurance, an insurance company). I had been supporting Rüdiger Esch at the presentation of his book *ELECTRI_CITY: The Düsseldorf School of Electronic Music*, which included a public discussion and an interview about the phenomenon of electro music from Düsseldorf. What could I say to the fan? I hadn't planned anything of the sort – indeed, had only just heard that Kraftwerk mark III was going to play an open-air concert at the Ehrenhof in Düsseldorf at the beginning of July 2017, with the group Air as support.

I replied, "I saw the lads in February 2013 in Düsseldorf in the K20 museum. I don't expect any novelties in July. But their 3D projections were fabulous!"

The young man told me that he had read my report on the subject in the online magazine *The Quietus* and that he was of the same opinion. I asked him what he meant by that. He explained that, in his opinion, there was only one Kraftwerk, namely Ralf, Florian, Wolfgang and Karl. Everything else that emerged later was only a surrogate product. I didn't say anything in reply; I had already said more than enough about it. I present my most recent report on the subject at the end of this chapter.

Another fan asked me how my performance in Birmingham the day before had gone, noting that unfortunately he hadn't been able to come because he had been caring for his mother. I declared that it had been a successful evening, that I enjoyed being in Birmingham and that my presentations in the UK were always very special – as they were also, incidentally, in Ireland and the rest of Europe. The programme had even been hugely successful in Mexico, Japan and the USA. It still gives me pleasure to be onstage and to play music. Like I said, 69 years old, dyed hair...

An Italian friend and DJ had tried some years ago to lure me into coming to Berlin to DJ electro music at the 103 Club. At first I had refused because I was not a DJ and did not have the ability to become one. At least, that was how I explained my refusal to him at the time. Since then, though, I have become quite good at it and have developed my own style, using ever more elaborate video recordings on the screen behind me; "the power of imagery", a visitor once remarked afterwards, the visuals making it impossible to take one's eyes off the screen. And the tracks, particularly the quite tough, industrial songs, are also great. The crowd gets positively intoxicated and doesn't want to let me stop at the end of the show. I like hearing comments like these; they spur me on to even greater improvement.

Recently I gave a private show for a man in London. He is a banker; his wife, a classy Sicilian, wanted to give her husband, a native German, my show as a 50th birthday present. Alessandra let on to me that her husband was a great Kraftwerk fan and that 'Neon Lights' was one of his favourite songs, and could I please play it in the show. I explained to the mistress of the house that this would not be suitable, since 'Neon Lights' was a pop song in a slow tempo; my dance-orientated show was performed at the high speed of 136 beats per minute. But I wanted Albrecht – her husband – to be pleased, and I started thinking about putting together a dance mix of 'Neon Lights'. This wasn't easy, but with the help of the Brazilian Alec Araujo, whom I got to know through the internet, I managed to achieve just that: I had Miriam Suarez completely re-record her vocals and adapted everything to suit the new tempo. Only a single sample of the original Kraftwerk song was left in the track, also adapted to the new speed, of course. These days the 'Neon Lights' dance mix is a song that I particularly look forward to, because it sounds so refreshingly different from the original and because I like Miriam's voice so much.

Actually, I don't play many songs by my former group, and when I do it is always the dance versions. Some of them work very well in this format: 'Home Computer', 'Expo 2000', 'Dentaku' and now also the 'Neon Lights' dance mix. Otherwise the songs

I play are from my own project or those of DJ friends of mine from here or abroad. I would, in particular, like to give Phil Fuldner a mention, as I have two of his songs in use. Also Michael Forza, Alex Smoke, Lutzenkirchen and, not least, Karl Bartos, my former colleague from Kraftwerk. The compilation of my tracks during the show resembles choreography – they become stronger and stronger, and more sonorous. During the last song I parade ironically onstage, with an anti-war film projected behind me, wearing a German spiked helmet, the type worn in the First World War. Spiked helmet, you may ask? I recommend that you read up about this on my website www.musiksoldat.de, following the link "Helmet" to find the explanation.

During all of my wonderful trips abroad – there have been many more than in my Kraftwerk days – I have made many contacts, colleagues with whom I now co-operate. At the moment I am working on my third album, to be titled, appropriately, *Collaborations*.

How did all this come about?

Well, my former involvement with Kraftwerk was fundamentally important to me and to my later identification process. On the one hand, we developed some fine things that went with our music, presented it on our travels, got to know the world and gained friends, which I benefit from today. On the other hand, for someone like me, or Karl, being part of Kraftwerk left a deep mark on us, and it can also be a stigma. It is hard, for example, to introduce journalists or our fans to new things. Often reviews of records begin with the words, "Does it sound like Kraftwerk?"

Who wants to hear that, when one has developed differently or further, or has become more modern? I myself have discovered the story-teller in me, as well as my voice, a skill that I enjoy using in my new songs. This can also be heard in *Collaborations*. My songs tell stories; I write the lyrics and develop the melodies, all in a way that I would never have believed possible. I am like an actor in a scene – you might remember that I was keen to become an actor as a boy, but my parents did not allow me to.

In spite of everything, or so it seems to me, I have achieved this in my music and onstage: I act a part. Every musician acts a part when he/she goes on stage – that is my opinion.

When I gave an interview at the end of 2014 to the online newspaper *Electronic Sound* in celebration of the 40th anniversary of the album *Autobahn*, it was a big deal for the magazine. I asked their boss, Mark Roland, to do something for me in return – I desperately needed new contacts in the UK for dealing with representation and booking matters. Mark made the connection between myself and a woman who works for his newspaper. Yvette is a Dane, loves electro music and has great contacts in the British press, BBC radio and with managers of clubs and festivals. After a few gigs in England things really started happening. She was keen to have a few of my new songs for marketing purposes. I told her that my new album was to be called *Eloquence* and that work on it was almost complete. Using various songs I had been producing with my partner Stefan Lindlahr in his Sonicfield Studio in Neunkirchen for years, I put together a 20-minute medley and sent it to Yvette. She forwarded it to Cherry Red Records and to PIAS Records and immediately received an offer from Cherry Red. That knocked my socks off. Something like that had been unthinkable in Germany for many years. In Germany, this is the kind of thing that happens:

At a meeting with Rüdiger Esch and a female A&R representative from the record label Grönland Records in Berlin I had handed over precisely the same medley, in the hope that Grönland might submit an offer for the German market. There was no offer of any kind. There was no refusal. Nothing. This was not very polite – not to reply at all. Obviously they couldn't be bothered with my music. But the British could, because – lickety-split – there were invitations to BBC Radio 6 Music's Radcliffe and Maconie show, to Hoxton FM with the mad Mr Normski, an invitation for a life interview at the popular Ditto Campfire Talk with Tom Bolton, and also invitations to other talk shows in London, Manchester, Brighton, Birmingham, Worthing, Dublin, Belfast and other cities.

354

My *Eloquence* album was graced with a distinctive cover by the German graphic designer Markus Luigs and is doing well. I have a contract in the USA with Cleopatra Records, who brought out my *Time Pie* album back in 1997. In America, the album got to Number 14 in the independent radio stations charts. I was really pleased about it, since I had never expected this to happen. For a full two months I received a list each week of US stations that had broadcast songs from my album, along with their in-house playlists; often my songs had come almost top of the lists.

Markus Luigs was authorised to use photos for the album cover of my old Halliburton suitcase (model Zero) that I had bought in 1975 on Fifth Avenue during my first US tour, for $700. In 1975, that was a fortune. The Halliburton was a golden suitcase made of aluminium that had since travelled around the world with me. It became important for establishing contacts as well as for my world view and for the themes on my later album, with which it had a connection. The little suitcase and its handle was a symbol for seizing opportunities, for advancement, for making contacts or for launching into something. The superb idea was realised aesthetically by Luigs, inside as well as outside. Cherry Red then brought out a double vinyl limited edition, and Markus Luigs created a suitable design for this as well. The transparent double vinyl editions were gone in a flash.

At this point my representative set up a Facebook page (www.facebook.com/musiksoldat) for my project and from then on uploaded news of my activities and short clips of my appearances, which my partner films whenever I go onstage anywhere in the world. I edit the scenes afterwards. I learned how to edit years ago, when a friend gave me an old Mac Pro and a few editing programs on a disc. My partner supplies the films, I do the editing; we are a good team.

What has given me pleasure most recently is international team play. As I don't have a band, I must work on my collaborative songs with artists from all over the world via the internet. They

355

send me a sound track and I make up a story to go with it. Then I write the lyrics, record the vocals and have my singer record her parts to fit in with my melody line. For example, for the chorus – which is the most important part of a pop song – when Miriam sings, I don't have a chance: hardly anyone does. Miriam Suarez is perfect for my projects. I am so glad that I met her in a music studio in Essen, where she was completing a practical course as a recording assistant.

I am in collaboration with Jack Dangers (San Francisco) from Meat Beat Manifesto; with Bon Harris (Los Angeles) from Shadow Bureau; with Anni Hogan (Liverpool), who was keyboard player in Marc Almond & The Mambas; with Ramon Amezcua (Tijuana) from the famous Mexican Nortec Collective. Currently I am working with the producers from U96 (Hamburg) on a song about the Hildebrand saga – a complicated old German text with a few original verses from the Hildebrand song. It is just about the most way-out thing I have ever done, and at this point the song hasn't even been released yet. It will cause a furore, I am sure, because nobody has ever done an electro song in ancient German before. I have worked with the band Tiny Magnetic Pets (Dublin) on a song about the radio, 'Radio On' and with the student Alexander Young (Worthing) from Northbrook College on 'Robo Boy'. At the moment I am working with Peter Dugall (Hebden Bridge) on the aforementioned song about the city of Birmingham.

In these collaborations, I always write the lyrics, record them and sometimes sing them via vocoder, developing additional melodies and at times letting Rüdiger Esch's young daughter sing some of the words. Cosi has a voice like a little angel – she is only nine! I can do all this comfortably from home; I don't need a large music studio. With the help of simple programs such as Garage Band, Virtual DJ and Ableton, it is all feasible. I find sounds that I think sound aesthetic on my Novation MiniNova synthesiser and edit them for the arrangements. The vocoder functions included on it are a big help. Sometimes the material goes back and forth between me and my online partners until the end mix is crowned. This kind of work gives me great satisfaction.

Much of it will appear on my next album, *Collaborations*. I hope that the co-operation between myself and my British record label will continue, just as I had hoped for it to continue back in 1997, when the EMI staff in Cologne so badly tricked me.

A few years ago I wrote a book with my partner about German folk living in the Rhineland, titled *Neben Mir: Rheinland Grotesken*. It contains 16 short stories about experiences and encounters with fellow human beings, some of them quite dreadful, which we had observed in our daily lives. The Rhineland should not only be well known for its colourful carnival parties.

I have often given readings from the book in Germany, but in the UK the readings tend to be from my autobiography – for example in the Tate Gallery in Liverpool, where I did a reading in the foyer on a podium on which a table with a microphone had been set up. The anteroom was crammed with listeners. During the lecture I noticed an old couple standing in the audience, listening attentively; the man was leaning on a stick. I couldn't let this stand. I interrupted my reading, stepped off the platform, grabbed a young man and went into the wings with him, found two chairs and pushed my way back through the audience with the helper and the chairs towards the old couple. I offered them the chairs to sit on, which they were very pleased about. After my reading I returned to the couple and enquired if they were Kraftwerk fans. "What do you mean?" the woman asked in surprise. I said that I had been reading stories about my former music group in Germany – Kraftwerk was the name of the band. "Ah," she replied, "it was so interesting listening to your life stories and you speak so nicely. We loved your lecture, thank you very much. We were just passing by and had nothing else to do this morning." I freely admit that these two old folks touched and amused me greatly. Readings give me pleasure; it is in these moments that I become an actor.

What else is there to report?

I had an encounter with Florian. Or rather, he with me – with my right shoulder, to be precise. How did it come about?

In May 2016 I had arranged to meet some friends in the Schumacher brewery in Oststraße in Düsseldorf for an evening meal. There were five of us. We were served hearty German food, as is customary in brew houses. After a couple of hours my partner nudged my knee under the table and whispered, "Isn't that your old pal Florian sitting over there behind you? Don't look over now. He's sitting opposite a gorgeous, dark-skinned woman and there is a pretty blonde girl sitting next to him." After a short while I turned my head ineffectually upwards and back, pretending to be admiring the ornaments on the ceiling of the inn. In doing so I recognised Florian at a small table quite close behind me, sitting with the two ladies who had been described to me.

The proximity of my ex-pal irritated me, I have to admit. I had been in trouble with him and his former partner as a result of my autobiography since 1999. I wanted to get out of the issue, to forget all these never-ending disputes, and hadn't the faintest idea, at first, how to do this elegantly today. My thoughts were racing round my mind. Should I simply stand up and walk over to the table? Might it be discourteous to disturb him in the presence of his company? The blonde girl was his daughter, that was clear to me, and how pretty she was! I had often seen Florian with a dark-skinned woman in the past. That was probably still the same woman sitting at the table behind me. Here I was, seated with my friends, nearly petrified, eating and drinking Altbier. I shoved the fork with the cold beef tartare dressed with anchovies, onions, paprika powder, capers and mustard almost mechanically into my mouth. My mind went back to the good times I had shared with Florian, about how often we original Kraftwerkers had come here after long studio sessions, especially in the summer, when we had sat outside in the yard behind the brewery building in the open air. We had often eaten cold platters here and drunk Altbier (apart from Karl); that is why the restaurant has become a legendary temple to me. It might well be the same for Florian; he too loves the Düsseldorfer Altbier and hearty food.

My friends were constantly whispering to each other. None of them knew Florian personally. None of them had ever met him or shook hands with him. They knew because of my book that we had had troubles and lawsuits. Suddenly I felt a hand on my right shoulder. I turned round and looked up. "Florian?" I said, pretending to be dumbfounded. "Hallo Wolfgang," he answered and smiled down at me. I stood up from my chair and greeted my pal properly, telling him that I liked his solo music very much. "Your 'Stop Plastic Pollution' is a great song," I went on. "It's wonderful that you are still making music, and how different it sounds to your previous music with Kraftwerk."

Florian refrained from making a comment. "You've put on quite a bit of weight," he replied instead, reaching out to stroke my belly, smiling broadly at me as he had done in the past, when he was in a good mood. There we were, the two of us, helplessly, wordlessly standing facing each other, 30 years after I had left Kraftwerk. I couldn't help myself; all of a sudden I put my arms around my friend and hugged him, whispering into his ear, "Thank you for the beautiful years with you both." Florian replied, "That was the best Kraftwerk time."

He lifted his cap to the others at the table and, with his women, took his leave of us, departing with a friendly "Have a nice evening." Markus, who was sitting at our table, had opened his iPhone a while ago and had taken a shot of this intimate moment.

After this encounter I was ready for a Killepitsch (a traditional "Schnapps"), as it had really stirred something up in me. At that moment everything seemed to have vanished into thin air – the lawsuits, all the previous misunderstandings and disputes. I would have liked to have agreed upon another longer meeting with Florian and to have offered him a musical collaboration. He had jotted his telephone number onto a beer mat in the brewery, and the very next day I sent him a short message, including our photo.

He's a model and he's looking good.

Florian actually became a male model in his old age, and he makes an extremely handsome one. It was my graphic designer who let me in on this development by sending me an assortment of pictures that he had seen in the business magazine *The Heritage Post*. Florian looks unbelievably attractive in male fashion garb provided by Habsburg, Haversack and Hobo. How the photographer, Lutz Hilgers, managed to get Florian to be his model remains a mystery. Now that he has split up with Ralf and the brand Kraftwerk, he looks relieved and free. He had always been a cool type, had worn special clothes and amazed us with his unequalled humour. My gratitude towards Florian was meant sincerely. Without my time in his group I could not have found my present identity. It changed my life. It was their modernity and desire to experiment that, in 1973, opened my senses to a new musical genre, without which I probably would have become an architect or a designer of furniture. Not bad, but not quite as full of adventure.

I don't think we had ever hugged each other in the past. But what we had was a lot of fun – as you can see, for yourself:

## It's No More Fun To Compute!
## Kraftwerk Live Review By Wolfgang Flür
## The Quietus, February 7th, 2013 07:39

In January 2013, the former robot went to the band's home town show in the Düsseldorf museum K 20 and sent us this report, a longer version of a piece originally published in Germany earlier this year.

It was early morning when I got into bed on Sunday 20th January. It had been many years since my last appearance with Kraftwerk in the summer of 1981 at Düsseldorf's Philips Hall. But on this night, thirty-two years later, I had met up with some friends, one from the Netherlands, two from England, one from Cologne and Rüdiger Esch, the bassist from the German industrial band Die Krupps. And we had gone to see Kraftwerk Mark III. In a museum!

Rüdiger had contacts at the main sponsor of this concert, the Düsseldorf Stadtwerke power plant, which produces our city's electricity. (Since when did Kraftwerk need sponsors, I wondered? As far as I remember they function economically. Automatically!) Rüdiger brought us into the gallery via a side door for VIPs – tres chic – so we didn't need to queue with the long row of fans in that minus-degree-night. We got a desirable, white all-access pass that allowed us to go anywhere in the hall – apart from the garage where the robots were. And inside the foyer, I immediately saw Emil Schult, my former friend and room mate at Berger Alley 9 [where Karl Bartos and Flür lived in the 1970s], crossing my path, looking very stressed and austere. He saw me – and looked away.

So, he was still in cahoots with Ralf. I understood why he didn't want to be recognised by me, after all the testimonies he had made against me and all that had happened at the Hamburg land court [Ralf and Florian tried to stop Flür publishing his memoirs in 2000].

Inside the huge hall it was stinky and muggy – there had been a show that night already, and we were to see the second one. The midnight special. We Germans call it the ghost hour.

And then came Kraftwerk Mark III. The music they made was very loud – so much so that I was afraid for my ears and of a brand-new level of tinnitus. But the sound was brilliant, crispy and digitally clear.

To the left of me and my friends was a group of English and Dutch fans, rampaging, drunk and bawling. The guys stank like Schnapps and bawled Kraftwerk lyrics along with Ralf and his vocoder-device. While she was dancing, a female member of their party kicked me hard on my left foot, so I shouted at her to be calm and well mannered. After all, we were in a museum, not a rock-concert arena. She apologised, but soon went on with bawling. The smell in that area was such a ghastly mixture – disgusting! I know why I normally avoid such events.

But the graphic projections in 3D were a hit. Sensationally clear and near. During 'Kometenmelodie' it felt like you could grab the space capsules coming out of the screen. During 'Musique Non Stop' the music notes I knew from so long ago came flying towards us, beautiful and smooth. I was able to grab one and put it in my jacket as a souvenir.

But I have to report that there was nothing else for me to admire that night.

So much I remembered had changed from the appearances we made during the 70s and the 80s, although I understand that today's Kraftwerk fans won't be able to sense this. But we used to move; these robots don't. The non-performance of Kraftwerk Mark III made me yawn; the concert went on too long. Thirty minutes less might have worked, perhaps. But this performance as Kraftwerk seemed to offer no joy to the four people who had to *be* Kraftwerk.

They didn't even look at each other. There was not one spark between the figures. No magnetism left. Coldness came over me. What had happened? Was it the effect of the two concerts, one after the other? Were they possibly overworked, or overwrought? Can robots generally be overwrought? Ralf seemed to me to be completely absent. His voice was thin, short of breath, and he looked broken. I have other images of Ralf in memory though – fortunately.

The passion was gone, the lights were out. I can imagine why Florian bade his farewell to the bondage and dictatorship of his original partner. He didn't want this any more, that's my view. One of my friends lent over during the show and said, "Listen Wolfgang, actually YOU should go and stand on the stage as the second figure from the right." Ralph from Cologne replied to him, in protest, "Are you crazy? Our Wolfi between those ghosts onstage? No way! He feels much better today than ever before – after all, he is free, right?"

I had to smile, because he was right. Then another of my companions – one a little younger than me – whispered this: "Those neoprene suits on those tummies...they look awkward, right? On top of that, they're sweating inside. And then they are standing for a long time. Two shows, one after the other... They could get varicose veins at their age."

I had to laugh loudly, and add: "Those plastic trousers already have the effect of surgical stockings. Maybe that's why they wear them."

Now we both had to laugh. Nevertheless, I find it pretty courageous that Ralf, one year older than me, stands on stages worldwide in a Spiderman costume. I can only hope that he has several for changing into during tours.

The whole spectacle appeared to me like a final farewell tour. The guy [Stefan Pfaffe] who replaced Florian three years ago has latterly been replaced by a figure whose name is hard to remember [Falk Grieffenhagen], and the turnover of music-workers is occurring quicker and quicker. At Ralf's age, if he has become Grot – the alerter of the machines in Fritz Lang's *Metropolis* – he may find it harder and harder to discover fresh cogs who agree to examination. In some ways, Kraftwerk's story has become a bit like Goethe's Zauberlehring, 'The Sorcerer's Apprentice'. The sorcerer activated something powerful all those years ago, and maybe now he can't stop it. The musique is Non-Stop. The Volkswagen runs and runs and runs and runs...

Last night, Kraftwerk Mark III certainly did something with effective technique. But is that always best?

After the concert, when the lights came on, things got crazy in the foyer. Quite a few people recognised and assembled around me, and wanted to have all sorts of things signed. Girls were there too – and these girls were young. Did we formerly have female fans? I cannot remember this...

To conclude, I can genuinely see how this was a superb night in many ways, and I loved the 3D-video projections. But however brilliant and perfect yesterday's spectacle was, all in all, I still must say:

It's no more fun to compute!

And it used to be fun. Onstage in the 70s and 80s, in that pioneering era, it felt good in our hearts as well as our heads. No visitor or fan could imagine it being that way yesterday. If the show was a film I'd think of it this way – as *Jaws* part III in 3D (without Florian/Spielberg).

The remaining commander should at least replace himself with a new construction ("everyone is replaceable," Ralf once said) and send those four fresh figures around the world (White Shark, part IV). Then he would not need to suffer. In fact, he looked stressed on stage, sad, endlessly lonely. So hard without his Flori...

I met this Flori recently, on a cross-road at Berlin Alley, while waiting for the green pedestrian light. Florian was passing by in a tiny British car. Noticing me, he threw a smile through his side window. I waved to him. His face looked peaceful and relaxed. He seemed to have escaped from the Kraftwerk stigma.

Like me.

# Discography

## With Kraftwerk

**ALBUMS:**

| | | |
|---|---|---|
| 1974 | *Autobahn* | EMI 7461532 |
| 1975 | *Radioactivity* | EMI 7461322 |
| 1977 | *Trans Europe Express* | EMI 741332 |
| 1978 | *The Man Machine* | EMI 7461312 |
| 1981 | *Computer World* | EMI 7461302 |
| 1986 | *Electric Cafe* | EMI 7464202 |

## With Yamo

**ALBUMS:**

| | | |
|---|---|---|
| *Time Pie* | EMI Electrola | 7243 8 54172 1 |

**VINYL CLUBMIX:**

| | | |
|---|---|---|
| 'Musica Obscura' | EMI Electrola | 7243 8 84669 67 |

**SINGLES:**

| | | |
|---|---|---|
| 'Stereomatic' | EMI Electrola | 7243 8 6229 2 1 |
| 'Guiding Ray' | EMI Electrola | 7243 8 622 60 2 0 |

## *With International Artists*

ALBUM:

| 2015 | Wolfgang Flür – Eloquence (Complete Works) | Cherry Red Records | SFELP 046D |